A Guide to Coding Compliance

Joanne M. Becker

A Guide to Coding Compliance

Joanne M. Becker

DELMAR
CENGAGE Learning™

Australia • Canada • Mexico • Singapore • Spain • United Kingdom • United States

A Guide to Coding Compliance
Joanne M. Becker

Vice President, Career and Professional
Editorial: Dave Garza

Director of Learning Solutions: Matthew Kane

Senior Acquisitions Editor: Rhonda Dearborn

Managing Editor: Marah Bellegarde

Product Manager: Jadin Babin-Kavanaugh

Editorial Assistant: Chiara Astriab

Vice President, Career and Professional
Marketing: Jennifer Ann Baker

Marketing Director: Wendy Mapstone

Senior Marketing Manager: Nancy Bradshaw

Marketing Coordinator: Erica Ropitzky

Production Director: Carolyn Miller

Production Manager: Andrew Crouth

Senior Content Project Manager:
Stacey Lamodi

Senior Art Director: Jack Pendleton

Technology Product Manager:
Mary Colleen Liburdi

Technology Project Manager: Patti Allen

For product information and technology assistance, contact us at
Cengage Learning Customer & Sales Support, 1-800-354-9706

For permission to use material from this text or product,
submit all requests online at **www.cengage.com/permissions**.
Further permissions questions can be e-mailed to
permissionrequest@cengage.com

2009 Current Procedural Terminology (CPT) © 2008 American Medical Association. All Rights Reserved.

Library of Congress Control Number: 2009928610

ISBN-13: 978-1-4354-3921-4
ISBN-10: 1-4354-3921-X

Delmar
5 Maxwell Drive
Clifton Park, NY 12065-2919
USA

Cengage Learning is a leading provider of customized learning solutions with office locations around the globe, including Singapore, the United Kingdom, Australia, Mexico, Brazil, and Japan. Locate your local office at:
international.cengage.com/region

Cengage Learning products are represented in Canada by Nelson Education, Ltd.

To learn more about Delmar, visit **www.cengage.com/delmar**

Purchase any of our products at your local college store or at our preferred online store
www.ichapters.com

NOTICE TO THE READER

Publisher does not warrant or guarantee any of the products described herein or perform any independent analysis in connection with any of the product information contained herein. Publisher does not assume, and expressly disclaims, any obligation to obtain and include information other than that provided to it by the manufacturer. The reader is expressly warned to consider and adopt all safety precautions that might be indicated by the activities described herein and to avoid all potential hazards. By following the instructions contained herein, the reader willingly assumes all risks in connection with such instructions. The publisher makes no representations or warranties of any kind, including but not limited to, the warranties of fitness for particular purpose or merchantability, nor are any such representations implied with respect to the material set forth herein, and the publisher takes no responsibility with respect to such material. The publisher shall not be liable for any special, consequential, or exemplary damages resulting, in whole or part, from the readers' use of, or reliance upon, this material.

Printed in the United States of America
1 2 3 4 5 6 7 12 11 10 09

Dedication

In dedication to my husband, Bill, and my beautiful daughters and grandchildren, who granted me the space to dream, the time to create, the support to finish, and the love to believe.

Table of Contents

Preface

Recently a colleague said to me, "I don't know why anyone stays in this business anymore." The "business" he was speaking of was that of delivering health care—primarily from a financial perspective. The massive complexity of laws, federal regulations, health insurance contracts, and billing requirements would seemingly require that someone be a doctor, lawyer, financial analyst, mathematician, and politician to understand them. Unfortunately, even those who write the regulations sometimes do not understand them, cannot explain them, or fully comply with them. Just when we think we have figured out the rules, they change! Even when we are confident we have done everything we can, we get denials or are audited, resulting in more lost revenue.

Although the figures vary, it is estimated that billions of health care dollars are lost annually to fraud. There are even figures that place the rate lost per hour—at $25 million! Unfortunately, many of the fraud cases that make the news releases are obvious infractions of the law, often indecent, entrenched in greed, and committed by the "ethically challenged." Health care fraud is not limited to health care providers. It also involves payers, managed care organizations, manufacturers of health care supplies, medical billing companies, and sometimes even the patient. Often overlooked is the consequence to the ordinary health care consumers, who entrust their lives to the system but become irrevocably harmed.

It is my belief that the majority of individuals involved in the delivery of health care are honest, sincere folks who truly want what is best for the patient. They do not look for loopholes or skate along the outside borders of compliance. They do their best to understand the laws and follow the guidelines. They never seek to get more than what is deserved or provided for but recognize that fair reimbursement is not only acceptable but justly deserved. This book is written for them.

At the heart of health care fraud and abuse is noncompliant coding and billing. Developing a strong coding compliance program is essential to instilling the appropriate processes to ensure compliance. Compliant coding and billing is more than just ensuring that the correct codes are submitted on a claim. Sometimes the compliant coding and billing *process* involves vast changes in how we operate, requiring changes in our behavior, culture, and habits. Developing an effective coding compliance process will not prevent outside audits or claim denials, however, but it can provide strong armor for defense and deterrence.

Untangling all the threads of regulations, rules, and laws can be understandably difficult. At times we can get so hung up in trying to manage all the information that we forget the obvious. Often, I am asked what should we do in a particular situation or how should we code a particular bill. The answer is: Just do it right! For example, if we have coded our claims following official coding guidelines, we will always be able to defend them. If the result is something we can honestly defend, then we probably have chosen the right answer.

Coding and billing compliantly cannot rest solely on the shoulders of those responsible for appending codes to claims and submitting them. The coding and billing is only as good as the documentation, which is only as good as the policies that are written to guide the creators and maintainers of the health care document. Compliant coding and billing is a collaborative effort that involves everyone in the health care organization—administration, health care providers, suppliers, vendors, finance, business services, health information management, and compliance. Failures in the compliance process are usually a result of breakdowns in the partnerships of the health care team and a lack of communication.

Even when everything works to perfection, we may still be faced with denials, questions of medical necessity, and allegations of inaccurate claim submission. Although we can do our best to ensure compliance in our facility, there are no guarantees that our outside partners, such as payers, share the same commitment to compliant coding and billing. Unfortunately, providers sometimes feel as if they are being held hostage: "Code and bill it like we want or no money!" There are many published guidelines on proper coding and laws that require that everyone follow them. From a compliance perspective, we are fully aware that we cannot code noncompliantly just to receive payment. Sometimes the only alternative left is to educate and reeducate our partners.

I am hopeful that the information contained in this text will provide the learner with assurance, insight, and instruction. In compliance, it is important to recognize that the answer to any particular question is not always black and white. In many situations there is not one obvious answer but, rather, a choice of alternatives. The case studies at the end of each chapter were written primarily to stimulate discussion for various options. Obviously, sometimes there are specific written laws that need to be followed, but each individual, real-life case is different, and the answer may not be the same in every situation.

To the student, I hope this book provides you an opportunity to gain valuable insight into the real day-to-day coding and billing issues that can develop. No doubt at some point in your career you will be faced with a coding or billing compliance issue. Come back to the examples, reflect on them, and go with your instinct. Someone once told me, "If it smells bad, it's probably rotten." It's amazing how often our gut instincts are right on target. Do not get discouraged!

This book was written with the understanding that the reader has at least a moderate or advanced concept of medical coding and billing. I have tried to include examples of compliance situations that will benefit both the physician and hospital coder. I welcome your suggestions and hope that you will share your coding and billing compliance examples for future editions.

Joanne M. Becker

OBJECTIVES

A *Guide to Coding Compliance* was written and developed for learners desiring an understanding of coding compliance guidelines and regulations. The text and instructor manual was developed to assist the student and educator in gaining a basic understanding of coding and billing compliance, while providing the experienced coding professional helpful insights into developing a coding compliance program. The case studies were developed with the intention of providing a mixture of professional and facility (hospital) coding and billing scenarios. The instructor manual and StudyWare™ CD-ROM help to reinforce the material presented in the text with answers to case studies, additional exercises and activities, and discussion points for the chapter reviews.

FEATURES OF THE TEXT

The following key features of this text are designed to facilitate learning and encourage understanding:

- **Learning objectives** and **key terms** identify main learning outcomes for each chapter.
- Practical **examples** provide immediate clarification of covered concepts.
- **Chapter Review** questions allow for self-testing and self-review.
- **Case Studies** provide real-life compliance scenarios that relate to both physician and hospital coding situations.

- End-of-chapter **References** provide resources for further exploration of topics and expansion of knowledge of industry standards, guidelines, and practices.

- The **Appendix** includes exercises that can be completed with the free trial of Ingenix's EncoderPro included in the back of the text.

DISCLAIMER

A Guide to Coding Compliance, 2010 edition, is based on the latest references available at the time of publication. Every reasonable effort has been made to ensure the accuracy of the information on these pages. This book does not replace legal counsel and will not prevent an audit or investigation. It serves only as a guide. The author and publisher make no representation or guarantee that this book will prevent differences in opinion or disputes with governmental agencies and health insurance payers. Advice and strategies contained within may not be applicable to every individual in every circumstance. The examples provided in this text are fictional and should not be inferred to represent any individual provider, unless otherwise noted.

The Web sites listed in this book were current and valid as of the date of publication. As Web addresses and the information on them change or disappear at any time, without notification, and without any particular cause, the user is encouraged to perform their own web searches to locate addresses that are no longer valid.

Readers should always consult professional counsel for specific legal, ethical, or clinical questions.

Supplements

STUDENT RESOURCES

The following resources were developed to help students review and retain the information covered in *A Guide to Coding Compliance*:

StudyWare™ CD-ROM

The free StudyWare™ CD-ROM in the back of the text acts as your own private tutor to help you learn the terms and concepts presented in *A Guide to Coding Compliance*. As you study each chapter, be sure to complete the activities for the corresponding chapter on the StudyWare™ for immediate reinforcement and assessment.

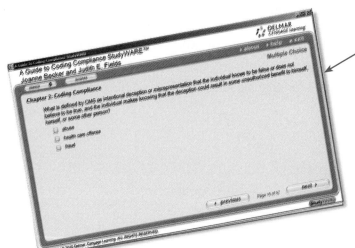

Chapter Quizzes

Do quizzes in Practice Mode to receive immediate feedback, or in Test Mode for immediate assessment. Print out your scores and submit to your instructor or as a personal record to see which subject areas you need to review.

Activities

Include Hangman and Concentration to help you build your vocabulary.

EncoderPro 30-Day Free Trial CD-ROM

The EncoderPro software included in the back cover of this textbook is presented as a 30-day free trial of Ingenix's powerful medical coding solution that allows you to look up ICD-9-CM, CPT, and HCPCS Level II codes quickly and accurately. This software can be used to assign codes to any exercise in the textbook. Be sure to check with your instructor before installing the EncoderPro software because the CD-ROM bundled with your book expires 30 days after installation.

Menus and Toolbars

EncoderPro contains a menu that expands to allow you to easily navigate the software. Click on a menu heading to select one of its options, such as View, Code Book Sections, etc. EncoderPro contains a toolbar with drop-down menus that allow you to select the ICD-9-CM, CPT, or HCPCS Level II coding system and new/revised/deleted codes and code book sections.

- Use the coding system drop-down menu on the far left to select a coding system. Then, enter a condition (e.g., diabetes) or procedure/service in the Search box. Click the Search button to view Tabular Results, which can be expanded, or click the "See index listing" to use the alphabetic index to locate a code.

- Use the drop-down list on the far right of the black toolbar to quickly access New Codes, Revised Codes, Deleted Codes, and Code Book Sections. Make a selection and click the View button to access the dialog boxes.

- EncoderPro's toolbar with clickable buttons allows you to use its unique features. Simply mouse over a button to view its title, and a brief description of the button will also appear in the status bar on the bottom left of the screen. Click on the button to use its function.

Features and Benefits of EncoderPro

EncoderPro is the essential code lookup software for CPT®, ICD-9-CM, and HCPCS code sets. It gives users fast searching capabilities across all code sets. EncoderPro can greatly reduce the time it takes to build or review a claim, and helps improve overall coding accuracy. If you decide to subscribe to the full version of EncoderPro, the following tools will be available to you:

- **Powerful Ingenix CodeLogic™ search engine.** Improve productivity by eliminating time-consuming code lookup in outdated code books. Search all three code sets simultaneously using lay terms, acronyms, abbreviations, and even misspelled words.

- **Lay descriptions for thousands of CPT® codes.** Enhance your understanding of procedures with easy-to-understand descriptions.

- **Color-coded edits.** Understand whether a code carries an age or sex edit, is covered by Medicare, or contains bundled procedures.

- **Quarterly update service.** Rest assured you are always using accurate codes. You can code confidently throughout the year with free code updates.

- **Great value.** Get the content from over 20 code and reference books in one powerful solution.

For more information about EncoderPro software, click on the Help menu from inside the free trial version, then select "Features by Product," or go to www.ingenixonline.com.

INSTRUCTOR RESOURCES

The following instructor resources, developed to provide instructors with the tools they need to teach and assess student progress, are available either on Instructor Resources CD-ROM (ISBN 1-4354-3925-2) or at the Online Companion Web site for *A Guide to Coding Compliance*:

- **Exam*View*® Computerized Test Bank** with more than 250 questions that you can use to create your own review materials or tests.

- **Customizable instructor support slide presentations** written in PowerPoint® with more than 200 slides that correlate to the chapters in the book.

- **Instructor's Manual** with answer keys to text and appendix exercises.

To receive the Instructor Resources CD-ROM, please contact your Delmar Cengage Learning Sales Representative. To access the instructor resources via the Online Companion site, go to http://www .delmarlearning.com/companions, and click on Allied Health in the left navigation menu. Then, scroll down to select *A Guide to Coding Compliance*. The user ID and password are available from your Sales Representative on request.

About the Author

Joanne M. Becker, RHIT, CCS, CPC, CPCI, is currently Associate Director in the Joint Office for Compliance at University of Iowa Health Care, Iowa City, Iowa. Ms. Becker has more than 25 years of experience in health information management including inpatient, outpatient and physician coding, as well as compliance, quality improvement and education. She was previously Program Coordinator of the Health Information Technology Program at Kirkwood Community College in Cedar Rapids, Iowa. There she taught classes on ICD-9-CM and CPT coding and reimbursement, health information technology, quality improvement, legal aspects, health statistics and health information management. Ms. Becker is also a consultant, specializing in coding reviews for hospital and professional services. She has presented numerous educational seminars on coding and coding compliance.

"In a moment of decision the best thing you can do is the right thing.
The worst thing you can do is nothing."

Theodore Roosevelt

Acknowledgments

The author and publisher would like to recognize the following reviewers for their invaluable feedback on this product:

Mary M. Cantwell, RHIT, CPC, CPC-I,
CPC-H, RMC
Instructor
Metro Community College
Omaha, Nebraska

Sheryl S. Chambers, CBCS
Medical Instructor
Indiana Business College
Terre Haute, Indiana

Marie T. Conde, MPA, RHIA, RHIT, CCS
Health Information Technology Program Director
City College of San Francisco
San Francisco, California

Michelle Cranney, MBA, RHIT, CCS-P, CPC
Virginia College Online
Birmingham, Alabama

Pat King, MA, RHIA
MIS System Program Coordinator
    and Adjunct Faculty
Baker College
Cass City, Michigan

Mary F. Koloski, CBCS, CHI
Health Insurance Billing & Coding Program
    Team Leader
Florida Career College
Clearwater, Florida

June M. Petillo, MBA, RMC
Instructor—Medical Assisting Program
Manchester Community College and Capitol
    Community College
Manchester, Connecticut, and Hartford,
    Connecticut
Project Manager—EMR
Women's Health USA
Avon, Connecticut

Julie Pope, CMA, CPC-I, CPC-H
ATA Career Education
Louisville, Kentucky

Angela P. Rein, BSHM, CPC, MAHS, CPC-H
Medical Billing and Coding Department
Chairperson
Sanford-Brown College
Collinsville, Illinois

Lori Warren, MA, RN, CPC, CPC-I, CCP, CLNC
Spencerian College, Medical Department
Co-Director, and
Medical Coding/Healthcare Reimbursement
Program Director
Louisville, KY

Coding and Billing:
Differences and Similarities

Objectives

At the completion of this chapter, the learner should be able to:

- Define coding and billing, describing their similarities and differences.
- Identify the purposes of coding and the importance of accuracy.
- Discuss ways that billers and coders can work cooperatively to enhance the quality of coding and limit coding compliance risks.
- Describe current quality health care initiatives that relate to coding.

Key Terms

adjudication

Ambulatory Patient Classifications (APCs)

ambulatory surgical setting (ASC)

Bertillon classification of causes of death

billing

coding

coding systems

Current Dental Terminology (CDT)

Current Procedural Terminology, 4th Edition (CPT-4)

Healthcare Common Procedure Coding System (HCPCS) (Level I CPT codes and Level II National Codes)

Health Insurance Portability and Accountability Act (HIPAA)

hospital-acquired conditions

ICD-9-CM Official Guidelines for Coding and Reporting

inpatient prospective payment system (IPPS)

International Classification of Diseases, 9th Revision, Clinical Modification (ICD-9-CM)

International Classification of Diseases for Oncology (ICD-O)

Medicare Severity Diagnosis-Related Groups (MS-DRGs)

never events

outpatient prospective payment system (OPPS)

Physician Quality Reporting Initiative (PQRI)

professional ethical standards

quality measures

relative value units (RVUs)

Systematized Nomenclature of Medicine—Clinical Terms (SNOMED)

Defining Coding and Billing

Coding and billing. Billing and coding. Are they the same? Is a coder the same as a biller? Can a biller be a coder?

The terms *coding* and *billing* are often used interchangeably. An Internet search on "coding and billing" yields hundreds of thousands of hits. Colleges, business organizations, and technical schools offer programs on medical coding and billing. Some programs offer extensive billing courses and limited coding; others concentrate on coding with limited courses on billing. Many programs offer certificates of completion, and professional associations offer credentials for coders and billers to become "certified." Medical billing companies promise to "help you get paid" or "get the reimbursement you deserve," indicating that a provider can get paid for every service every time. Are there compliance risks when coding and billing are treated the same?

The differences between coding and billing may best be understood by examining how the information, particularly coding information, is created and used. The American Hospital Association (AHA) defines medical **coding** as assigning "a numeric value to medical diagnoses, procedures and surgery, signs and symptoms of disease and ill-defined conditions, poisoning and adverse effects of drugs, complications of surgery and medical care." Coding can mean translating medical documentation (terms and phrases) into a numeric code (sometimes an alphanumeric code). The documentation can range from a single word or phrase to a patient's entire hospital inpatient stay. Coders will often say that coding is not black and white—there is not always one right answer. Some describe coding as an art, in that successful coding requires interpretation, application of facts and data, analysis, and some sleuthing skills.

Most commonly, coding refers to the **International Classification of Diseases, 9th Revision, Clinical Modification (ICD-9-CM)** and the **Healthcare Common Procedure Coding System (HCPCS) (Level I CPT codes and Level II National Codes),** where CPT stands for Current Procedural Terminology. These **coding systems** are used by physicians, hospitals, home health agencies, nursing homes, rehabilitation centers, and other providers. These systems are the basis for physician and hospital reimbursement, quality review, and statistical and benchmarking data. Several other classification systems exist, including the **International Classification of Diseases for Oncology (ICD-O), Current Dental Terminology (CDT),** and the **Systematized Nomenclature of Medicine—Clinical Terms (SNOMED–CT).** Coding systems such as the ICD-O and SNOMED are not used for reimbursement but rather to collect specialized health care data. Coders must understand the mechanics and coding guidelines of the manuals they utilize, along with the numerous regulations that involve coding.

Medical **billing** requires transferring necessary information from the coded data to claims for reimbursement. Billing involves managing and filing claims, preparing insurance forms, processing payments, and working denials. A biller is usually keenly aware of payer-specific instructions for properly filed claims, including coverage issues.

When a claim has successfully gone through the process of **adjudication** (been processed and paid), it is sometimes thought that the billing, and therefore also the coding, was correct. This is not necessarily true. The payer may not have systems in place to identify coding and billing errors. That fact alone, however, is not justification for incorrect coding and billing. As will be discussed in subsequent chapters, Medicare makes it clear that it is the provider's responsibility to submit claims accurately and to ensure that the coding and billing are correct.

To further illustrate the difference between coding and billing, consider the following examples:

CASE 1: A coder at an oncology office assigns the diagnosis codes V58.11, "Encounter for antineoplastic chemotherapy," and 202.86, "Lymphoma of intrapelvic lymph nodes." The coder lists the V58.11 as diagnosis one, and 202.86 as diagnosis two. Prior to submission to the payer, the claim is reviewed in the billing office. The staff member in the billing office believes that the payer will reject the claim if the V-code is listed as the first diagnosis and resequences the diagnosis codes so the V-code is listed secondarily. The claim is submitted to insurance and paid. Is the coding correct on the claim? Has the claim been properly adjudicated? Has there been any fraudulent activity? Who, if anyone, is at fault?

CASE 2: A patient is involved in a motor vehicle accident and sustains multiple injuries. The physician notes in the history and physical that the patient has hypertension and a history of alcohol abuse, both currently being managed and treated. The coder assigns the codes for the injuries, along with diagnoses 401.9, "Hypertension," and 305.00, "Alcohol abuse." The claim is sent to the payer and is denied because of the presence of the alcohol abuse code. When questioned by the billing office for the reason for the denial, the representative from the insurance company states that the claim will be paid if the alcohol abuse code is removed. The billing office asks the coder to remove the code from the claim so it can get paid. The coder argues that the code should not be removed, since it was documented by the physician and is a condition currently being treated. Should the coder remove the alcohol abuse code? Is there a risk of fraudulent activity? Who, if anyone, would be out of compliance?

Answers to these actual case examples are not simple or straightforward. A professional, certified coder relies on the **ICD-9-CM Official Guidelines for Coding and Reporting,** follows professional standards of ethics, and considers coding compliance risks when assigning codes. These guidelines, discussed in greater detail in a later chapter, have been approved by the American Hospital Association (AHA), the American Health Information Management Association (AHIMA), the Centers for Medicare & Medicaid Services (CMS), and the National Center for Health Statistics (NCHS). The guidelines are required under **Health Insurance Portability and Accountability Act (HIPAA)** regulations.

The biller is aware of the multiple payer-specific instructions for claims processing. Many billers also belong to professional associations and abide by **professional ethical standards.** Billers understand the importance of compliant billing under HIPAA and numerous regulatory claim submission guidelines. The payer's main interest may not be tied to official coding guidelines, coding and billing professional standards, or even HIPAA, but instead may be most concerned that it pay for only those services defined as "covered" under the beneficiary's health insurance plan. Many large payers are actively involved in health care initiatives designed to lower the cost of health care and promote its quality and safety.

There are obviously many close ties between coding and billing. The greatest differences often appear when billing becomes exceedingly aggressive. This occurs when emphasis is placed on doing whatever it takes to get a claim paid or submitting claims before all the necessary information is available to submit accurate coding information. Providers need to understand that not every service that is ordered and performed is considered medically necessary or is covered by Medicare or other third-party payers. Some services are considered inherent in other procedures or "bundled." Problems are intensified when a payer lacks an understanding of official coding rules or chooses not to follow them. Misinterpreting coding guidelines, coverage policies, and billing rules can place the provider at risk for submitting inaccurate claims. Coders and billers are often placed in the precarious ethical position of coding compliantly or following payer guidelines that sometimes conflict with official coding guidelines. The problem is further compounded when different payers have different billing requirements.

In most health care institutions, the coding and billing functions are performed in different departments. Generally, "coders" do not perform "billing," and "billers" do not perform "coding" functions. Unfortunately, these two departments do not always communicate well with each other, which can create tension and increases compliance risks. In the past many coders felt that they did not need to understand the billing requirements, and the billing staff felt they needed to know little about coding. But increasingly complex coding and billing requirements, and tough penalties for inaccurate claim submission, require that the departments communicate and collaborate with each other. For example, it is important that the billing department share denial and resolution information with the coding staff so they can be aware of possible coding errors. Many of the top reasons for claim denial relate to coding issues including modifier usage, unbundling, and medical necessity. Likewise, coders should communicate to billers the reasons for use of specific codes which can be beneficial when billers respond to payers on issues of denials and adherence to coding guidelines.

Although these functions occur in different departments, which can sometimes hinder the communication process, it is important that the functions of each department be clearly defined. As mentioned earlier, coders generally do not perform billing functions, and billers generally do not perform coding functions. It would not make good business sense to have coders assign codes to diagnoses and procedures only to have them changed in the billing office. Claim issues that involve coding issues should be resolved by the coder. Consider the following case examples:

CASE 1: A biller in a physician's office receives payer denials with a reason code indicating that some of the services reported on the claim are bundled. The biller assumes that appending a modifier will clear the edits and appends modifier 59, "Distinct procedural service," to all the procedure codes. The claim is reprocessed and paid. The misapplication of modifier 59 results in overpayment to the physician, requiring repayment to the patients and payers.

CASE 2: A biller in a hospital business office is aware that many non-Medicare payers do not like unspecified HCPCS Level II drugs. Claims with these codes are usually returned to the provider indicating that another code should be used, or detailed information is required. The coder in the oncology department assigned an unlisted HCPCS code, specifically, J3590, "Unclassified biologics," for treatment of senile macular degeneration of the retina, according to coverage instructions provided by the local Medicare contractor. The biller assumes the unlisted HCPCS code will be denied and on further review of the medical record, changes the code to J9035, "Bevacizumab." The claim is submitted and denied because of lack of medical necessity. Noting that an Advance Beneficiary Notice (ABN) was not secured from the patient, the charges are written off by the hospital.

In both of these cases, claims were not adjudicated properly because of a lack of communication between the coder and the biller. In the first case, the coder should have assisted the biller in the proper application of modifier 59. In the second case, the coder could have explained to the biller that the unlisted HCPCS code was the appropriate code assignment according to Medicare coverage guidelines, and the claim would have met medical necessity and been properly paid.

Payer-specific guidelines complicate the coding and billing guidelines when their guidelines differ from standard coding practice. This in turn can complicate the roles of the coder and the biller. Figure 1-1 identifies how five different payers require modifier 50, "Bilateral procedure," to be reported on the claim form.

One can easily see that coding for just a single modifier can be confusing when different payers have different reporting requirements. If the coder is asked to code "per the payer guidelines," that will require the coder to know with a high degree of certainty the patient's payer status. However, if the coder is asked to code bilateral procedures according to the coding guidelines, he or she will likely code the appropriate CPT code with modifier 50, "Bilateral procedure," appended. The billing office will have the responsibility to submit the claim information in the manner required by the payer so reimbursement can be appropriate. In most health care settings, coders should not be expected to know every payer's requirements for every possible billing scenario. Likewise, billers should not be expected to know all the coding guidelines and whether the codes submitted are based on the provider's documentation. Exceptions exist, of course, especially in smaller health care facilities, where a single individual will wear both the coder and biller hats.

Payer	Modifier 50 Usage	Number of Units	Example
Payer 1	CPT/HCPCS code with modifier 50	1 unit	69436-50 (1 unit)
Payer 2	CPT/HCPCS code on two line items with LT/RT	1 unit for each line item	69436-LT (1 unit) 69436-RT (1 unit)
Payer 3	CPT/HCPCS code on two line items, one with LT, one with modifier 50	1 unit for each line item	69436-LT (1 unit) 69436-50 (1 unit)
Payer 4	CPT/HCPCS code on two line items, with RT and LT and one item with modifier 50	1 unit for each line item	69436-RT (1 unit) 69436-50 LT (1 unit)
Payer 5	CPT/HCPCS code with modifier 50	2 units	69436-50 (2 units)

Figure 1-1 Payer Comparison of Modifier 50 Billing Requirements. *SOURCE: 2009 CPT © 2008 American Medical Association. All rights reserved. CPT is a registered trademark of the American Medical Association.*

The Importance of Coding Accuracy

Aside from the problem of fraudulent billing and coding and the risk of financial loss, why should we be concerned about the accuracy of the coding? To answer this question, we need to appreciate the integration of coding with health care data.

Health care information directly affects a number of sectors. A report by the Quality Assurance Project, a research group supported by the U.S. Agency for International Development's (USAID) Bureau for Global Health and Country Missions, suggests that the quality of health care data produced has a direct impact on the overall performance of health care delivery systems and ultimately, the population's health care status. Improving the quality of health care information improves the quality of health care provided in a community.

Coded data, that is, data derived from claims in the form of ICD-9-CM diagnosis and CPT/HCPCS codes, are used not only in adjudication of claims but also for health care statistics and policy planning. Coding information is used by health care organizations, epidemiologists, researchers, health care insurers, consumers, and others.

Coded data are used for clinical, financial, informational, and /consumer reasons. The integration of electronic information systems has enabled data to be used in a variety of ways. Clinically, coded data can assist physicians who use automatic warning systems to alert them to potentially adverse drug interactions or allergic reactions. Coded data can also be used in clinical decision-support systems. For example, a physician may be alerted when a patient is a tobacco user (ICD-9-CM diagnosis code 305.1) so that tobacco cessation counseling can occur. An electronic alert may be generated when a physician is prescribing medications for a patient with comorbid conditions. Additionally, coded data are used as clinical communication between providers. Many health record formats include problem lists with diagnoses listed, along with ICD-9-CM diagnosis codes. These codes are often used for ordering diagnostic tests.

Accurate coding data are essential for proper reimbursement, and federal regulations require accurate coding. Stiff penalties are assessed for fraud and abuse. One of the problems associated with linking coding with reimbursement is that the primary coding systems (ICD-9-CM and CPT) were not created for this purpose. Diseases were classified as early as the mid 1500s when burial information contained in church and public logs provided details on the causes of death. These records were intended to monitor diseases such as the bubonic plague. The International Classification of Diseases (ICD) traces its origins to the early 1900s and to the **Bertillon classification of causes of death** (Jacques Bertillon [1851–1922]), long before Medicare and Blue Cross/Blue Shield! ICD was created to list and classify diseases and causes of death for statistical purposes. CPT was created in 1966 because no other coding system existed at the time that adequately described physician services in the outpatient setting. CPT was used to communicate information for actuarial and statistical purposes and in a limited reimbursement role. CPT was not used on health care claims until 1983, when it was adopted as part of the Health Care Financing Administration's (HCFA) Common Procedure Coding System (HCPCS) for reporting services under Part B for Medicare services. Although both systems have evolved over the years, the systems cannot fully describe every health care service in every situation. For example, not every diagnostic condition can be exactly translated into an ICD-9-CM diagnosis code, nor can every procedure or service performed be explained completely by a CPT code. In those situations when an unlisted CPT code or a "not elsewhere classified" (NEC) diagnosis code is used, problems sometime arise with proper adjudication of the claim. But the unlisted, not elsewhere classified, or nonspecific code may still be the correct code to apply according to the classification system.

As will be discussed in later chapters, accurate coding is essential for proper reimbursement and for determining medical necessity. For some diagnostic tests and procedures, only specific ICD-9-CM diagnosis codes are considered medically necessary. Inaccurate coding of the procedure or the diagnosis can lead to unnecessary denials and lost reimbursement.

Accurately coded diagnoses and procedures are also important for financial rate setting and future reimbursements. Payment rates are often based on historical coded data. For example, payments for Medicare inpatient services in the **inpatient prospective payment system (IPPS)** are based on a number of factors, including wage indexes, cost of labor, and geographic factors. The payment system formula uses these factors as well as others to determine proper future payments for **Medicare Severity Diagnosis-Related Groups (MS-DRGs)**, which are based on ICD-9-CM diagnosis and procedure codes.

In the outpatient setting, Medicare payment rates are based on a similar formula but are more dependent on the CPT procedure code. In the **ambulatory surgical center setting (ASC)**, the payment rate for calendar year 2008 was 65% of the **outpatient prospective payment system (OPPS)** payment rates. Hospital outpatient rates are based on groups called **Ambulatory Payment Classifications (APCs).** Services in each APC are clinically similar in terms of the resources they require. For physician reimbursement, payment rates are based on three components: (1) **relative value units (RVUs),** (2) conversion factors, and (3) geographic practice cost indices. All these components are used in calculating a physician payment related to a specific CPT code. Both systems are heavily dependent on accurate CPT coding to reflect appropriate costs.

Billing information that includes costs and codes is used in future rate setting, making it essential that coding be accurate so the most accurate rate setting amount can be obtained. Coded data are also used to help identify fraudulent coding and billing practices. Today's coding is being translated into rate-setting data for tomorrow.

Linking Coding Accuracy with Data Quality

In recent years, coding has become increasingly important in reporting **quality measures.** In the 1999 report *To Err Is Human: Building a Safer Health System,* the Institute of Medicine (IOM) stated that **hospital-acquired conditions** and other medical errors may be responsible for as many as 98,000 deaths annually, the costs of which total $29 billion. Reports from the Centers for Disease Control and Prevention (CDC) estimate that approximately 1 in 10 hospitalized patients will acquire an infection after admission, with cost estimates of up to $6.7 billion annually. *(Economics and Preventing Hospital-Acquired Infection,* by Nicolas Graves, available at www.cdc.gov.)

The Deficit Reduction Act of 2005 (DRA) requires adjustments in payment to hospitals for inpatient services when patients develop certain hospital-acquired conditions. The conditions must meet the following definitions:

a. Are high cost or high volume or both,

b. Result in the assignment of a case to an MS-DRG that has a higher payment when present as a secondary diagnosis, and

c. Could reasonably have been prevented through the application of evidence-based guidelines.

Such measures are intended to link the quality of care provided to Medicare beneficiaries and payment for services. Under the Hospital-Acquired Condition (HAC) initiative, Medicare no longer pays hospitals at a higher rate for increased costs of care that result when a patient is harmed by one of several conditions that the patient did not have on admission. These conditions are determined to be reasonably preventable by following generally accepted guidelines. The conditions are reported by ICD-9-CM diagnosis codes. See Figure 1-2 for a listing of these conditions.

Another quality measure establishes uniform national policies that will prevent Medicare from paying for certain serious, preventable errors in medical care. These are termed **"never events"** and consist of the following:

- Wrong surgical or other invasive procedure performed on a patient

- Surgical or other invasive procedure performed on the wrong body part

- Surgical or other invasive procedure performed on the wrong patient

Whereas the hospital-acquired conditions affect payments to hospitals for inpatient stays, the "never events" affect payment to hospitals, physicians, and any other health care provider or supplier involved in the erroneous surgery or invasive procedure.

The 2006 Tax Relief and Health Care Act (TRHCA) (Public Law 109-432) established a physician quality reporting system. CMS developed the **Physician Quality Reporting Initiative (PQRI)** measures as a financial incentive for eligible providers to report quality measures. Physicians who report these measures receive a financial incentive of 1.5% of the total allowed charge for covered services payable under the Physician Fee Schedule (2008 figures). PQRI measures are reported with CPT, HCPCS, and ICD-9-CM diagnosis codes. Figure 1-3 lists some examples of PQRI measures.

Another incentive program for providers is the E-Prescribing Incentive Program, which provides monetary incentives for physicians who utilize electronic prescribing systems. All these measures are intended to increase patient safety and improve quality of care. With the increasing focus on associating quality reporting with payment, the responsibility for ensuring accurate coded data also increases dramatically.

Coded data are also used to provide information for benchmarking, research, improving the quality of health care, and evaluating health care systems. Although the use of health care data for such uses is sometimes controversial, many agree that quality health data can be beneficial, as when a population with a particular disease or condition is studied. Such research may lead to understanding of environmental or biological causes and may identify methods of early detection, preventive measures, and treatment.

Health data registries, including those that monitor cancer, birth defects, and strokes, rely heavily on coded data. Disease, operating, and physician indexes use coded data that are important for research, patient care, budgeting, benchmarking, and long-range planning.

Coded data also have a human element as individuals seek easier access to their own personal health information. Many providers use electronic health information systems that allow patients such access. An individual's health care data may include coded data that are shared with multiple providers, compiled into health information systems, and included on claims data. Inaccurate coding on claims can

Category	Condition	ICD-9-CM Code(s)
Serious preventable events	Object left in during surgery Air embolism Blood incompatibility	998.4 (CC) 998.7 (CC) 999.1 (MCC) 999.6 (CC)
Catheter-associated infections	Catheter-associated urinary tract infections	996.64 (CC) and *excludes* the following from acting as a CC/MCC: 112.2 (CC), 590.10 (CC), 590.11 (MCC), 590.2 (MCC), 590.3 (CC), 590.80 (CC), 590.81 (CC), 595.0 (CC), 597.0 (CC), 599.0 (CC)
Pressure ulcers stages III & IV	Pressure ulcers	707.23 (MCC) 707.24 (MCC)
Vascular catheter-associated infection	Vascular catheter-associated infection	999.31 (CC)
Surgical site infection	Mediastinitis after coronary artery bypass graft (CABG) surgery Surgical site infection following certain orthopedic procedures Surgical site infection following bariatric surgery for obesity	519.2 (MCC) and one of the following procedure codes: 36.10–36.19 996.67 (CC) 998.59 (CC), and one of the following procedure codes: 81.01–81.08, 81.23–81.24, 81.31–81.83, 81.83, 81.85 *Principal Diagnosis:* 278.01 998.59 (CC), and one of the following procedure codes: 44.38, 44.39, or 44.95
Falls and trauma	Fractures, Dislocations, Intracranial injuries, Crushing injuries, Burn, Electric shock	Codes within these ranges on the CC/MCC list: 800–829 830–839 850–854 925–929 940–949 991–994
Staphylococcus aureus septicemia	*Staphylococcus aureus* septicemia	038.11 plus 995.91, 998.59, 999.3
Thrombosis and embolism	Deep vein thrombosis (DVT)/ pulmonary embolism (PE) following certain orthopedic procedures	415.11 (MCC) 415.19 (MCC) 453.40–453.42 (MCC), and one of the following procedure codes: 00.85–00.87, 81.51–81.52, or 81.54
Manifestations of poor glycemic control	Certain Diabetic Complications	250.10–250.13 (MCC) 250.20–250.23 (MCC) 251.0 (CC) 249.10–249.11 (MCC) 249.20–249.21 (MCC)

Figure 1-2 Hospital-Acquired Conditions. Inpatient prospective payment system (IPPS) hospitals will not receive additional payment for cases in which one of the selected conditions was not present on admission. The case will be paid as though the secondary diagnoses were not present. *SOURCE: Courtesy of the Centers for Medicare Services, www.cms.hhs.gov.*

result in inappropriate denial of payment and partial or total loss of coverage. There are reported cases in which patients were refused health insurance because of coded information in their claims data history. Unfortunately, sometimes the coded information was in error.

Consumers of health care depend on the medical coding and billing information to be accurate. Complex regulations, various pricing calculations, negotiated costs, and a lack of standardization lead

Acute Episode of Care

CHEST PAIN

Measure #54: Electrocardiogram Performed for Non-Traumatic Chest Pain

- **Reporting Description:** Percentage of patients aged 40 years and older with an emergency department discharge diagnosis of non-traumatic chest pain and an applicable CPT Category II code for each episode of non-traumatic chest pain occurring during the reporting period

- **Performance Description:** Percentage of patients aged 40 years and older with an emergency department discharge diagnosis of non-traumatic chest pain who had a 12-lead electrocardiogram (ECG) performed

Eligible Cases:

Patient aged ≥ 40 years on date of encounter	23
AND	
Place of Service (POS) = Emergency Dept (23)	**AND**
AND	
Discharge diagnosis of non-traumatic chest pain (ICD-9)	413.0, 413.1, 413.9, 786.50, 786.51, 786.52, 786.59
AND	**AND**
Patient encounter during reporting period (CPT)	99281, 99282, 99283, 99284, 99285, 99291

Management of Chronic
Conditions

DIABETES

Measure #1: Hemoglobin A1c Poor Control in Type 1 or 2 Diabetes Mellitus

- **Reporting Description:** Percentage of patients aged 18 through 75 years with diabetes mellitus and an applicable CPT Category II code reported a minimum of once during the reporting period

- **Performance Description:** Percentage of patients aged 18 through 75 years with diabetes mellitus who had most recent hemoglobin A1c greater than 9.0%

Eligible Cases:

Patient aged ≥ 18 and ≤ 75 years on date of encounter	250.00, 250.01, 250.02, 250.03, 250.10, 250.11, 250.12, 250.13, 250.20, 250.21, 250.22, 250.23, 250.30, 250.31, 250.32, 250.33, 250.40, 250.41, 250.42, 250.43, 250.50, 250.51, 250.52, 250.53, 250.60, 250.61, 250.62, 250.63, 250.70, 250.71, 250.72, 250.73, 250.80, 250.81, 250.82, 250.83, 250.90, 250.91, 250.92, 250.93, 648.00, 648.01, 648.02, 648.03, 648.04
AND	
Diagnosis of diabetes mellitus (ICD-9)	**AND**
AND	97802, 97803, 97804, 99201, 99202, 99203, 99204, 99205, 99211, 99212, 99213, 99214, 99215, 99304, 99305, 99306, 99307, 99308, 99309, 99310, 99324, 99325, 99326, 99327, 99328, 99334, 99335, 99336, 99337, 99341, 99342, 99343, 99344, 99345, 99347, 99348, 99349, 99350, G0270, G0271
Patient encounter during reporting period (CPT or HCPCS)	

Figure 1-3 Examples of Physician Quality Reporting Measures. *NOTE: Entire measures are not listed; only specific portions that address coding are presented. SOURCE: Centers for Medicare & Medicaid Services, Coding for Quality: A Handbook for PQRI Participation, http://www.cms.hhs.gov/PQRI/31_PQRIToolkit.asp*

to billing errors. Although estimates of claim errors vary, their increasing number has created an industry devoted just to helping consumers review their medical bills and detect billing errors. Consumers are often frustrated by the lack of answers to questions about the billing and coding on their claims, often hearing different answers from providers and payers. Many coders and billers can relate a conversation with a patient who told them, "The insurance company said you coded it wrong!"

Summary

Coding and billing have many overlapping characteristics but some differences as well. Both the coder and biller need to appreciate the importance of accurate health care data beyond just getting an individual claim paid. The demand for professional coding and billing professionals is increasing. Demand for accurate claims data by governmental entities, health care providers, the health care industry, and individuals is also increasing. The need for accurate coding data is essential for reimbursement and for quality health care data.

Coders and billers can develop an appreciation of each others' roles when there is open communication between the departments. Discussing coding and billing issues in an environment that encourages collaboration can reduce coding and billing compliance risks.

Chapter Review

1. Describe the importance of quality medical data in relationship to the quality of health care in a given population.

    _____

    _____

    _____

2. Define *medical coding.*

    _____

    _____

    _____

3. Define *medical billing.*

    _____

    _____

    _____

4. Identify common classification systems used in coding for reimbursement.

    _____

    _____

    _____

5. A claim that has been successfully adjudicated means that the claim is accurate. Identify whether this is a true or a false statement, and give your reasoning.

    _____

    _____

    _____

6. Explain the risks of "aggressive" billing, and identify potential compliance issues that may arise when coding and billing are not distinct.

    _____

    _____

    _____

7. Visit the Web site of the National Institutes of Health (NIH) (www.nih.gov) or of the Centers for Disease Control and Prevention (www.cdc.gov). Review a recent news release or research article addressing a specific health care finding or study. Identify how coding may have been used to generate the findings and the importance of accurate coding in this example.

_____

_____

_____

8. Conduct an Internet search of medical coding and billing certification programs. Compare and contrast at least two programs, including prerequisites, program content, cost, certification, continuing-education requirements, and professional ethical standards. Are the programs "coding" or "billing" programs or both? What are the strengths and weaknesses of each?

_____

_____

_____

9. Investigate one of the quality initiatives currently supported by Medicare (www.cms.hhs.gov). Is reimbursement tied to the quality initiative? Describe the importance of accurate coding in the quality initiative.

_____

_____

_____

10. Write a policy statement for a health care facility on how claim issues involving coding and billing issues should be resolved. For example, if a claim is denied for apparent coding reasons, who should resolve the issue?

_____

_____

_____

Case Studies

Case Study 1

The hospital billing office notices a sudden increase in the number of units of a certain pharmaceutical that are being reported and billed. Further investigation reveals that the pharmacy's software billing system has been inaccurately calculating the units for the drug. A review of past claims that were billed with this drug shows that there may have been problems with the number of units billed for the past six months.

1. What steps should be taken to correct the billing error?

   _____

   _____

   _____

2. Will the provider need to notify the payers involved?

   _____

   _____

   _____

3. What are the compliance risks?

   _____

   _____

   _____

Case Study 2

During a coding review, it is found that a patient inadvertently had a coded diagnosis of HIV infection, ICD-9-CM diagnosis code 042, listed as a secondary diagnosis. The documentation does not support the diagnosis. The reviewer assumes that the coder made a keying error, as the patient did have a documented diagnosis of injury to the femoral vein, ICD-9-CM diagnosis code 904.2.

1. What steps should be taken to correct the coding?

   _____

   _____

   _____

2. Does the patient or payer need to be contacted?

   _____

   _____

   _____

3. What are the compliance risks?

_____

_____

_____

Case Study 3

The coders in a large physician group practice apply CPT modifier 50, "Bilateral procedure," to codes indicating that a bilateral procedure was performed. For example, the coders will enter 69436-50 into the billing system for a bilateral tympanostomy. The billing office staff know that certain payers require bilateral codes to be listed on two separate line items, with modifier 50 appended only to the second listed code. The biller changes the 69436-50 to 69436 and 69436-50.

1. Are the biller's actions appropriate?

_____

_____

_____

2. Is the coding compliant?

_____

_____

_____

3. What are the compliance risks?

_____

_____

_____

Case Study 4

A payer does not consider unlisted CPT procedure codes to be covered services. Therefore, the payer will either require the provider to change the coding to be paid or will change the code to a lesser-priced procedure in the same code category.

1. What are the provider's options?

_____

_____

_____

2. Should the provider change the coding?

_____

_____

_____

3. Has the payer acted compliantly?

_____

_____

_____

4. What are the compliance risks and who is responsible?

_____

_____

_____

Case Study 5

A hospital coding department has a goal of coding and abstracting inpatient records within five days of discharge. The hospital's chief financial officer believes the coding should be completed within three days of discharge, regardless of whether the documentation of the discharge summary, history and physical, and operative reports have been completed.

1. What are the potential compliance and financial risks of this policy?

_____

_____

_____

2. What is a reasonable time frame for coding?

_____

_____

_____

References

American Hospital Association. *The importance of coding.* Web site: http://www.ahacentraloffice.org

Centers for Medicare & Medicaid Services. Acute inpatient PPS. Web site: http://www.cms.hhs.gov/AcuteinpatientPPS

Centers for Medicare & Medicaid Services. 2008 *Coding for quality handbook.* Web site: http://www.cms.hhs.gov/PQRI/31_PQRIToolkit.asp

Centers for Medicare & Medicaid Services. Hospital outpatient PPS. Web site: http://www.cms.hhs.gov/hospitaloutpatientPPS

Centers for Medicare & Medicaid Services. Physician quality reporting initiative. Web site: http://www.cms.hhs.gov/pqri

Garvin, Jennifer, PhD, RHIA, CPHQ, CCS, CTR, FAHIMA, and Mark Weiner, MD 2006. Uses of coded and administrative data: Implications for code assignment and research. Chicago: American Health Information Management Association. Web site: http://www.ahima.org

Health information system module. In Islam, Mursaleena (Ed.). (2007). *Health systems assessment approach: A how-to manual* (pp. 11–11 and 11–12). Submitted to the U.S. Agency for International Development in collaboration with Health Systems 20/20, Partners for Health Reform*plus*, Quality Assurance Project, and Rational Pharmaceutical Management Plus. Arlington, VA: Management Sciences for Health. Web site: http://www.healthsystems2020.org/content/resource/detail/528/

Institute of Medicine. (1999, November). *To err is human: Building a safer health system.* Web site: http://www.iom.edu/?id=12735

Rational Pharmaceutical Management Plus Center for Pharmaceutical Management Sciences for Health. (2007, February). *Health systems assessment manual: A how-to approach.* Web site: http://www.qaproject.org

Health Systems Assessment Approach—A How-To Manual, published by the Quality Assurance Project. Web site: www.qaproject.org

Coding Compliance

Objectives

At the completion of this chapter, the learner should be able to:

- Define health care fraud and abuse.
- Discuss the purpose of the False Claims Act and its impact on coding professionals.
- Describe the purpose of the Health Insurance Portability and Accountability Act of 1996 (HIPAA) and its impact on coding compliance.
- Define key terms including *upcoding, unbundling,* and *coding "creep."*
- Identify the key attributes of the Anti-Kickback Statute and the Stark law.
- Identify the sources of "official" and "unofficial" coding advice.
- Recognize the importance of the HIPAA Transactions and Code Set Regulations, identifying valid code sets and penalties for misuse.
- Describe the purpose of the National Correct Coding Initiative (NCCI) edits and correlation to compliant coding.

Key Terms

abuse	downcoding	Office of Inspector General (OIG)	*qui tam*
Administrative Simplification	False Claims Act	official code sets	Stark law
Anti-Kickback Statute	fraud	Public Law 104–191, Health Insurance Portability and Accountability Act (HIPAA)	unbundling
clustering	medically unlikely edits (MUEs)		upcoding
coding and billing advice	National Correct Coding Initiative (NCCI) edits		

Defining Fraud and Abuse

News reports of both alleged and actual health care fraud have been plentiful in recent years. Long before Public Law 104-91, the Health Insurance Portability and Accountability Act (HIPAA) was enacted in August 2006, the federal government was actively investigating reports of fraud and abuse in health care. Indeed, many of these investigations directly influenced the HIPAA regulation that includes specific legislation designed to reduce the amount of health care fraud.

Health care programs, payers, and providers may be subject to allegations of fraud. This includes physicians, physical therapists, psychologists, podiatrists, dentists, hospitals, nursing homes, assisted living centers, home health care, durable medical equipment suppliers, pharmacies, insurance companies, billing services, and even patients themselves. Health care fraud investigation is not limited to Medicare claims. Fraudulent schemes have been identified and prosecuted on behalf of Medicaid programs and commercial payers as well. It has been estimated that 10% of the annual $2 trillion health care industry is involved in fraudulent activity.

Consider the following examples:

- A physician was found to have provided excessive narcotic prescriptions, including OxyContin, to patients in exchange for which the patients agreed to have unnecessary nerve block injections. The physician also insisted that patients schedule visits weekly, which in some cases rendered the patients addicted to the drugs he prescribed. The physician's actions directly resulted in the death of two of his patients. The physician was convicted of 57 counts of health care fraud, including two counts of health care fraud resulting in death, which carries a mandatory life prison sentence.

- A podiatrist was indicted on 43 counts, including filing false claims, wire fraud, and health care fraud for allegedly submitting false claims for diabetic shoes provided to Medicare patients. The false claims totaled more than $500,000.00. The physician faces up to 20 years of prison time if convicted.

- A dentist pleaded guilty to health care fraud, admitting that he filed false claims to commercial payers for dental services that were never performed. For example, claims showed that four impacted wisdom teeth were extracted, but only two were actually taken out. The dentist was also charged with performing unnecessary procedures. The dentist was ordered to pay restitution and was sentenced to 3 years' probation.

- A billing service was found guilty of overbilling Medicare and other governmental payers by millions of dollars from 1992 to 1995. The scheme involved billing for more than 100 emergency physician groups that spanned 33 states. The billing service, founded and owned by a physician, was charged with regularly upcoding claims and billing for services more extensive than those actually provided by physicians. The federal government and individual states collected millions of dollars from the billing service and the physician groups who utilized the services of the company. The suit was initially filed under terms of the *qui tam* provisions of the False Claims Act, which is explained in the following section.

The False Claims Act

The **False Claims Act** was enacted in the United States in 1863 and is sometimes referred to as the "Lincoln law." During the Civil War the government found that its contractors were often corrupt and becoming "proverbially and notoriously rich."

In an investigation of the goods and services purchased by the Union Army, it was noted that:

> For sugar, [the government] often got sand; for coffee, rye; for leather, something no better than brown paper; for sound horses and mules, spavined beasts and dying donkeys; and for serviceable muskets and pistols, the experimental failures of sanguine inventors, or the refuse of shops and foreign armories.

Congress enacted the False Claims Act with President Lincoln's strong support. The act allows private individuals (referred to as "relators") to bring suit on their own behalf as well as on behalf of the government in issues related to fraudulent or false claims. These are referred to as *qui tam* or *whistle-blower* actions. *Qui tam* is an abbreviation of the Latin phrase *"qui tam pro domino rege quam pro sic ipso in hoc parte sequitur,"* which means, "who as well for the king as for himself sues in this matter." The False Claims Act established three important principles: (1) it allowed individuals the right to bring suit on questions of fraud; (2) it provided monetary rewards for disclosure of information; and (3) it provided the government with additional means of monitoring its internal contractors.

Even the False Claims Act itself is not immune to abuse, however. It became apparent in the 1940s that private individuals were taking advantage of the act by disclosing information that was already known to the government or already investigated. In 1943 an amendment allowed the government to take over a *qui tam* action. It also reduced the relator's recovery from 50% to 25% if the government did not step in, or 10% if the government did take over the case. Furthermore, the amendment increased the relator's burden of proof. These amendments greatly reduced the number of *qui tam* actions that were brought to the courts.

As a result of the reduced number of claims filed and an increase in highly publicized contractor fraud cases, more amendments were enacted in the 1980s. The 1986 amendment increased the monetary penalties to three times the amount of damages and increased the penalty per claim from $2000 to $5000–$10,000 per false claim. The amendment included provisions that attorney fees be included and paid by the defendant. There were also whistleblower safeguards including protection against firing or other forms of retaliation, and provisions for reinstatements and back pay. Although further amendments to the False Claims Act are currently being debated, the act has essentially been successful. Since 1986, billions of dollars have been recovered by the Medicare program, a large number of which resulted from *qui tam* actions.

The False Claims Act provides liability for certain acts committed by an individual who:

- Knowingly presents, or causes to be presented, to an office or employee of the United States Government . . . a false or fraudulent claim for payment or approval;

- Knowingly makes, uses, or causes to be made or used, a false record or statement to get a false or fraudulent claim paid or approved by the government;

- Conspires to defraud the government by getting a false or fraudulent claim allowed or paid;

- Has possession, custody, or control of property or money used, or to be used, by the government and intends to conceal the property or delivers less property than the amount for which the person received money;

- Is authorized to make or deliver a document certifying receipt of property used, or to be used, by the government and intending to defraud the government, makes or delivers the receipt without completely knowing that the information on the receipt is true;

- Knowingly buys, or receives as a pledge of an obligation or debt of an obligation or debt, public property from an officer or employee of the government . . . who lawfully may not sell or pledge the property;

- Knowingly makes, uses, or causes to be made or used, a false record or statement to conceal, avoid, or decrease an obligation to pay or transmit money or property to the government.

The False Claims Act defines "knowing" and "knowingly" to mean that "a person, with respect to the information—(1) has actual knowledge of the information; (2) acts in deliberate ignorance of the truth or falsity of the information; or (3) acts in reckless disregard of the truth or falsity of the information and no proof of specific intent to defraud is required" (31 USC 3729[b]).

The real examples of illegal cases noted at the beginning of this chapter are obvious and egregious forms of health care fraud and deception. Many would agree that such actions are not part of the normal operations for the majority of health care providers. These examples constitute **fraud,** which is defined by the Centers for Medicare & Medicaid Services (CMS) as:

> "the intentional deception or misrepresentation that the individual knows to be false or does not believe to be true, and the individual makes knowing that the deception could result in some unauthorized benefit to himself/herself or some other person" (Medicare Program Integrity Manual Exhibits, www.cms.hhs.gov).

But what about less-flagrant situations than the ones noted earlier? Can a provider be found guilty of fraud resulting from a computer error that accidentally duplicated a charge on a claim? Is a coder guilty of fraud if a code is transposed when entered into the billing system?

Consider the following scenario: The documentation in the medical record indicates that a diagnostic colonoscopy was performed (CPT code 45378). The coder mistakenly inputted the code for a colonoscopy with a snare polypectomy (CPT code 45385). The polypectomy procedure is reimbursed at a higher rate than the diagnostic procedure. Has the coder committed fraud?

The definition of fraud from *Black's Law Dictionary,* 6th edition is:

> "A false representation of a matter of fact, whether by words or by conduct, by false or misleading allegations, or by concealment of that which should have been disclosed, which deceives and is intended to deceive another..."

Elements of the legal definition of fraud include:

- False representation of a present or past fact

- Suppression of truth

- "Bad faith"

- Intentional deceit

- Obtaining advantage over another by false suggestions or by suppression of the truth

The following are examples of fraud per Medicare taken from the *Medicare Program Integrity Manual,* Chapter 4, Benefit Integrity:

- Incorrectly reporting diagnoses or procedures to maximize payments.

- Billing for services not furnished or supplies not provided. This includes billing Medicare for appointments that the patient did not keep.

- Duplicate billing, for example, billing both Medicare and the beneficiary for the same service, or billing both Medicare and another insurer in an attempt to receive payment twice.

- Altering claim forms, electronic claim records, or medical documentation to obtain a higher payment amount.

- Soliciting, offering, or receiving a kickback, bribe, or rebate.

- Paying for a referral of patients in exchange for ordering diagnostic tests and other services or medical equipment.

- Unbundling or "exploding" charges.

- Completing Certificate of Necessity (CMNs) for patients not personally and professionally known to the provider.

- Participating in schemes that result in higher costs or charges to the Medicare program.

- Billing for "gang visits." For example, a physician visits a nursing home and bills for 20 nursing home visits without furnishing specific services to individual patients.

- Misrepresenting dates and descriptions of services furnished or the identity of the beneficiary or the individual who furnished the service.

- Billing noncovered or nonchargeable services as covered items.

- Repeatedly violating the participation agreement, assignment agreement, and the limitation amount.

- Using another person's Medicare card to obtain medical care.

- Giving false information about provider ownership in a clinical laboratory.

- Using the adjustment payment process to generate fraudulent payments.

Health Insurance Portability and Accountability Act of 1996

The **Administrative Simplification** provisions of HIPAA (Title II) require that the Department of Health and Human Services (HHS) develop national standards for electronic health care transactions. HIPAA also addresses the security and privacy of health data. The purpose of HIPAA is to promote standardization and efficiency in the health care industry. Additionally, the law was enacted to provide consumers with greater access to health care insurance and to protect the privacy of health care data.

Under HIPAA, a "health care offense" is defined as "a violation of, or a criminal conspiracy to violate, any provisions of a health care benefit program, which includes health care fraud, embezzlement, false statements, and obstruction." The statute applies to persons or entities that "know or should know" that an offense has occurred. The HIPAA definition of "should know" "means that a person with respect to information—(A) acts in deliberate ignorance of the truth or falsity of the information; or (B) acts in reckless disregard of the truth or falsity of the information, and no proof of specific intent to defraud is required" (42 USC1320a-7a[i], as amended by subsection [h][2]). Furthermore, a person "who engages in a pattern or practice of presenting or causing to be presented a claim for an item or service that is based on a code that the person knows or should know will result in a greater payment to the person than the code the person knows or should know is applicable to the item or service actually being provided" is subject to civil monetary penalties. The act discusses fraudulent activities similar to those in the preceding legal definition, including making false pretenses, representations, statements, or promises.

The issue of intent has been used to distinguish between health care *fraud* and health care *abuse.* **Abuse** is defined as the lack of intent to deceive. The *Medicare Program Integrity Manual* defines abuse as "billing Medicare for services that are not covered or are not correctly coded." The CMS Web site includes another definition: "payment for items or services that are billed by mistake by providers, but should not be paid for by Medicare." The Medicaid program offers a definition that includes practices that are not consistent with sound business or medical practice and that may result in unnecessary cost to the Medicaid program. It also includes reimbursement for services that are not medically necessary or those that fail to meet professionally recognized standards of health care.

Whether intentional or not, providers must disclose and return any overpayments to Medicare that result from mistaken or erroneous claims (42 USC 1320-7b(a)(3)). The **Office of Inspector General (OIG)** publishes a Supplemental Compliance Program Guidance for Hospitals, which notes that unintentional misapplication of coding and billing guidelines may also give rise to overpayments or liability for providers that have developed a pattern of inappropriate billing. Because the OIG and the Department of Justice (DOJ) aggressively investigate health care fraud for the Medicaid program, such disclosures should also include state Medicaid programs.

Fraudulent Coding and Billing

Investigations of health care fraud and abuse have yielded dozens of examples of fraudulent coding and billing schemes. Some of the most common examples include the following:

- Billing for services not rendered
- Providing insufficent or no documentation to support that a service was performed
- Upcoding
- Unbundling
- Making inappropriate referrals or self-referrals
- Falsifying claim information or giving false information
- Billing for services that are not covered or not medically necessary

Billing for services that have never been performed is an obvious fraudulent practice, yet this is an all-too-common occurrence. Facilities that link charges to orders are especially susceptible. For example, if a charge is linked to a specific lab test that is ordered but not on the actual completed service, the charge may be included on the claim. Items that are ordered may not be carried out for a number of reasons (for example, change in physician orders or patient condition). If the charge is linked to the final report or at the conclusion of the lab test, the charge is more likely to be appropriate. Fraud can also exist when the provider is unable to provide documentation that supports the service billed, even though it may indeed have been performed. The phrase "not documented, not done" applies in this case. Documentation that is incomplete or illegible can also lead to improper coding.

The OIG's Compliance Program Guide for Hospitals states:

> Hospitals should also review their outpatient documentation practices to ensure that claims are based on complete medical records and that the medical record supports the level of service claimed. . . . Coding from incomplete medical records may create problems in complying with this claim submission requirement. Moreover, submitting claims for services that are not supported by the medical record may also result in the submission of improper claims.

Similar language is also found in the (⋯ ⋯-group physician
practices: "written standards and proced⋯ ⋯based on
medical record documentation."

Upcoding involves coding services⋯ ⋯rvice performed
or coding a more intensive procedure ⋯ ⋯etimes called
"coding creep" or "DRG creep." In mc⋯ ⋯formed, but an
inaccurate code is used to report the⋯ ⋯oding. The following
are some common examples of upc⋯

- A physician performs and dc⋯ ⋯) service that
  includes an expanded probl⋯ ⋯cal decision making of
  low complexity. According t⋯ ⋯However, the service
  is coded and billed to 992⋯ ⋯d examination and
  medical decision making⋯

- A 20–30 minute individu⋯ ⋯umented but coded as a
  45–60 minute service.

- A patient presents to t⋯ ⋯hysician applies a splint
  and recommends that⋯ ⋯pedic clinic for definitive
  treatment. The emergency ⋯ ⋯care, rather than the
  splinting service, resulting in higher re⋯

- A dentist provides nitrous oxide as an analgesic but ⋯ ⋯ges on the claim for a general
  anesthetic.

- A patient with chronic obstructive asthmatic bronchitis is admitted into the hospital with
  pneumonia. Several cultures are obtained to determine the bacterial source of the pneumonia,
  but none of the tests are conclusive. The physician documents that the patient is at risk for
  aspiration. The coder assumes that the patient has aspiration pneumonia and assigns the
  diagnosis code 507.0, "Aspiration pneumonia." As a result, the hospital is reimbursed at a
  higher DRG rate than appropriate because the appropriate pneumonia diagnosis code, 486,
  "Pneumonia, unspecified," was not used.

Although not commonly considered fraudulent billing, **downcoding** by a health care provider may be
considered a fraudulent incentive practice. Often, this is unintentional. For example, the physician may
not fully understand the coding guidelines for accurately applying evaluation and management levels.
Some providers downcode from fear of retaliation from payers and auditors. Providers may downcode
for some patients, and not others, based on sympathy for the patient or the patient's inability to pay.
Although not frequently prosecuted, this practice is strongly discouraged and could be considered
fraudulent by providing unfair incentives to elicit patients. Such practices have obvious repercussions
on the finances of the provider.

To further illustrate downcoding as an unfair incentive practice, consider the following
example:

National coverage guidelines exist for Medicare patients undergoing routine foot/nail care. Because
there is typically no Medicare payment associated with routine foot care, Clinic A decides to
routinely write off the service. In actuality, it is providing this as a free service to Medicare patients.
Meanwhile Clinic B is also aware that Medicare does not pay for routine foot care. It presents an
Advance Beneficiary Notice (ABN) (discussed later in the text) to its Medicare patients, thereby
making the services patient liability. Clinic A may be found guilty of violating the Anti-Kickback
Statute by soliciting patients (the Anti-Kickback Statute is discussed later in this chapter),
whereas Clinic B is appropriately following the guidelines for noncovered Medicare services.

Another type of downcoding occurs when third-party payers reduce the payment to providers by changing codes to a lower-paying or less complex code than was reported. For example, some payers may automatically downcode an evaluation and management code based on the diagnosis submitted. Some cases have been challenged in the courts, such as *Love v. Blue Cross Blue Shield Association et al.*, which was settled in 2007. In that case, a number of major commercial health insurers were found to have improperly denied or reduced payments to physicians by inappropriately bundling, downcoding, or rejecting claims. Remarkably, some provider agreements with payers may even allow such a practice. It is important that provider agreements with payers outline any downcoding issues and the payer's compliance with coding guidelines. It is also important that health care providers regularly review claim reimbursement to ensure that the provider's payment is appropriate.

"Clustering" is a practice that may involve both upcoding and downcoding. This practice involves coding one or two middle levels of services (such as evaluation and management services) exclusively, under the philosophy that some will actually be higher and some lower. The belief is that the services will average out over a period of time. This practice results in overcharging (upcoding) some patients while undercharging (downcoding) others.

Unbundling or "exploding" charges commonly refers to fragmenting or coding a packaged or bundled service or procedure based on its individual components. Unintentional unbundling is often a result of misunderstanding of the coding guidelines. However, unbundling can be intentional when the purpose is to receive additional reimbursement for services that should have been packaged. The following are examples of unbundling of services:

- The physician performs and documents a colonoscopy. The documentation indicates that a polyp was removed by snare technique. The physician assigned CPT code 45378 for the diagnostic colonoscopy, and 45385 for the polypectomy by snare technique. The therapeutic colonoscopy (45385) includes the diagnostic colonoscopy (45378), so separate reporting of both services is inappropriate.

- An electrolyte panel is ordered and performed. The electrolyte panel (CPT code 80051) includes carbon dioxide, chloride (blood), potassium (serum), and sodium (serum). The laboratory bills for the electrolyte panel and an additional potassium (serum) test (CPT code 84132). Because the panel includes the potassium (serum) test it is inappropriate to separately bill for an additional potassium (serum) test unless the test was ordered and performed separately at a different time.

- A bilateral mammography is ordered and performed (CPT code 77056). The radiologist inappropriately reports the bilateral service as 77055 RT and 77055 LT. Because a code exists for the bilateral service, that code should be utilized rather than two unilateral codes.

- A physician performs an operation that has a 90-day global period. The surgical global period typically includes the procedure, anesthesia (local infiltration, digital block, or topical anesthesia), one related evaluation and management (E/M) service that occurs after the decision for surgery, immediate postoperative care, writing notes and dictating operative reports, evaluating the patient postanesthesia, and typical postoperative follow-up care. The physician sees the patient in the office two weeks following surgery and bills the E/M service (no additional problems or complications are documented). The physician has unbundled the surgical package by separately billing for the follow-up care.

- An ENT physician performs a septoplasty and submucous resection of inferior turbinates. During the global period, the physician sees the patient and performs a diagnostic nasal endoscopy procedure to check and remove any postsurgical clots. The physician appends modifier 79,

"Unrelated procedure or service by the same physician during the postoperative period." The endoscopy procedure is considered a routine postoperative service that follows many sinus surgeries. Thus, use of the modifier to unbundle the diagnostic endoscopy is not appropriate.

Over the past few years, health care fraud settlements and judgments have accounted for the majority of dollars returned to the federal government. The nonprofit organization Taxpayers Against Fraud (www.taf.org) estimated that in 2006, for every $1 invested in health-related enforcement activities, $15 was returned to the government. Individual states have also enacted laws to prevent health care fraud. The Omnibus Deficit Reduction Act of 2005 provides financial incentives to states that pass False Claims Acts.

Falsifying claim information or giving false information commonly includes incorrect billing practices. According to Medicare this is the most frequent kind of health care fraud. Violators may include providers, beneficiaries, and employees of providers. For example, a service provided entirely by a nurse is billed as though it were provided by a physician. In another case a hospital receives inappropriate MS-DRG reimbursement because the hospital fails to accurately report the patient's discharge disposition. (Under the MS-DRG [Medicare Severity Diagnosis-Related] system, reimbursement to a hospital may be different if the patient was transferred to another acute care hospital versus discharged to a nursing facility or to home.)

Billing for services that are not covered or not medically necessary includes falsifying information to make services appear to be medically necessary. Billing Medicare for services that are not medically necessary is a violation of the False Claims Act. For instance, a radiology service is ordered and performed for a patient, but the documentation does not support a diagnosis that would be considered covered under a local or national coverage decision. The claim is nonetheless submitted with a diagnosis that is covered, and reimbursement is made. In another case covered diagnoses are listed on a requisition or encounter form but not supported in the medical record documentation. In these two examples, the documentation is incomplete or lacking sufficient detail to support medical necessity. The procedure provided may actually be considered medically necessary, but medical necessity is not supported in the patient's medical record. Medical necessity, discussed in detail in Chapter 4, is defined by Medicare in several publications such as the *Medicare Benefit Policy Manual,* the *Medicare National Coverage Decision Manual,* and various program transmittals.

Health care providers are not the only entities that can fall under health care fraud and abuse schemes. Third-party payers, especially those that process claims for government-sponsored plans, may also be guilty of committing health care fraud. Examples include automatically downcoding or bundling services, failing to pay for medically necessary services, failing or refusing to recognize CPT modifiers, providing false or misleading information on denial guidelines, refusing to disclose fee schedules, failing to respond to beneficiary inquiries, and failing to pay claims within the contractual time periods.

Even patients may commit health care fraud by falsifying documents to obtain Medicare coverage or using another beneficiary's name and Medicare card.

The Anti-Kickback Statute and the Stark Law

Inappropriate referrals or self-referrals fall under two complex anti-kickback and self-referral statutes known as the **Anti-Kickback Statute** (Section 1128B of the Social Security Act, 42 USC § 1320a-7b) and the **Stark law** (Section 1877 of the Social Security Act, 42 USC § 1395nn). The Anti-Kickback Statute makes it a criminal offense to knowingly and willfully offer to pay, solicit, or receive any payment or to induce or reward referrals of items or services reimbursed by the Medicare program. The Stark law is a Medicare payment rule named after Representative Fortney "Pete" Stark (Dem.,

California). Generally, the Stark law prohibits a physician from making any referral to another provider or health service if the physician (or an immediate family member) has a financial or compensation relationship with that provider or health service. The intent of the Stark law is to prevent billing Medicare for services that resulted from self-referrals or kickbacks. For example, if a physician is part owner of a rehabilitation clinic, the physician may not refer a Medicare or Medicaid patient to that rehabilitation clinic and bill for the service. Other prohibited financial arrangements include leasing office space below market rates or being reimbursed for services above market rates. Common areas of risk are physician practices that provide clinical laboratories, X-ray facilities, and other ancillary businesses that offer services to Medicare beneficiaries. Many laboratory and radiology services (including both technical and professional components) are considered services for which the physician self-referral prohibition applies. CMS publishes annually the list of CPT and HCPCS codes that apply to physician self-referral prohibition. There are some exceptions for in-office ancillary services, such as the availability of other such services in the area. Interestingly, another exception is e-prescribing and electronic health record software. These exceptions were made in an effort to encourage physician use of these technologies.

Violations of the Stark law include civil monetary penalties of up to $100,000 for each violation and possible exclusion from the Medicare program. The DOJ has prosecuted violations of the Stark law under the False Claims Act. The Stark law, including the recent Phase III final rule, is highly complex legislation, and legal counsel should be obtained for advisory opinions.

Penalties for Fraudulent Billing and Coding

There are several federal, state, and local agencies that participate in efforts to investigate health care fraud in addition to the CMS, the OIG, and the DOJ. These include the Food and Drug Administration (FDA), the Federal Bureau of Investigation (FBI), the Drug Enforcement Agency (DEA), and the Internal Revenue Service (IRS). Other private agencies include the National Health Care Anti-Fraud Association (NHCAA), the National Insurance Crime Bureau (NICB), the Blue Cross and Blue Shield Association (BCBSA), the American Association of Retired Persons (AARP), and the Coalition Against Insurance Fraud. Given that health care expenditures total more than $2 trillion per year, it is easy to see why these influential agencies are motivated to investigate potential fraud and abuse cases.

All cases of potential Medicare fraud are referred to the OIG for review and any potential criminal or civil actions, including monetary penalties (restitution and fines) or other sanctions. Violations may include imprisonment for certain violations. Administrative sanctions such as suspension or exclusion from the Medicare program may be imposed. Exclusion from the Medicare program means that no payment is made for items or services furnished by the excluded entity. The extent of the exclusion period is made based on a variety of factors including the seriousness of the offense and the effect of the exclusion on the delivery of health care services in the community. Other sanctions include suspension of payments, expanded prepayment review, recovery of improper payments, and referral to state licensing boards or medical/professional societies.

Civil monetary penalties may be imposed and are dependent on the specific violation. Under HIPAA, a penalty of $5000–$10,000 per false item or service provided and treble damages can be assessed. The amount of the penalty is based on a variety of factors including the nature of the offense, the degree of culpability of the person against whom the penalty is imposed, a history of prior offenses or sanctions, and the financial condition of the entity. Other considerations may include whether the provider developed a corrective action plan or took immediate action against the responsible violator.

CMS notes that organizations that exercise "reasonable diligence" and make efforts to monitor and correct problems are unlikely to be subject to civil or criminal penalties. "Good faith efforts will go a long way as you work toward HIPAA compliance," according to CMS. However they also add, "if the covered entity does not respond to CMS, fines could be imposed as a last resort."

The Coding Rules: Understanding the Official Guidelines and Coding Advice

There are numerous billing and coding commercial products on the market that promise to help providers "get the reimbursement you deserve." These include newsletters, books, audio-seminars, live conferences, and high-priced consultants. An Internet search of the preceding phrase in quotations yielded more than a million hits! Certainly, there is nothing wrong with receiving legitimate reimbursement for services provided or correctly coding and billing to ensure accurate payments. But the saying "If it seems too good to be true, it probably is" may apply to some **coding and billing advice**. Because of the risks associated with coding noncompliantly, caution should be exercised when considering the advice of every self-proclaimed expert that promises to increase reimbursement.

HIPAA—specifically, the Final Rule on the Standards for Electronic Transactions (45 CFR Parts 160 and 162, published August 17, 2000)—includes clarification on the use of medical code sets. The intent of the regulation was "to improve the efficiency and effectiveness of the health care system" and "to adopt national standards for electronic health care transactions." The purpose of standardizing code sets is to:

- Improve the cost efficiency and effectiveness of the health care system;

- Standardize the collection of data needed for claim submission and research;

- Meet the needs of the health data standards user community, including health care providers, health plans, and health care clearinghouses;

- Be consistent and uniform with other HIPAA standards and with other private and public section health data standards to the extent possible;

- Have timely development, testing, implementation, and updating procedures;

- Be precise and unambiguous but as simple as possible; and

- Keep data collection and paperwork burdens on users as minimal as feasible.

Prior to the regulation, payers could require the use of "local" codes (HCPCS level III Codes) or codes developed specifically for reporting services for their beneficiaries. The HIPAA rule on electronic transactions eliminated the use of local codes. The code set regulations clarify the use of other medical code sets that include the following:

- ICD-9-CM, Volumes 1 and 2 (including the ICD-9-CM Official Guidelines for Coding and Reporting), is the required code set for diseases, injuries, impairments and other health problems and their manifestations, and causes of injury, disease, impairment, or other health problems.

- ICD-9-CM, Volume 3: Procedures (including the ICD-9-CM Official Guidelines for Coding and Reporting) is the required code set for reporting procedures or other actions by hospital inpatients as reported by hospitals.

- The National Drug Code (NDC) is the required code set for drugs and biologics.

- The Code on Dental Procedures and Nomenclature is the code set for dental services.

- The combination of HCPCS and CPT-4 is the required code set for physician services and other health care services.

- HCPCS is the required code set for other substances, equipment, supplies, and other items used in health care services primarily representing items, supplies, and nonphysician services not included in the CPT-4 codes.

The Final Rule also includes the ICD-9-CM Official Guidelines for Coding and Reporting. Note that every covered entity, that is, every provider (hospital, physician, nursing home, etc.), payer, and health care clearinghouse is required to follow the ICD-9-CM Official Guidelines for Coding and Reporting. These guidelines are approved by the four parties that make up the cooperating parties for ICD-9-CM and include CMS, NCHS, AHA, and AHIMA. The guidelines are updated periodically but not necessarily annually. In most cases, revised guidelines become effective on October 1st of the year they are published. As noted previously, the guidelines are required for all covered entities under HIPAA, which generally includes all providers.

It is important to note that the ICD-9-CM coding manual named as the **official code set** in the regulations (Volumes 1, 2, and 3) is the coding manual on display on the maintainers' Web sites. Coding books are published and sold under various titles by many different companies and professional associations. Some ICD-9-CM coding books include additional definitions under the codes, legislative citations, tables, charts, and color-keyed notations. These additions are not part of the official ICD-9-CM volumes. Care should be exercised when purchasing code books to ensure they support compliant coding.

See Table 2-1 for a further breakdown of the official code sets as named under the HIPAA transactions and code set regulations.

Although it is important to note the inclusion of the ICD-9-CM Official Coding Guidelines, it is also necessary to point out that the final rule specifically states, "We do not name guidelines for other code sets." Generally speaking, this means that no other "official" guidelines exist for the other code sets, such as CPT-4 and HCPCS. This creates obvious problems with consistency in interpretation in use of these code sets. For example, different payers may have different interpretations on the use of CPT modifier 59, "Distinct procedural service." Because there are no "official" guidelines regarding the use of CPT-4 codes and modifiers in the regulations, providers are often at the mercy of the payer's interpretation, even though this may mean coding differently for patients based on their payer status or differently from the maintainers' published advice. The problem is further compounded when the maintainers of the code sets fail to provide coding guidance and tell providers that they should follow the guidance from the payer on the use of the codes and modifiers. The omission of official guidelines for all the code sets would appear to be at odds with the purpose of HIPAA standardization.

Violations of the HIPAA Transactions and Code Sets Regulations occur when:

- The complainant receives a noncompliant HIPAA transaction from another covered entity.

EXAMPLE: A provider submits claims with invalid CPT/HCPCS codes or invalid NPI (National Physician Identifier) numbers.

- The complainant sent a compliant HIPAA transaction to a covered entity, but the claim is being rejected.

Table 2-1 Official Code Sets under HIPAA Legislation

Health Care Service	Coding Reference	Maintainer
Physician services	Current Procedural Terminology (CPT) for reporting services and procedures; ICD-9-CM Volumes 1 and 2 for reporting diagnostic information, including the ICD-9-CM Official Guidelines for Coding and Reporting.	CPT is maintained and distributed by the American Medical Association (AMA). ICD-9-CM Volumes 1 and 2 are maintained by the National Center for Health Statistics (NCHS).
Dental services	The Code on Dental Procedures and Nomenclature (The Code), published as CDT.	Maintained and distributed by the American Dental Association (ADA).
Inpatient hospital services	International Classification of Diseases, 9th edition, Clinical Modification (ICD-9-CM), Volume 3 for reporting services and procedures; ICD-9-CM Volumes 1 and 2 for reporting diagnostic information, including the ICD-9-CM Official Guidelines for Coding and Reporting.	ICD-9-CM Volume 3 is maintained and distributed by the Centers for Medicare & Medicaid Services (CMS). ICD-9-CM Volumes 1 and 2 are maintained by NCHS.
Outpatient hospital services	Current Procedural Terminology (CPT) for reporting services and procedures; ICD-9-CM Volumes 1 and 2 for reporting diagnostic information, including the ICD-9-CM Official Guidelines for Coding and Reporting.	CPT is maintained and distributed by the AMA. ICD-9-CM Volumes 1 and 2 is maintained by NCHS.
Other health-related services	Health care Financing Administration Common Procedure Coding System (Level II of HCPCS).	Maintained and distributed by the U.S. Department of Health and Human Services (HHS).
Drugs	National Drug Codes (NDC).	Maintained and distributed by HHS, in collaboration with drug manufacturers.
Other substances, equipment, supplies, or other items used in health care services.	Health Care Common Procedure Coding System (HCPCS) (Level II).	Maintained and distributed by HHS.

EXAMPLE: A provider submits a health care claim with valid CPT/HCPCS codes, but the payer rejects the valid codes or requires the use of nonvalid codes. Note that a payer must *accept* the claim, but acceptance of a claim is not a determination to pay a claim.

- A covered entity to which the complainant sends data or from which the complainant receives data has a noncompliant companion guide. A companion guide provides detailed instructions to providers on the submission of electronic claims. Specifically, the companion guide may not conflict with established HIPAA guidelines that address the use of specific fields on the claim form.

EXAMPLE: A diagnosis code (ICD-9-CM) is required on the CMS-1500 claim form in field 21. A payer may not require that this field be used to report procedures, such as CPT codes.

Anyone may file a HIPAA transaction and/or code set complaint. The individual(s) filing the complaint must be able to provide details of the complaint. Complaints may be filed electronically through the use of the Administrative Simplification Enforcement Tool (ASET) system that can be accessed through the CMS Web site at www.cms.hhs.gov/. Complaints may also be made in writing to the Office of E-Health Standards & Services (OESS) at the Centers for Medicare and Medicaid Service HIPAA Enforcement Activities, Complaint Submission, PO Box 830, Baltimore, Maryland, 21244-8030.

Penalties for noncompliance with the Transactions and Code Sets Regulations vary. The civil monetary penalty for violating transaction standards can range from $100 per person per violation up to $25,000 per person per violation within a single calendar year.

Federal Regulations

Many instances of coding instruction and guidance, along with other regulations and directives, can be found in federal government documents such as CMS transmittals and manuals, on Medicare contractor Web sites, and in the *Federal Register.* For example, CMS publishes guidance on the specific use of modifiers and consultation services reported with CPT codes 99241–99255. Commercial payers and medical and coding societies may also publish advice on the use of codes. Whereas the HIPAA Transactions and Code Sets Regulations include administrative simplification and standardized code sets, the coding advice published by the various organizations is not always consistent. Some even conflict with the official coding guidelines for ICD-9-CM. Consider the following advice published by a Medicare contractor in a local coverage decision on trigger point injections:

ICD-9 codes 729.0, 729.1, and 729.4 are commonly used to indicate myofascial syndrome and are not associated with specific muscles in the table below; therefore, documentation must be maintained noting the anatomic location of the injection site(s) [such as]

720.1	Serratus anterior; Serratus posterior; Quadratus lumborum; Longissimus thoracis; Lower thoracic iliocostalis; Upper and lower rectus abdominus; Upper lumbar iliocostalis; Multifidus; External oblique; McBurney's point
723.9	Trapezius (upper and lower); Sternocleidomastoid (cervical and sternal); Masseter; Temporalis; Lateral pterygoid; Splenii; Posterior cervical; Suboccipital
726.19	Scaleni, Subscapularis; Levator scapulae; Brachialis; Deltoid (anterior and posterior); Middle finger extensor; Rhomboid, Infraspinatus/Supraspinatus; First dorsal interosseous; Pectoralis major and minor; Supinator; Latissimus dorsi

---

The advice includes additional codes and muscle sites that would be considered medically necessary for trigger point injections. The obvious problem is that the ICD-9-CM nomenclature does not associate the listed muscles with these specific codes.

To further illustrate the problem with the Medicare contractor's advice, consider the following example:

The health record documentation states that the patient has serratus anterior muscle pain. Following ICD-9-CM coding conventions, the coder assigns this to ICD-9-CM code 729.1, "Myalgia and myositis, unspecified." The Medicare contractor however has assigned serratus anterior muscle pain to a different code, 720.1,"Spinal enthesopathy." The contractor's advice conflicts with official coding guidelines and coding conventions. The provider and coder believe that the patient's serratus anterior muscle pain is a covered condition according to the policy but are in the risky compliance situation of having to choose between coding accurately or coding to receive reimbursement. Unfortunately, the issue of medical necessity, which appears to have been met, is overlooked.

The National Correct Coding Initiative Edits

The **National Correct Coding Initiative (NCCI) edits** were developed by CMS to control improper payments for bundled services and "to promote national correct coding methodologies." CMS states they developed the NCCI policy based on coding instructions developed by national societies, coding conventions defined in the AMA's CPT manual, CMS national and local coverage decisions, and a review of current coding practices. The edits are updated quarterly and are managed by Correct Coding Solutions, LLC, an independent contractor to CMS. The NCCI edits were originally developed for Part B services but have been part of the Outpatient Code Editor (OCE) or hospital facility Part B services since 2000. As a result, there are two sets of edits, one that determines payment for hospital outpatient services and one that determines payment for physician services. Many third-party payers have also adopted the NCCI edits in determining bundling payments.

Column 1 CPT	Column 2 CPT	Effective Date	Deletion Date	Modifier
50020	37202	2002 10 01		1
50020	44950	2002 04 01		0

Figure 2-1 Example of Column 1/Column 2 Edits. *SOURCE: National Correct Coding Initiatives Table (version 14.2), http://www.cms.hhs.gov/NationalCorrectCodInitEd/*

The NCCI edits utilize two different types of edits: Column 1 and Column 2 edits and mutually exclusive edits (see Figure 2-1). Column 1 and Column 2 edits are used to describe services that identify a comprehensive code and a component code. The component code is usually bundled with the comprehensive code, and payment is for the comprehensive code only. A modifier indicator of 0 or 1 indicates whether a modifier can be used to "break" the NCCI edit. For example, CPT code 50020, "Drainage of perirenal or renal abscess, open," is a Column 1 code. CPT code 37202, "Transcatheter therapy, infusion other than for thrombolysis," is a Column 2 code. Code 50020 is the comprehensive code, and 37202 is considered a component of 50020. The code pair is identified by 1, which means that modifiers may be used if appropriate to break the edit. If both procedures are reported and no modifier is applied, payment will be based on the 50020 code only. However if a modifier, such as modifier 59,"Distinct procedural service," is applied to the Column 2 code (37202), payment may be made on both services.

The use of any modifier that breaks the NCCI edit is determined by the actual circumstances of the case and guidelines for appropriate modifier application. In the preceding code pair example, if the thrombolysis and the drainage of the abscess were different sites or different encounters, applying modifier 59 to the 37202 code would be appropriate. However, if the thrombolysis and the drainage of the abscess were of the same site and during the same operative episode, modifier 59 and payment for the thrombolysis would not be appropriate.

In another coding pair involving the drainage of the abscess, CPT code 50020 and CPT code 44950, "Appendectomy," the indicator is 0, which means that no modifier may be reported if both procedures of the code pair were performed together on the same date of service. In this case payment will be made on only one of the services. In these instances payment is usually made on the Column 1 code, which may or may not have the higher reimbursement or associated costs.

The term *mutually exclusive* generally refers to procedures that are not normally or reasonably performed on the same patient during a single operative episode. One example of mutually exclusive code pairs is procedures that are performed by two different methods. For example, an open cholecystectomy and a laparoscopic cholecystectomy are considered mutually exclusive. In Figure 2-2, the code pair 16030, "Debridement of partial-thickness burns, large," and 16025, "Debridement of partial-thickness burns, medium," are considered mutually exclusive. The modifier indicator is 0, which means no modifier is allowed, and payment will be made on the Column 1 CPT code only. CPT codes 17000 and 11056 are also considered mutually exclusive, but a modifier may be appended if appropriate.

Column 1 CPT	Column 2 CPT	Effective Date	Deletion Date	Modifier
16030	16025	1996 01 01		0
17000	11056	1998 04 01		1

Figure 2-2 Example of Column 1/Column 2 Edits for Mutually Exclusive Code Pairs. *SOURCE: National Correct Coding Initiatives table (version14.2), http://www.cms. hhs.gov/NationalCorrectCodInitEd/*

In many cases the NCCI edits are logical; that is, the code pairs represent procedures that are not commonly performed together or should never be reported together. It is important to recall that the NCCI edits were created by Medicare to control improper payment for services that are commonly performed together. Therefore, it is generally understood that the payment for two services that are identified in an NCCI edit is already considered in the comprehensive code. Additional reimbursement is appropriate only when the definition of the modifier applied, such as modifier 59, "Distinct procedural service," is true (e.g., separate site, separate encounter).

However, the questions of payment bundling by CPT codes and application of coding guidelines are not always clear and distinct. Consider the following two procedures: Hysteroscopy, surgical with polypectomy (CPT code 58558) and Hysteroscopy with endometrial ablation (CPT code 58563). The NCCI edits consider these procedures mutually exclusive, meaning that the polypectomy is always considered a component of the endometrial ablation (no modifier is allowed). However, neither the CPT manual nor *CPT Assistant* (companion newsletter to the CPT manual) contains guidance or information that would prohibit coding the procedures together. As mentioned earlier in the chapter, no official guidelines exist for code sets other than ICD-9-CM. Coders often follow the instructions of payers in the absence of official guidelines and/or rely on advice from the maintainers of the code set. This can lead to inconsistent coding practices across various payers. It is especially critical that coding policies exist to address these situations. (Coding policies will be discussed in a later chapter.) It is also important that coders understand the NCCI edits so that modifiers are applied correctly, and appropriate reimbursement is received.

Along with the NCCI edits, CMS also instituted claim edits known as Medically Unlikely Edits (MUEs). These edits indicate the ideal or maximum number of units that should be reported for any HCPCS code rendered by a single provider to a single beneficiary on the same date of service. For example, the MUE value for CPT code 20552, "Injection(s); single or multiple trigger point(s), 1 or 2 muscle(s)" is one. In another example, the MUE value of CPT code 70450, "Computer tomography, head or brain; without contrast material" is three. Additional units of service for these procedures would result in denial of the additional services. CMS publishes most of the MUE values on its Web site, but does reserve the option to keep some MUE values confidential.

Coding Advice from Professional Societies and Associations

Medical and specialty societies and other professional associations often provide their members with coding advice. This information is often extremely helpful to their respective members and can assist coders with specific coding issues. It is important to note, however, that these instructions, although sometimes valuable, are not necessarily "official." Many coders in physician offices can relate a time when their physicians attended a national conference and returned with coding advice that was finally going to ensure payment for that one particular service that was always being denied by the payer! Any coding advice needs to be carefully reviewed for compliance with the official coding guidelines and existing payer instructions. In cases of fraud and abuse, the responsibility of accurate coding and billing rests with the health care provider, not with the provider of bad advice.

Chapter Review

1. Provide an example of health care *fraud* and one of health care *abuse*, specifically related to the coding and billing processes.

   _____

   _____

   _____

2. Discuss the origins of the False Claims Act and its current impact on coding and health care reimbursement.

   _____

   _____

   _____

3. Provide at least five examples of violations of the False Claims Act related to coding and billing.

   _____

   _____

   _____

4. Research the OIG Web site at www.oig.hhs.gov and review a recent article related to health care fraud and abuse (see "News Room"). Discuss the violation as it relates to coding and billing.

   _____

   _____

   _____

5. A hospital intends to implement a new program for hospital patients and visitors in an effort to resolve patient complaints. The hospital will provide $10 gift cards to patients and visitors who experience inconveniences such as excessive wait times (greater than 30 minutes), cancelled appointments, delayed meals, excessive noise, housekeeping or dietary concerns, television set not working, or loss of personal items. The gift card would not be redeemable for cash or for items purchased at the hospital, for example, in the hospital gift store. Does this arrangement violate the Anti-Kickback Statute? (The OIG provided an advisory on this case, which is published on the OIG Web site.)

   _____

   _____

   _____

6. Provide coding examples of upcoding, unbundling, and coding creep.

_____

_____

_____

7. A coder in a dermatology office has questions on the proper CPT coding of allografts. What references would assist the coder in answering these questions?

_____

_____

_____

8. For the dermatology example in question 7, what reference should the coder seek to determine Medicare coverage on allografts?

_____

_____

_____

9. Review a local coverage decision published by a Medicare contractor, paying particular attention to the coverage guidelines and coding and documentation instructions. Does the policy adhere to official coding guidelines?

_____

_____

_____

10. Review any NCCI code pair and determine if the bundling is supported in coding guidelines published by the maintainers of the code set (e.g., AMA for CPT).

_____

_____

_____

Case Studies

Case Study 1

A hospital has offered area physicians free coding services in exchange for admitting or referring patients to the hospital.

1. Is this practice a violation of the Anti-Kickback Statute or the Stark law?

    _____

    _____

    _____

2. How should coders respond to requests to perform coding services in this situation?

    _____

    _____

    _____

Case Study 2

A physician performs a knee arthroscopy with medial meniscus meniscectomy (CPT code 29881) and chrondroplasty of the articular cartilage in the lateral compartment (CPT code 29877).

1. What code(s) should the coder select for this procedure performed on a non-Medicare patient?

    _____

    _____

    _____

2. What code(s) should the coder select for this procedure if performed on a Medicare patient?

    _____

    _____

    _____

3. If the coding is different for the Medicare and non-Medicare patients, is it compliant?

    _____

    _____

    _____

Case Study 3

To complete the billing process quickly, a coder in a physician's office has been instructed to code from the encounter/billing form only, not from the physician's documentation. The coder notices that one particular physician consistently checks the same CPT code, 99245, "Office consultation with a comprehensive history, examination, and medical decision making of high complexity." The coder is concerned that the physician may be upcoding.

1. What steps should the coder take to ensure that the coding is compliant?

    _____

    _____

    _____

2. If it is determined that the physician was upcoding, what legal risks does the physician face?

    _____

    _____

    _____

3. Would the upcoding be considered fraud or abuse?

    _____

    _____

    _____

Case Study 4

A Medicare contractor has published education on its Web site for the proper use of modifiers. Regarding modifier 59, "Distinct procedural service," the contractor states that modifier 59 should not be used for any "code combination not appearing in the CCI edits." In other words, the use of modifier 59 should be used only to break a CCI edit, not in any other situation.

1. Is this guidance accurate?

    _____

    _____

    _____

2. Is the advice official?

_____

_____

_____

3. Are providers required to follow the advice given by the contractor?

_____

_____

_____

Case Study 5

A coding supervisor attends a national coding conference on neoplasm coding titled "Understand the Complex World of Neoplasm Coding Now!" There she learns from a well-known national speaker that neoplasm codes, such as 174.9, "Malignant neoplasm of the breast, unspecified," should be coded for five years from the date of the patient's diagnosis. After that period of time, the appropriate history of cancer code, for example, V10.3, "Personal history of malignant neoplasm of the breast," should be used.

1. Is this coding advice correct?

_____

_____

_____

2. Should the facility adopt this advice in its coding policies?

_____

_____

_____

3. What is the rule for coding current and history of malignant neoplasms?

_____

_____

_____

Case Study 6

A commercial payer refuses to accept unlisted CPT procedural codes, referring to them as unacceptable "dump codes." When the coder is asked by the business office to review the coding, the coder states that the procedure is appropriately coded using the unlisted procedure code. The billing person then contacts the payer and is told again by the payer that the claim cannot be processed with an unlisted CPT procedure code, and the provider will need to submit a different code to be paid for the service.

1. What options are available to the provider?

    _____

    _____

    _____

2. What should the coder do in this circumstance?

    _____

    _____

    _____

3. Has either party committed fraud or abuse?

    _____

    _____

    _____

4. If the codes are changed, will either party be committing fraud or abuse?

    _____

    _____

    _____

Case Study 7

A third-party payer is requiring hospitals to report ICD-9-CM procedure codes (Volume 3 ICD-9-CM procedure codes) for hospital (facility) outpatient procedures. They are also requiring the CPT-4/HCPCS codes.

1. Has the payer violated the HIPAA Transactions and Code Sets Regulations?

_____

_____

_____

2. What action, if any, should coders and the provider take?

_____

_____

_____

References

American Medical *Association. (2007). Current procedural terminology 2008. Chicago: AMA Press.*

Centers for Disease Control and Prevention. *ICD-9-CM Official Guidelines for Coding and Reporting,* Effective October 1, 2008. Retrieved July 17, 2008, from http://www.cdc.gov/nchs/datawh/ftpserv/ftpICD9/icdguide08.pdf

Centers for Medicare & Medicaid Services. Benefit integrity. In *Medicare program integrity manual,* Chap. 4. Retrieved from http://www.cms.hhs.gov/manuals/downloads/pim83c04.pdf

Centers for Medicare & Medicaid Services. (2002, November). CMS HIPAA Electronic Transactions & Code Sets Information Series: 1. HIPAA 101 for health care providers' offices. Retrieved from http://www.cms.hhs.gov/EducationMaterials/Downloads/HIPAA101-1.pdf

Centers for Medicare & Medicaid Services. (2003, May). CMS HIPAA Electronic Transactions & Code Sets Information Series: 10. Enforcement of HIPAA standards. *Retrieved from* http://www.cms.hhs.gov/EducationMaterials/Downloads/Enforcement.pdf

Centers for Medicare & Medicaid Services. (2004, January 23). CMS questions and answers. ID 2612: Who can file a Health Insurance Portability and Accountability Act of 1996 (HIPAA) complaint? Last updated on 3/18/2009. Retrieved from https://questions.cms.hhs.gov/cgi-bin/cmshhs.cfg/php/enduser/std_alp.php?p_sid=*HLxb3Aj&p_lva=&p_li=&p_accessibility=0&p_redirect=&p_page=1&p_cv=&p_pv=&p_prods=0&p_cats=&p_hidden_prods=&prod_lvl1=0&p_search_text=2612&srch_btn_submit=%C2%A0%C2%A0%C2%A0Search%C2%A0%C2%A0%C2%A0&p_new_search=1&p_search_type=answers.search_nl

Centers for Medicare & Medicaid Services. (2009, April 9). *National Correct Coding Initiative policy manual for Medicare services.* Retrieved from http://www.cms.hhs.gov/NationalCorrectCodInitEd/

Department of Health and Human Services, Office of Inspector General. (2007, November). *Department of Health and Human Services and the Department of Justice health care fraud and abuse control program annual report for FY 2006.* Retrieved from http://www.oig.hhs.gov/publications/docs/hcfac/ hcfacreport2006.pdf

Department of Health and Human Services, Office of Inspector General. (2000, April 26). *Health care programs: Fraud and abuse; revised OIG civil money penalties resulting from Public Law 104-19142. Federal Register, 65(81), 24400–24401.*

Department of Health and Human Services, Office of Inspector General. (2000, October 5). OIG compliance program for individual and small group physician practices. *Federal Register, 65*(194), 59434–59452.

Department of Health and Human Services, Office of Inspector General. (2005, January 3). OIG supplemental compliance program guidance for hospitals. *Federal Register; 70*(19), 4858–4876.

Federal Bureau of Investigation. (n.d.). *Financial crimes report to the public fiscal year 2006.* Retrieved from http://www.fbi.gov/publications/financial/fcs_report2006/financial_crime_2006.htm

Health Insurance Portability and Accountability Act of 1996, Public Law 104-91, 104th Congress (August 21, 1996). Retrieved from http://hippo.findlaw.com/hipaa.html

Legal Information Institute. (n.d.). U.S. Code collection: Title 31, Subtitle III, Chapter 37, Subchapter III, Section 3729; False Claims. Retrieved from http://www4.law.cornell.edu/uscode/uscode31/ usc_sec_31_00003729—000-.html

The Importance of Documentation

Objectives

At the completion of this chapter, the learner should be able to:

- Discuss the link between good documentation and accurate coding.
- Explain the purpose of a clinical documentation improvement program.
- Describe the main purpose of the encounter form, discussing risks associated with relying on encounter forms solely for coding.
- Discuss the pros and cons of using templates.
- Identify compliance risks associated with cutting and pasting in the electronic medical record.
- Identify the correct process for making corrections in both the traditional paper medical record and the electronic health record.
- Evaluate the purpose of the coding query and identify the components of a properly constructed query.

Key Terms

clinical documentation improvement program

clinical documentation specialists

cloning of medical records

Comprehensive Error Rate Testing Program (CERT)

correction of errors in medical records

electronic medical record (EMR)

encounter forms

queries

templates

Documentation as the Key Resource

Whether medical records are electronic or in the traditional paper record format, their underlying purpose has remained constant over time. The health record serves as a necessary vehicle for continuity of patient care. Additionally, health care documentation is used to assess quality and appropriateness of care, to provide clinical data for research, to procure reimbursement, to support medical necessity, and to provide data for public reporting.

Historically health care documentation and data were used primarily for continuity of patient care, research, and for legal purposes. Since the onset of prospective payment systems, the False Claims Act, and the Health Insurance Portability and Accountability Act (HIPAA), health care data are constantly being reviewed, particularly for measures of health care quality and medical necessity. Poor documentation often results in poor patient outcomes and negatively affects health care data quality. Conversely, as discussed in this and previous chapters, improving the quality of health care data has a direct impact on the improvement of health care quality. All too frequently the media report on medical errors that resulted in the death of or injury to patients. Costs of medical errors in hospitals are estimated at more than $30 billion annually. However, not all medical errors are a result of incompetence or inadvertent human error; many are due to incomplete, illegible, or missing documentation.

An obvious outcome of poor documentation is inaccurate reimbursement. Poor documentation can affect the provider's reimbursement and result in increased staffing time to work denials and rejections. If the documentation cannot be produced to support a service being billed, the service is technically nonbillable (not documented; not done). If the documentation is incomplete, medical necessity may be questioned and accurate codes cannot be assigned. Although many health care providers utilize some form of medical necessity software or claim scrubber to identify services that are not medically necessary and to identify obvious coding errors, these software systems are usually used after the documentation has been completed, and there is little opportunity to improve or correct missing documentation.

Just as good documentation is important for health care quality, so is it necessary for accurate coding and billing. A coder may have all the necessary education, certifications, and understanding of coding conventions and billing rules needed to accurately assign codes, but if the documentation is poor or mediocre, then the quality of the coding will also suffer. Coding can be only as good as the documentation. The better the documentation, the more accurately will it reflect the patient's diagnoses and services provided.

The Center for Medicare & Medicaid Services (CMS) has identified through its **Comprehensive Error Rate Testing Program (CERT)** review several areas of coding errors. Figure 3-1 represents coding errors found for Part B (physician services) on audit of CPT code 99233, "Subsequent hospital care."

The percentage of errors found on the CERT review is striking. There is probably no single factor that explains the high error rates, but one factor may be that many physician offices do not employ certified coders. In offices that do have certified coders, the documentation is often not available at the time of coding. This is especially true for hospital inpatient services. Providers visit patients in the hospital, relaying to their office billing staff the names of the patients they saw and provide the billing code(s). A note is placed in the hospital's medical record, but it is often not available to the coding staff at the physician's office. During a coding audit, an outside auditor reviews the hospital's documentation against the code the physician billed. Although the errors may be coding errors, they are also documentation errors in that the documentation did not support the service that was billed.

Problem Code: CPT Code 99233

Fiscal Year	Number of Lines Reviewed	Number of Lines Questioned	Percent of Lines in Error
1996	217	115	53.0%
1997	416	128	30.8%
1998	457	114	24.9%
1999	187	102	54.5%
2000	449	220	49.0%
2001	338	142	42.0%
2002	228	174	76.3%
2003	709	435	61.4%
2004	768	391	50.9%
2005	1,079	474	43.9%
2006	1,102	440	39.9%
2007	1,157	532	46.0%

Figure 3-1 Problem Code: CPT Code 99233. CMS has recognized problems with certain procedure codes, including 99233, "Subsequent hospital care." The physician should typically spend 35 minutes with the patient and perform at least two of these key procedures: a detailed interval patient history, a detailed examination, and/or medical decision making of high complexity. *SOURCE: Improper Medicare Fee-for-Service Payments Report,* http://www.cms.hhs.gov/apps/er_report/edit_report_1.asp?from=public&reportID=6

In most cases, medical record documentation does not need to be lengthy to support the services performed or to effectively communicate the care provided. Clear and concise documentation is paramount over pages of duplicated or cut-and-pasted information. Key factors in good documentation include the following:

- The reason for the encounter or admission. It is often surprising that the physician's documentation does not state the reason why the patient is being seen. Most commonly this information is included in the chief complaint and pertinent history. Another key element is documenting whether the patient is being seen for a new problem, an established problem, a consultation, or a follow-up.

- On hospital admission, the level of care. The admission order should state "admit to inpatient" or "admit to observation." Failure to document the level of care can lead to inappropriate code assignment for the provider (for example, inpatient versus observation) and questions of medical necessity for the hospital services.

- Inclusion of all diagnoses and procedures performed. Listing all pertinent diagnoses is especially important to reflect medical necessity and complexity. Daily documentation for an inpatient should include key diagnoses and services ordered and reviewed. The discharge summary should include a synopsis of the patient's entire stay, including diagnoses that were ruled out, diagnostic tests that were ordered, results, and discharge plans.

- Proper documentation of office procedures. Many physicians are aware that the hospitals in which they perform surgeries or procedures have specific documentation requirements for dictating surgery and procedure notes. These same rules should carry over to the office setting. When procedures are performed in the office, the documentation should clearly describe the procedure that was performed, including the patient's outcome and response to the procedure.

Documentation is essential for safeguarding and optimizing patient care and to providing legal protection for the provider. There are numerous legal case examples in which insufficient documentation led to adverse patient outcomes and/or unfavorable legal judgments. Consider the following real case examples:

EXAMPLE 1: A urologist saw a patient with an abnormal prostate. The physician determined during the physical exam that the patient had a nodule. The initial prostate specific antigen (PSA) result was normal. The patient returned some time later complaining of urinary frequency. The PSA was slightly elevated, but the physician felt the rising PSA was due to prostatitis and prescribed medication. The physician instructed the patient to return in three months for a repeat PSA check. The physician noted the follow-up plan on a lab slip in the record but not in the progress notes. When the patient returned in three months with another symptom (scrotal cyst) the physician did not recheck the PSA level, as indicated in the follow-up from the previous visit. Later, a biopsy was performed that indicated an aggressive form of prostate cancer that had metastasized to the lymph nodes. The plaintiff in this case argued that had a PSA check been performed sooner, the cancer might have been detected before it spread to the lymph nodes. Appropriate documentation in the progress notes would probably have reminded the physician to recheck the patient's PSA level at the patient's next scheduled visit.

EXAMPLE 2: Following a workplace injury, a patient was referred to a physician, who diagnosed a low back strain and radicular pain. The physician failed to document any objective medical findings to support the diagnoses but prescribed Valium for the patient to take "as needed for muscle spasms." Owing to the lack of supporting documentation of objective findings, the patient's compensation benefits were denied.

EXAMPLE 3: A patient in a skilled nursing facility had an established sacral ulcer. There was sufficient documentation of the sacral ulcer and care provided for it, but there was no documentation from nursing staff or physicians that other vulnerable areas, such as the heels, were inspected for skin breakdown. The patient was subsequently discharged from skilled care and received home health services. The home health nurse found a new lesion on the patient's left heel, which ultimately contributed to complications, and the patient had to undergo a below-the-knee amputation of her left leg. The health care providers argued that it was not their practice to document the absence of pressure ulcers on areas of the body where none existed. However, the court found that the documentation should have indicated that the heels had been inspected and no evidence of a pressure sore had been found. The nursing facility was found negligent.

Clinical Documentation Programs

As noted previously, poor or incomplete documentation can have a negative impact on reimbursement and may not support medical necessity for diagnostic and therapeutic services. The appropriateness of a patient's hospital stay may also be questioned. As a result, many hospitals have established **clinical documentation improvement programs** and utilize **clinical documentation specialists (CDSs)** to ensure that documentation supports the medical necessity of inpatient stays and captures the appropriate diagnosis-related group (DRG). These individuals are typically nurses or experienced certified coders who review documentation while the patient is still an inpatient. CDSs are likely to be staffed in the case management, utilization review, or health information management department.

The key factor to a successful clinical documentation improvement program is collaboration among physicians, coders, and the clinical documentation specialists. Organizational support to see the project through to completion is also necessary. Some documentation programs have failed in facilities that did not have the support of one or more key departments, including administration, nursing, coding, and clinical staff. Enlisting a physician champion will help garner the support of other physicians. If nurses are clinical documentation specialists it is important that they understand basic coding guidelines and the coder's thought process in selecting codes. For example, even though both the nurse and the coder may see a diagnosis that is clinically indicated in the documentation, the coder cannot assign the code unless it is documented by the physician.

Coding compliance issues sometimes arise when the clinical documentation program is too focused on DRG assignment rather than on improving documentation. For example, placing emphasis on documentation that supports only complications and comorbidities is inappropriate. Chart documentation that consistently states that every patient has acute blood loss anemia, a bacterial pneumonia, or acute respiratory failure can raise red flags to outside auditors. The clinical documentation specialist should try to ensure that all documentation is complete and accurate, not just documentation that results in higher reimbursement to the hospital.

When the clinical documentation specialist and the coder disagree about the final coded DRG, it is important to discuss the differences. Considerations should include official coding guidelines, present-on-admission criteria, and documentation policies. The findings of neither the clinical documentation specialist nor the coder should be considered final without a discussion about the variances. As many coders realize, coding is not always black and white. Nevertheless, the documentation may not clearly indicate an exact diagnosis in every case. Sometimes the clinical evidence does not provide the physician with a reason for a patient's respiratory failure or the cause of an infection in a patient with multiple comorbidities. In some situations it may be necessary to utilize an independent third party, such as the coding compliance manager, to help resolve coding differences. Regardless, the coder should not be instructed to code strictly based on the clinical documentation specialist's recommendations.

The Encounter Form

Encounter forms, or *superbills,* serve many purposes. Foremost, they communicate services that the provider has performed. They also assist the office staff in scheduling future appointments or referrals, identifying further tests that should be performed, and facilitating efficient claims processing. Encounter forms often list the common procedures, along with appropriate CPT/HCPCS codes, performed by the physician or group. They may also provide a listing of common ICD-9-CM diagnosis codes. Encounter forms are generally considered administrative records and are not filed in the patient's health care record.

The encounter form should never be a replacement for the provider's documentation. Coding and billing errors can result from relying solely on the encounter form for coding accuracy. The provider's documented progress notes must support the services billed, not the encounter form.

Consider the following documentation from a physician who sees a Medicare patient for abdominal symptoms:

> The patient noticed some feelings of progressive abdominal distention that started one week ago. This morning he started having progressive abdominal pain, especially located in the right lower quadrant. No radiation; pain 7/10. No nausea or vomiting. He had no blood in the stools or melena. The patient did not eat this day, but he has a normal appetite. The patient notes some blood in the urine and difficulty urinating. No fevers or chills. Otherwise the patient denies chest pain, headache. He has some shortness of breath on movements. His pain is sharp. The patient also has bilateral skin lesions on the anterior side of his shins that appeared a few days ago, and he relates them to poison ivy. The patient said that these lesions are better today.
>
> IMPRESSION: Right lower quadrant pain. Hematuria. Difficulty urinating. Poison ivy dermatitis. Shortness of breath.

The physician orders a number of blood and urine tests as well as a CT urogram for evaluation of the patient's hematuria and difficulty of urination. The physician checks the diagnosis "abdominal pain" on the encounter form. The charges for all services are billed to Medicare, but the CT urogram and many of the lab tests are denied for medical necessity, since the claim included only the nonspecific diagnosis code of abdominal pain—ICD-9-CM code 789.00, which was the code checked on the encounter form. Had the claim included all the diagnoses from the physician's documentation, the payer would have reimbursed the services appropriately when the claim was initially submitted. This would have saved staff time in determining the reasons for the denials and allowed more prompt payment for the services.

As noted earlier, the encounter form is generally considered an administrative form that is not part of the patient's health record. In audit situations, or when a payer requests copies of medical record documentation to support services that were billed, it is the provider's documentation (i.e., progress notes, history, and physical examination) that is submitted to verify the services, not the billing form. If coding is being based primarily on the encounter form, periodic audits should be conducted to ensure that the diagnoses and services noted in the provider's documentation match the services and diagnoses noted on the billing form.

An effective encounter form will allow the provider ample free space to record services and diagnoses not included on the encounter form. Providers should understand that if the service provided or specific diagnosis is not identified on the form, a diagnosis or service that is "close enough" is not compliant.

Encounter forms must be updated annually, reflecting current codes. Because coding changes occur at different times of the year (October 1 for ICD-9-CM, and January 1 for CPT-4 and many HCPCS Level II codes) inventory of these forms should be monitored closely. Outdated forms should never be used, as they may result in inaccurate coding, delays in claims processing, and claim denials.

Templates and the Electronic Medical Record

Never before has health care documentation been more scrutinized or more demanded. As documentation is increasingly being used to provide evidence and support for health care services a major drive is underway toward the **electronic medical record (EMR)**. Many providers welcome the electronic record as they look for ways to decrease the administrative burdens of documentation creation and maintenance. Technology is often viewed as the solution to repetitive notes and time-consuming documentation requirements.

Templates, especially those associated with the EMR or the electronic health record (EHR), are viewed as both money- and time-savers. In some cases electronic templates have replaced provider dictation. In others, templates have been developed with a combination of dictation, direct entry, or handwritten entries. Templates are also credited with improving patient safety and reducing medical errors, as many electronic templates have the capability of recognizing clinical indicators such as drug interactions and disease protocols. The creation of templates, however, has created some concern among medical associations and several Medicare contractors. The following notice was published on a Medicare contractor's website:

> "With the advent of increasingly popular Electronic Medical Record (EMR) templates, comes an increased risk of noncompliance, as well as potential patterns of fraud and abuse. . . . If not properly used, they may also lead to **"cloning" of medical records.** When medical records have nearly identical documentation, the medical necessity of the services is questionable. Misleading or providing false information can occur. Physicians may copy and paste a patient's information from one day to the next without modifying the record to reflect all changes in the patient's status. If the physician copies and pastes without editing, a patient's physical exam or medical decision making may not be a true reflection of that patient for that service . . . Medical record cloning may cause documentation for many beneficiaries to be remarkably similar as well, leading to some confusion regarding patient care among specialties for consultation, as well as among other health care professionals. It could also lead to excessive billing at the higher ends of E/M codes. Medicare Contractors are noting increasing frequency of cloned records. Each E/M service should stand alone. When no documentation differences are noted for several services for one beneficiary or for services for multiple beneficiaries, there may be a question for potential fraud. . . .
>
> . . . [C]loning of records will most likely lead to denial of services due to lack of medical necessity and may lead to investigation of potentially fraudulent practices" (Pinnacle Business Solutions).

Many EMR systems allow for cutting and pasting. Other terms for this function include *copy and paste, copy and forward, carry forward*, and *cloning*. The function actually predates electronic computer systems, dating to the 1960s when manuscript editors would literally cut paragraphs from a manuscript with scissors and physically paste them onto another page or in another section. Computer makers later developed functions using keyboard strokes, pop-up menus, or toolbar buttons to cut and paste or copy and paste text or other data. Today these features are used in health care records to reduce the redundancy of some documentation. However, some of these practices can damage the integrity and trustworthiness of the record.

Cutting and pasting, or copying and pasting, can be risky documentation practices, especially when it is evident that documentation is worded exactly like or similar to previous entries. For example, it is usually quite evident in an inpatient record that copying and pasting has occurred if a patient's physical exam is the same day after day. One would expect to see daily changes in the patient's vital signs and health condition. Copying and pasting the patient's medical history and physical examination findings is inappropriate. The following are other key principles regarding the cutting or copying and pasting functions that should be included in documentation policies:

- Any copying and pasting activity should require the author's approval and authentication of the accuracy of the copied material

- Documentation that has been copied and pasted from another document should be clearly identified and easily distinguished from new and added documentation

- Providers should summarize any lab data, pathology, and radiology reports that are copied into their documentation rather than just copying the information itself

- Electronic health record documentation should be regularly audited to assess the use or misuse of copying practices

The use of templates and copying and pasting can lead to assigning more complex codes than would be expected, for example, a higher level evaluation and management (E/M) service. The medical record documentation needs to state individual facts, findings, and observations, which are sometimes not easily integrated into templates. The frequent use of templates can result in every patient's documentation looking very similar, if not exactly the same. The personal care and treatment provided a patient must be included in the patient's documentation. Coding and documentation should be regularly reviewed to ensure that the use of templates is not resulting in inadvertent overcoding.

Corrections in the Health Record

It is inevitable that at some point clinical documentation may need to be corrected, amended, or clarified. It is important that providers documenting in the medical record are aware of the appropriate laws, regulations, and policies concerning corrections to the health record. Policies covering documentation guidelines should minimally include the following:

- Specific documentation requirements for clinical and administrative purposes, such as the following:
  - All clinical notes will be dictated and transcribed.
  - Electronic health record templates for physical examinations will be used.
  - The patient will complete or update a medical history form at each visit, which will be incorporated into the medical record.
  - The patient's problem list will be reviewed by the provider at each visit, with the provider noting any changes.
- Policies addressing individual responsibility and accountability for the accuracy and integrity of information in the health record:
  - Prohibiting the entry of false information.
  - Outlining the consequences for falsification of information.
  - Educational requirements addressing falsification of information and security.
- Corrections, amendments, and clarifications to the medical record:
  - Who is allowed to make corrections?
  - How are corrections made?

Changes in the medical information in the EMR as well as in the traditional paper medical record need to be carefully addressed in policy. Written policies and procedures should be developed with consideration of CMS guidelines, state and local laws, hospital and provider bylaws, and accreditation standards. Regulations and standards that outline specific documentation requirements include the following:

The Medicare Conditions of Participation for Hospitals	Section 482.24(c)(1) states that "All entries must be legible and complete, and must be authenticated and dated promptly by the person (identified by name and discipline) who is responsible for ordering, providing, or evaluating the service furnished."
Joint Commission Standards	The Joint Commission provides guidelines for proper authentication of medical record entries. There are also standards for protection of data and information from loss, destruction, or tampering.
State Laws	Many states have enacted laws that address electronic signatures and authentication of medical record information.

Within the EMR, a method to amend, correct, or clarify information must be accessible to the proper owner of the document, which in most cases is the original author. The author should be clearly identified, as well as the date the amendment was made. The information that is being amended or corrected should be clearly addressed. The ability to create and/or amend documentation by users other than the original author should be avoided.

Documentation policies should include specific procedures for correcting errors in the medical record. The error should never be completely erased, blacked out, or written over. Steps commonly followed for correction of errors include the following:

- Draw a line through the entry. Make sure that the inaccurate information is still legible.

- Write "error" by the incorrect entry and state the reason for the error in the margin or above the note if room.

- Sign and date the entry.

- Document the correct information. If the error is in a narrative note, it may be necessary to enter the correct information on the next available line, documenting the current date and time and referring to the incorrect entry.

Correction of errors in computerized or EMRs should follow the same basic rules. The notation that is in error should not be completely erased or deleted but outlined in such a way as to distinguish it as an error. Some electronic systems allow the incorrect material to be lightly shaded, although still visible. Other systems allow the word *error* to be watermarked over the incorrect information. Some systems do not allow any changes to the original text, only addendums. Whatever the method, the system should have the ability to track corrections or changes that are made to the record. The person making the change should be clearly identified. If a hard copy of the EMR is maintained, the hard copy should also be corrected.

Mandatory educational requirements are necessary to ensure provider understanding of documentation guidelines and to reinforce the importance of data quality. Frequently, local and national coverage decisions, along with CMS transmittals that address coverage issues, include specific details on documentation requirements. These requirements, along with accreditation documentation requirements, need to be reviewed regularly and included in the organization's policies and procedures.

Querying: A Process within a Process

One piece of advice that coders often hate to hear is, "Query the physician." Perhaps this is because they understand that as much as they dislike writing and sending queries, physicians generally dislike answering them. But queries should be regarded part of the standard health care operating process, meant to improve the accuracy of coding and documentation.

A **query** is "a question posed to a provider to obtain additional, clarifying documentation to improve the specificity and completeness of the data used to assign diagnosis and procedure codes in the patient's health record." AHIMA. "Managing an Effective Query Process" *Journal of AHIMA* 79, no. 10 (October 2008): 83–88. Many practice guidelines, including the American Health Information Management Association's Standards of Ethical Coding, include expectations that involve provider queries:

> "Coding professionals should consult physicians for clarification and additional documentation prior to code assignment when there is conflicting or ambiguous data in the health record."

Queries may be appropriate in the following situations:

Illegibility	The reader cannot determine the provider's assessment.
Completeness	The provider does not indicate the clinical significance of an abnormal test result.
Clarity	The provider documents a diagnosis, usually a symptom, without a statement of a cause.
Consistency	There is a disagreement between two or more providers with respect to a diagnosis.
Precision	Clinical reports or a clinical condition suggests a more specific diagnosis.

Although the documentation may be very clear to a clinical provider, the coder cannot assume the medical context or act as a physician when assigning codes. Only codes that are clearly supported in the documentation can be reported. This is sometimes difficult to convey to providers, especially when the clinical situation seems obvious. Consider this example:

EXAMPLE: A patient undergoes a left hemicolectomy for severe diverticulosis. Three days following surgery the physician documents that the patient's hemoglobin is 9.0 G/DL. The documentation does not indicate specifically that the patient has "anemia."

Many physicians would probably give coders a long, hard stare over their eyeglasses if the coder asked in this situation, "Does the patient have anemia?" However, from the coder's perspective and according to official coding guidelines, the diagnosis of anemia cannot be assigned by the coder based on lab values alone, but only on the physician's documentation of "anemia." In the preceding example, the coder should query the physician as to whether the patient has anemia *and* if it is related to the patient's surgery. This information is important in assigning the accurate anemia code.

Responses to queries should be timely and yet respectful of provider schedules and availability. Coders should ensure that the medical record, including all provider documentation, has been thoroughly reviewed before relying on a physician query. A proper review of other resources such as coding and coverage guidelines may also be beneficial before sending a query.

If the query form has been designed to be part of the medical record, a response on the form alone may be satisfactory. However, if the form is not part of the formal medical record, the documentation in the medical record should be amended to support the additional changes. The response may be documented in the progress notes, discharge summary, or other form in the medical record. Handwritten queries on scratch paper or sticky notes should be avoided.

Queries should be written in language that is neither leading nor based solely on any reimbursement ramifications. Examples of inappropriate queries follow:

EXAMPLE 1: The patient was admitted in respiratory distress and placed on oxygen. Please document that the patient has respiratory failure.

EXAMPLE 2: You have documented that the patient has pneumonia and difficulty swallowing. If you document that the patient has aspiration pneumonia, the hospital will receive a higher DRG payment.

In both these examples, the query is clearly leading the provider to a specific diagnosis. The query should state the clinical facts but allow the provider the opportunity to make a clinical determination. Consider this example of an appropriately worded query:

EXAMPLE: Per the documentation, the patient was admitted with acute exacerbation of chronic obstructive pulmonary disease and pneumonia. There was also concern about increased sputum production and the possible risk of aspiration pneumonia, given the patient's esophageal stricture. The patient was also started on empiric IV antibiotic treatment. Please indicate the type of pneumonia that was being treated.

Formatting queries to yield only a yes or no answer should be avoided. Such questions may lack specific detail in the medical record documentation to support the change. For example, asking a question such as, "Does the patient have gram-negative pneumonia?" may garner a quick yes or no answer, but the clinical data may not fully support the diagnosis.

Clinicians may respond to queries verbally, but the diagnosis should be clarified in the paper or electronic medical record. Remember that all codes assigned must be supported by the documentation, and evidence that a coder spoke to a physician who provided clarification on the documentation is not sufficient evidence to support code assignment.

Queries should:

- Be written clearly and concisely, using specific clinical documentation;
- Discuss clinical facts from the medical record;
- Be based on the treatment, evaluation, and monitoring of services;
- Allow physician to document specific diagnosis(es); and
- Be signed by the person writing the query and the provider answering the query.

The query process can be performed concurrently or retrospectively. When performed concurrently, the documentation at the time of discharge is more accurate, and delays in coding can be avoided. An effective clinical documentation program, as utilized in many hospital settings, should develop an effective and efficient concurrent query process.

To achieve good documentation, organizations must educate physicians as well as other professionals on the importance of documenting medical necessity. Medical staff bylaws should include requirements that documentation support medical necessity, discharge planning, and services performed. Bylaws should include requirements for timely documentation and responses to queries. Emphasis should be placed on the requirement that documentation be appropriate and complete before claims are submitted. The documentation should be appropriately organized and legible. Accurate and complete medical record documentation directly affects coding accuracy and helps ensure compliant claim submission.

Chapter Review

1. Describe the key factors in good documentation.

    _____

    _____

    _____

2. Review the ICD-9-CM Official Guidelines for Coding and Reporting. According to the guidelines, what role does accurate documentation play in the assignment of codes?

    _____

    _____

    _____

3. List at least three pros and cons of using templates.

    _____

    _____

    _____

4. Write a policy statement for making corrections in the medical record.

    _____

    _____

    _____

5. Identify key components of a properly constructed provider query.

    _____

    _____

    _____

6. Queries are not necessary for every discrepancy or unclear issue in the medical record. Identify a situation in which a query may be appropriate.

    _____

    _____

    _____

7. Discuss why a verbal response to a query, rather than a written response, is not the preferred method of responding to a provider query.

_____

_____

_____

8. Provide an example of how cutting and pasting could lead to inappropriate code assignment.

_____

_____

_____

9. Discuss the role of the clinical documentation specialist.

_____

_____

_____

10. Why would a diagnosis marked on an encounter form, and not in the progress note, not support medical necessity?

_____

_____

_____

Case Studies

Case Study 1

A physician's office utilizes the codes selected on superbills for coding claims. The office is able to bill the physician's claims within 24 hours following a patient encounter. The physician's documentation is often not complete at the time of coding and billing.

1. Discuss any potential problems the physician may encounter with regard to supporting medical necessity and accuracy of claims.

_____

_____

_____

Case Study 2

A hospital coder notices that physicians often document on admission that the patient has urosepsis/ UTI. The subsequent progress notes reflect the same diagnoses, but on the discharge summary, the physician documents "septicemia." The clinical documentation specialist notes that the working DRG is for septicemia.

1. Discuss how the coder should approach this situation and any potential compliance risks.

_____

_____

_____

Case Study 3

A patient is scheduled to undergo an elective surgery in the hospital. The physician documents in the hospital's medical record that the patient has diabetes mellitus, Type II, and that perioperatively the patient's insulin will need to be stabilized. The coder sends a query to the physician stating, "Please document uncontrolled diabetes in this patient's record."

1. Discuss whether this is a valid query and suggest alternatives.

_____

_____

_____

Case Study 4

An elderly patient is admitted into the hospital with a history of CVAs and pneumonia. Chest x-rays reveal right upper lobe opacities that are consistent with aspiration pneumonia. The patient undergoes swallowing studies and is scheduled for PEG placement. The physician also treats the patient with gram-negative IV antibiotics.

1. Write a properly formatted query to the physician regarding possible aspiration pneumonia.

_____

_____

_____

Case Study 5

A coder sends a query to a physician, but the physician fails to respond. The coder contacts the physician two additional times but receives no response.

1. How should the coder proceed with the unresolved question?

_____

_____

_____

References

AHIMA e-HIM™ Work Group: Guidelines for EHR Documentation Practice. (2007, January). Guidelines for EHR documentation to prevent fraud. Appendix C: Steps to prevent fraud in EHR documentation [Electronic version]. *Journal of AHIMA* 78(1), 65–68.

AHIMA e-HIM Work Group on Maintaining the Legal EHR. (2005, November–December). Update: Maintaining a legally sound health record—Paper and electronic (Electronic version). *Journal of AHIMA*, 7(10), 64A–L.

AHIMA House of Delegates. (2008, September). *American Health Information Management Association standards of ethical coding.* Retrieved July 17, 2008 from http://library.ahima.org/xpedio/groups/public/documents/ahima/bok2_001166.hcsp?dDocName=bok2_001166

American Health Information Management Association. (2008). *Copy functionality toolkit.* Retrieved from http://www.ahima.org/infocenter/documents/copy_functionality_toolkit.pdf

Pinnacle Business Solutions. (2008, July 17). Electronic medical records may lead to decreased payment. Retrieved from http://www.lamedicare.com/provider/viewarticle.aspx?articleid=6194

TMF Health Quality Institute, the Quality Improvement Organization Support Center for the Hospital Payment Monitoring Program. (*2006,* January; revised 2008, March). *Hospital Payment Monitoring Program (HPMP) compliance workbook.* Retrieved from http://hpmpresources.org/Tools/tabid/93/Default.aspx

Tully, Melinda (Mel), and Withrow, Esq., Scott C. (2008, February 25). Successful physician queries. ADVANCE for Health Inf*ormation Professional*s. Retrieved from http://health-information.advanceweb.com/editorial/content/editorial.aspx?cc=108461

Coding and Medical Necessity

Objectives

At the completion of this chapter, the learner should be able to:

- Define medical necessity.
- Discuss the purpose of national and local coverage determinations.
- Explain the process of developing national and local coverage determinations.
- Discuss appropriate Advance Beneficiary Notice (ABN) presentation and requirements.
- Identify necessary requirements for billing under medical necessity guidelines, including proper use of modifiers and charge submission.
- Discuss the challenges of compliant coding under medical necessity, including the impact on the patient and the provider.
- List compliance activities that identify potential risk areas, and provide steps to resolution.

Key Terms

ABN modifier GA

ABN modifier GY

ABN modifier GZ

Additional Documentation Request (ADR)

Advance Beneficiary Notice (ABN)

automated review

CMS Medical Review Program

In re: Managed Care Litigation

LCD Reconsideration Process

local coverage determinations (LCDs)

medical necessity

Medicare administrative contractors (MACs)

national coverage determinations (NCDs)

NCD reconsideration process

preauthorization

precertification

program safeguard contractors (PSCs)

Quality Improvement Organizations (QIOs)

recertification

Defining Medical Necessity

Determining **medical necessity** and having good documentation are key elements of compliant coding and billing. Defining medical necessity can be a problem, since physicians, payers, individual states, insurance commissions, laws, the courts, and even the patient may define medical necessity differently. Physicians are often surprised to learn that not everything they order is considered "medically necessary" under a payer's definition. With these differences of opinion in the definition, the final determination of medical necessity is sometimes made in the courts, by a local Medicare contractor, third-party payer, or an individual physician.

Payers may apply medical necessity determinations *generally*, meaning they have made a general determination for all beneficiaries on the definition of medical necessity. For example, a payer may state patients covered under Plan A must have a specific diagnosis for a positron emission tomography (PET) scan to be considered covered. No exceptions are made based on a patient's medical condition. Some payer plans, however, define medical necessity in terms of what is medically necessary for a particular patient, based on the clinical indications at the time. This definition is also applied in many court cases.

One recent national court case involved Aetna, CIGNA, Health Net, Prudential, Anthem/WellPoint, and Humana managed care organizations (***In re: Managed Care Litigation***). Physicians and medical societies sought class action alleging that the companies conspired to improperly deny, delay, or reduce payment to more than 900,000 physicians in violation of the Racketeering Influenced and Corrupt Organizations (RICO) Act. Many of the defendants settled out of court. Part of the complaints included failing to pay for "medically necessary" services as allowed under beneficiary plans. The settlements, among other things, included clarification of the definition of medical necessity. Expiration dates are included in the settlements, however, which means that in the future the companies are not legally bound to follow the definitions of medical necessity as outlined in the court action.

The health care provider or supplier must be aware of the various definitions of medical necessity whether they are defined by the payer, the government, or the courts. Failure to do so can result in reduced payment, no payment, and even allegations of fraud.

Although the definition can vary, most agree that medical necessity must:

- Be generally accepted medical practice

- A medical standard of the community

- Be widely accepted

Prior to the settlement of *In re: Managed Care Litigation* it was commonplace that many managed care organizations included cost into the medical necessity definition or, at least, the application of medical necessity. In the American Medical Association's (AMA) Model Managed Care Contract, medical necessity is defined as:

Health care services or procedures that a prudent physician would provide to a patient for the purpose of preventing, diagnosing, or treating an illness, injury, disease, or its symptoms in a manner that is (a) in accordance with generally accepted standards of medical practice; (b) clinically appropriate in terms of type, frequency, extent, site, and duration; and (c) not primarily for the economic benefit of the health plans and purchasers or for the convenience of the patient, treating physician, or other health care provider.

It is no surprise that the AMA's definition clearly includes language that prohibits using cost as a factor, since it is the AMA's position that cost criteria should not be used in medical necessity determinations.

Medicare makes reference to medical necessity when addressing services that are "reasonable" and "necessary." According to Section 1862(a)(1)(A) of the Social Security Act, Medicare will not cover services that "are not reasonable and necessary for the diagnosis or treatment of illness or injury or to improve the functioning of a malformed member." Chapter 13 of the *Medicare Program Integrity Manual,* Section 5.1(C), allows Medicare contractors to determine whether services are considered reasonable and necessary based on the following criteria:

- The service is safe and effective;

- The service is not experimental or investigational (exception: routine costs of qualifying clinical trial services with dates of service on or after September 19, 2000, which meet the requirements of the clinical trials national coverage determinations (NCDs) are considered reasonable and necessary); and

- The service is appropriate, including the duration and frequency that is considered appropriate for the service, in terms of whether it is:
  - Furnished in accordance with accepted standards of medical practice for the diagnosis or treatment of the patient's condition or to improve the function of a malformed body member;
  - Furnished in a setting appropriate to the patient's medical needs and condition;
  - Ordered and/or furnished by qualified personnel;
  - One that meets, but does not exceed, the patient's medical need; and
  - At least as beneficial as an existing and available medically appropriate alternative.

Medicare generally does not provide coverage for services that are considered routine or screening. However, it provides an exception to the definition of "reasonable" and "necessary" for some screening and preventive services including the following:

- Pneumonococcal, influenza, and hepatitis B vaccines are covered if they are reasonable and necessary for the prevention of illness.

- Hospice care is covered if it is reasonable and necessary for the palliation or management of terminal illness.

- Screening mammography is covered if it is within frequency limits and meets quality standards.

- Screening Pap smears and screening pelvic exams are covered if they are within frequency limits.

- Prostate cancer screening tests are covered if they are within frequency limits.

- Colorectal cancer screening tests are covered if they are within frequency limits.

- One pair of conventional eyeglasses or contact lenses is furnished subsequent to each cataract surgery with insertion of an intraocular lens.

As indicated previously, payers may reduce or deny payment based on their definition of medical necessity. Some commercial payers allow for payment on services when **precertification** or **preauthorization** has been obtained. The terms are often used interchangeably and generally include a process whereby the insurance company is notified before a service is rendered or a patient is admitted into the hospital. The precertification may be the responsibility of either the health care provider or the patient (or patient's family). Many insurance companies include a list of CPT codes, services, or admission types (such as elective surgery) that require precertification before payment will be made. Failure to obtain precertification does not automatically default to patient liability. In some payer contracts and payment policies, the liability rests with the provider.

One problem associated with precertification is that many insurance companies require a specific ICD-9-CM diagnosis or CPT code to describe the service that is going to be performed. Often, the actual final diagnosis may be different based on the physician's documentation, clinical findings, or testing results. The proposed procedure may also change based on the clinical findings. For example, a CT scan of the abdomen/pelvis may be planned, but because of unusual findings a more extensive CT scan or additional test may be warranted. If the provider does not obtain precertification for the more extensive procedure or additional procedure, payment may be denied. It would be noncompliant to code the precertified test if a different test was actually performed. The official coding guidelines must be followed when coding for precertified services.

CMS uses **national coverage determinations (NCDs)** and **local coverage determinations (LCDs)** to describe medical necessity and coverage for Medicare beneficiaries. Other third-party payers may also develop coverage policies that outline coverage benefits.

National and Local Coverage Determinations

In the following section we discuss the development and application of CMS coverage policies and the importance of accurate coding.

CMS is required by law (under the Social Security Act) to pay for only those services that are reasonable and medically necessary. Providers may bill Medicare only for services that are considered covered; billing for services that are not covered is considered fraud under HIPAA.

CMS develops NCDs to define coverage guidelines and medical necessity for medical items, services, treatments, procedures, or technologies. NCDs are located in the *National Coverage Determinations Manual,* available on the CMS website.

When developing coverage decisions and medical policies, CMS may utilize an independent group, the Medicare Evidence Development & Coverage Advisory Committee (MedCAC) to provide expert advice on specific clinical topics. The committee reviews medical literature, makes technology assessments, and provides advice on the effectiveness and appropriateness of medical items and services. The committee meets approximately six times per year with meetings announced in the *Federal Register.*

CMS Medical Review Program

CMS contracts with carriers, fiscal intermediaries, and **program safeguard contractors (PSCs)** to perform medical review functions and to identify billing errors. This process is known as the **CMS Medical Review Program**. The entities involved in the program are generally referred to as *contractors.* Not all contractors perform all the same functions; some may have a contract to perform only data analysis. Issues that deal with quality of care are generally not the responsibility of medical review contractors; those issues remain with **Quality Improvement Organizations (QIOs) or Medicare Administrative Contractors**.

The goal of the Medical Review Program is to "reduce the payment error rate by identifying and addressing billing errors concerning coverage and coding made by providers." Contractors analyze and evaluate data to identify potential coding and billing problems. Local Medicare Contractors may develop LCDs to address specific issues.

An LCD is written to specify whether a service is covered (medically reasonable and necessary) and to provide specific documentation and coding instructions. The LCD should also explain how contractors will review claims to ensure they meet Medicare's requirements.

Contractors write and publish LCDs to provide guidance to the public and providers within a specified geographic area. Contractors with jurisdiction over other regions may develop similar policies, but they are not required to do so. Different contractors within the same geographic region (Part A and Part B) are not required to share policies or have similar policies. This can create confusion among providers and beneficiaries when a particular service may be considered covered for the Part B (physician) service but not covered for the Part A (hospital) service. However, under the Medicare Modernization Act of 2003, Medicare is required to combine Part A and Part B administration activities into 15 **Medicare Administrative Contractors (MACs)**. CMS has until October 2011 to transition all current contractor workloads to new MAC authorities. The MACs are required to consolidate all the LCDs of its member states and select the least restrictive LCD. The new MAC LCDs should address both Part A and Part B services.

Although a contractor may develop an LCD on any procedure/service, there are certain instances in which development or revision of a policy is required. Contractors *must* develop LCDs when an item or service has been identified that is never covered under certain circumstances, and they wish to establish an automated review. The contractor's claims processing software automatically reviews the claims and can issue an automated denial. Contractors may implement an automated review when there is:

- A clear policy that serves as a basis for the denial, or

- A review based on a medically unlikely edit, or

- No timely response is received in response to an **Additional Documentation Request (ADR)** letter.

Existing local coverage policies must be revised when new NCDs, coverage provisions in interpretative manuals, or program instructions are published. All revisions and developments should occur within 90 days of published national changes. Contractors must also revise LCDs within 120 days of an update to ICD-9-CM or CPT/HCPCS codes.

Contractors *may* develop LCDs when medical review indicates a widespread problem or a service has been identified as high-dollar or high-volume. Other reasons for developing LCDs include assuring beneficiary access to care, the occurrence of frequent denials of a specific service (or anticipation of frequent denials), and the assumption by a new contractor of the workload of another contractor.

LCDs are developed on the basis of NCDs, coverage in interpretative manuals, or contractor reviews. NCDs are binding on all Medicare contractors, fiscal intermediaries, quality improvement organizations, Medicare Choice organizations, and PSCs. Within 30 days of issuing an NCD, contractors are required to inform providers of the NCD in a provider bulletin or on the contractor's website. When reviewing claims, contractors must apply guidelines established in NCDs.

As mentioned previously, CMS may consult with MedCAC in establishing NCDs. Providers, vendors, and the general public may also request the development or revision of an NCD. The entire process may take several months, with a period allowed for public comment. Figure 4-1 outlines the process for creating an NCD.

Prior to finalizing an NCD, CMS prepares a Coverage Decision Memorandum. The memorandum informs the public that CMS has concluded its analysis, outlines implementation plans, and provides background information. Although decision memoranda are not binding on contractors, CMS encourages contractors to consider them in their reviews. The following are some examples of national coverage decisions:

- Acupuncture

- Anticancer chemotherapy for colorectal cancer

- Artificial hearts and related devices

Medical National Coverage Process
• A formal request to the Centers for Medicaid & Medicare Services (CMS) is made in writing. There are two types of formal requests:
◦ One track available only to aggrieved parties (defined as "individuals entitled to benefits under Part A, or enrolled under Part B, or both, who are in need of the items or services that are the subject of the coverage determination").
◦ One track available to anyone, including aggrieved parties, other beneficiaries, and manufacturers.
• The formal request letter and supporting documentation is submitted electronically (unless there is good cause for only a hard copy submission).
• The requestor identifies the request as a "formal request for an NCD" or a "formal request for reconsideration."
• The requestor states the benefit category or categories of the Medicare program to which the requestor believes the item or service applies.
• Upon acceptance of a valid request, CMS notifies the requestor and posts a tracking sheet on its website announcing review of the issue.
• The tracking sheet provides information for public participation, gathering additional information, and time frames.
• A decision memorandum is developed within 90 days.
• The national coverage decision is prepared and issued as a manual instruction or other document such as a program memorandum, ruling, or Federal Register notice.
• Payment changes or other system changes dictated by the NCD instructions are effective within 180 calendar days of the first day of the next full calendar quarter that follows the date of the decision memorandum.
• The decision memorandum and payment change can take up to 270 days from the date a formal request for an NCD is accepted for review by CMS.

Figure 4-1 Summation of the National Coverage Determinations Process. *SOURCE: Federal Register,* Volume 68, No. 187, Friday, September 26, 2003).

- Cytogenetic studies
- Diagnostic Pap smears
- Gastrophotography
- Home blood glucose monitors
- Infusion pumps
- Laser procedures
- Pancreas transplants
- PET scans
- Treatment of obesity
- Vertebral artery surgery

Local coverage determinations must be written so as not to conflict with national coverage determinations or policies. Similar to the development of an NCD, the LCD should be based on strong clinical evidence, including published research studies and scientific data. Medical opinion from consultations with medical associations and other health care experts should also be sought.

LCDs from all contractors must be written in a standard format and include specific mandatory items, including the indications and limitations of coverage, applicable CPT, HCPCS, and ICD-9-CM codes and reasons for denial. Contractors may include restrictive language in the development of an LCD, but only when strong clinical evidence exists. Restrictive language (also referred to as "absolute words") includes phrases such as "is never covered" or "is only covered for. . . ." When a policy has been written using restrictive language, claims may be denied via **automated review**, meaning that the claim will be automatically denied, even when supporting documentation is included with the claim. Contractors are not required to make any exceptions or give individual consideration based on evidence when applying LCDs. If a policy is written with less restrictive language, such as "not usually medically necessary," the contractor cannot use automated review if documentation is submitted with the claim in a prepay review. If a national policy includes words such as "never" or "only if," the local policy must also include the more restrictive language.

Many LCDs include guidelines regarding coding provisions. Policies may provide a list of covered diagnoses including specific ICD-9-CM codes. Inclusion of the code on the claim does not automatically guarantee coverage, however, and the service must still meet the "reasonable and necessary" conditions.

Unfortunately, many local and national policies that include coding instructions are not written by coding professionals. Local coverage determinations that include specific codes and coding instructions should not conflict with the official coding guidelines. For example, it would not be appropriate for the LCD to state that an E-code be first-listed. Although most LCDs are not so obviously inaccurate, some policies do instruct providers on sequencing, selection of combination codes, the use of manifestation codes, and other coding instructions. If the coding instructions in the policy conflict with the official coding guidelines, and therefore HIPAA, the contractor should be contacted and asked to correct the policy. If the contractor refuses, the provider should contact the regional office or follow the instructions for filing a HIPAA complaint.

Contractors are required to review all policies at least annually. Additionally, contractors must publish and maintain draft and final policies on the CMS website.

Prior to releasing a final LCD, contractors must allow a minimum comment period of 45 days. Providers, associations, vendors, manufacturers, beneficiaries, and caregivers may comment on draft versions of LCDs. Local Medicare contractors may not elicit comments on NCDs. It is important that providers utilize the comment period to review and respond to draft local coverage decisions. After a policy becomes final, it becomes much more difficult to change or amend the policy.

In some instances revisions to LCDs do not require a comment period. These include revisions that "liberalize" the policy, corrections of a typographical or grammatical error (assuming it does not substantially change the LCD), addition of clarifications, updating of diagnosis and procedures codes, and issuance of an LCD for "compelling reasons" (a highly unsafe procedure).

In addition to the 45-day comment period, contractors must provide open meetings to discuss draft policies. Contractors must give equal consideration to comments received whether written or provided at the open meeting. After the comment period has ended and comments have been considered, a final policy is published. The new or revised policy usually includes an effective date, which is the date when all claims will be applied to the LCD. A new LCD may not be implemented retroactively. Contractors are required to provide necessary education on applying the conditions outlined in LCDs.

Providers and other interested parties may request revisions to final LCDs through the **LCD Reconsideration Process**. Contractors must include on their websites instructions for submitting reconsideration requests. Contractors cannot accept reconsiderations for the following:

- NCDs
- Coverage provisions in interpretative manuals

- Draft LCDs

- Template LCDs, unless or until they are adopted by the contractor

- Retired LCDs

- Individual claim determinations

- Bulletins, articles, training materials; and

- Any instance in which no LCD exists, that is, requests for the development of an LCD.

A request for reconsideration cannot conflict with an established NCD. Changes to national coverage decisions are requested through the **NCD reconsideration process**, which is outlined on the CMS website.

The requirements for LCD reconsideration are the same as for development of a new LCD. That is, the reconsideration must be based on:

- Published authoritative evidence derived from definitive randomized clinical trials or other definitive studies

- General acceptance by the medical community (standard of practice), as supported by sound medical evidence based on:

  - Scientific data or research studies published in peer-reviewed medical journals;

  - Consensus of expert medical opinion (i.e., recognized authorities in the field); or

  - Medical opinion derived from consultations with medical associations or other health care experts.

Many contractors also state that any published evidence must be "new" evidence that has been published since the last time the LCD was updated. The guidelines for reconsideration make it apparent that it is important for providers to review and provide comment on policies when they are in the draft stage, rather than waiting until they become final.

It is important to note that not all CMS medical necessity guidelines are published in local or national coverage determinations. Coverage guidelines are also published in CMS interpretative manuals, including the *Medicare Carriers Manual* (MCM) and the *Medicare Intermediary Manual* (MIM). CMS often utilizes transmittals, *MLN Matters* (formerly *Medlearn Matters*) articles, and articles published by the contractor to provide coverage instructions.

When determining medical necessity, it is important that the provider reference the correct LCD or NCD. As noted previously, there are multiple policies for multiple different regions of the country. Policies may vary from state to state and with physician (Part B services) and facility (Part A services). It is important to ensure that the policy being referenced is correct for the date of service in question, as policies change frequently, and that if a medical necessity software product is used, that the vendor has loaded the appropriate coverage policies.

Advance Beneficiary Notices of Noncoverage (ABNs)

When the provider determines that a Medicare beneficiary will receive a service that is considered not medically necessary or noncovered (as defined in local or national coverage determinations or other coverage manuals) the patient should be presented with an **Advance Beneficiary Notice (ABN)** of noncoverage (see Figure 4-2).

(A) **Notifier(s):**

(B) **Patient Name:** _____   *(C)* **Identification Number:** _____

ADVANCE BENEFICIARY NOTICE OF NONCOVERAGE (ABN)

<u>*NOTE*</u>: If Medicare doesn't pay for *(D)*_____ below, you may have to pay.

Medicare does not pay for everything, even some care that you or your health care provider have good reason to think you need. We expect Medicare may not pay for the *(D)*_____ below.

*(D)*_____	*(E)* Reason Medicare May Not Pay:	*(F)* Estimated Cost:

WHAT YOU NEED TO DO NOW:

- Read this notice, so you can make an informed decision about your care.
- Ask us any questions that you may have after you finish reading.
- Choose an option below about whether to receive the *(D)*_____listed above.
    - **Note:** If you choose Option 1 or 2, we may help you to use any other insurance that you might have, but Medicare cannot require us to do this.

(G) OPTIONS: Check only one box. We cannot choose a box for you.
❑ **OPTION 1.** I want the *(D)*_____ listed above. You may ask to be paid now, but I also want Medicare billed for an official decision on payment, which is sent to me on a Medicare Summary Notice (MSN). I understand that if Medicare doesn't pay, I am responsible for payment, but **I can appeal to Medicare** by following the directions on the MSN. If Medicare does pay, you will refund any payments I made to you, less co-pays or deductibles.
❑ **OPTION 2.** I want the *(D)*_____ listed above, but do not bill Medicare. You may ask to be paid now as I am responsible for payment. **I cannot appeal if Medicare is not billed**.
❑ **OPTION 3.** I don't want the *(D)*_____listed above. I understand with this choice I am **not** responsible for payment, and **I cannot appeal to see if Medicare would pay.**

(H) **Additional Information:**

This notice gives our opinion, not an official Medicare decision. If you have other questions on this notice or Medicare billing, call **1-800-MEDICARE** (1-800-633-4227/**TTY**: 1-877-486-2048).

Signing below means that you have received and understand this notice. You also receive a copy.

(I) **Signature:**	*(J)* **Date:**

According to the Paperwork Reduction Act of 1995, no persons are required to respond to a collection of information unless it displays a valid OMB control number. The valid OMB control number for this information collection is 0938-0566. The time required to complete this information collection is estimated to average 7 minutes per response, including the time to review instructions, search existing data resources, gather the data needed, and complete and review the information collection. If you have comments concerning the accuracy of the time estimate or suggestions for improving this form, please write to: CMS, 7500 Security Boulevard, Attn: PRA Reports Clearance Officer, Baltimore, Maryland 21244-1850.

Form CMS-R-131 (03/08)   Form Approved OMB No. 0938-0566

Figure 4-2 CMS Advance Beneficiary Form (CMS-R-131). *Courtsey of www.cms.hhs.gov*

The ABN provides an opportunity to the beneficiary to make informed health care decisions about whether to receive an item or service that might be denied as not reasonable and necessary. If the provider expects payment for the items or services to be denied by Medicare, the beneficiary must be advised *before* the item or service is furnished. To be "personally and fully responsible for payment" means that the beneficiary will be liable to make payment "out of pocket", through other insurance coverage, through a state Medicaid program, or self-pay. Nearly all health care providers must notify patients of noncovered services, including physicians, nonphysician providers, hospitals, hospice providers, skilled nursing facilities, home health agencies, and suppliers. The Medicare ABN form may be used only for Medicare patients. A provider must use a different form to provide a non-Medicare beneficiary a notice of noncoverage.

A provider may be held financially liable for noncovered services when a Medicare contractor has published specific requirements for coverage, and the patient does not meet the definition of medical necessity. In cases where the provider believes that the service may not be covered as reasonable and necessary, an acceptable advance notice of Medicare's possible denial of payment must be given to the patient. The patient's signature on the ABN form allows the provider to bill the patient for the service that is considered not medically necessary. Therefore, the ABN represents a choice to the patient: to receive the service and likely be liable for the charges or to refuse the service and therefore not pay for it. An ABN should be presented to the patient *only* after the provider has determined that it is nearly certain that Medicare will not pay for the service. If the provider does not perform this investigation, it may be subjecting the patient to an uninformed, inappropriate choice. For example, a radiologist who requires every Medicare beneficiary to sign an ABN for CT scans may be presenting the beneficiary with a choice to refuse or to pay for the service when in fact the patient has a condition that meets the definition of medical necessity. Considering that they may be faced with paying thousands of dollars for the scan, patients may elect not to have the test that would have met the definition of medical necessity and could diagnosis a potentially life-threatening condition.

A provider who consistently fails to present ABNs to its beneficiaries, even accepting provider liability for the services, may be seen as offering "free" care or inducements, which may be considered fraudulent. Medicare contractors are encouraged to identify providers who do not present ABNs to their patients and investigate them under anti-kickback statutes.

When considering whether a patient should be presented with an ABN, Section 50.2.1 of the *Medicare Claims Processing Manual* states:

- If the user expects Medicare to pay, an ABN should **not** be given.

- If the user "never knows whether or not Medicare will pay," an ABN should **not** be given.

- If the user expects Medicare to deny payment, the next question is: On what basis is denial expected?

If the provider fails to obtain an ABN, the patient cannot be billed, and the cost is provider liability. An ABN may never be given routinely, that is, for every Medicare patient and for every service. However, an ABN is never required in an emergency or urgent care situation.

The ABN must be verbally reviewed with the beneficiary or his or her representative. It would be inappropriate to include the ABN in a packet of forms that a patient may routinely sign without providing adequate explanation. The beneficiary must receive the ABN far enough in advance of the service to allow for consideration of other options and to make an informed decision. For example, it would be inappropriate to deliver an ABN to a patient once he or she has been prepped for surgery or placed or attached to diagnostic or treatment equipment. This requirement does not strictly prohibit the delivery of a notice after a beneficiary has entered an examination room or is ready to receive certain services or items. If a situation arises during a service when the provider sees a need for a previously unforeseen service and it is expected that Medicare will not pay for the service, it is permissible to present the beneficiary with an ABN, provided the patient is capable of understanding (e.g., the patient is not under anesthesia).

The provider who is receiving reimbursement for an item or service is responsible for obtaining the ABN. This can be problematic, especially for ancillary services such as laboratory, pathology, and radiology services. Often, the patient presents with an order from the physician's office, and the testing facility is unsure whether an ABN has been obtained. In some cases the testing facility may not even see the patient, as in cases in which a pathology sample has been sent to a lab. The lab is ultimately liable for obtaining an ABN for its service if the staff thinks Medicare will not pay. However, the testing facility may seek additional history from the ordering physician before performing the test.

The patient should be given a copy of the form, with the original maintained by the provider. The ABN form is technically an "administrative" form and does not need to be filed in the patient's health record. However, the form should be available when requested from the Medicare contractor or in making a determination of medical necessity.

The ABN must be "hand-delivered" to the beneficiary. If items or services are furnished by telephone order, mail order, or over the Internet, ABNs still need to be executed in advance of furnishing the item or service by other means, such as mail, fax, or online form. Telephone notice alone to the beneficiary or his or her representative is not sufficient.

Medicare beneficiaries may be presented only with the official form approved by the Executive Office of Management and Budget (OMB). Any other form is considered invalid. The official OMB form may be used only for Medicare patients. Independent laboratories, physicians, practitioners, hospitals (outpatient services), and suppliers must use the official form. Other notices of noncoverage for home health agencies and other specific circumstances are available on the CMS website.

Limited customization of the form is permitted. A notification that does not meet the official ABN requirements may be ruled defective and does not serve to protect the provider. The following are some specific ABN requirements:

- The page may be either letter- or legal-sized but must be reproduced on a single page.

- The provider's logo may be at the top of the notice, replacing the blank (A) if necessary. The logo must include the address and telephone number of the provider. More than one provider's logo may be included in the title section, as long as it clear whom the beneficiary should respond to for questions.

- The form may be typed or handwritten but be large enough to read, using at least a 12-point font. Italics cannot be used, nor any font that is difficult to read. The Medicare Claims Processing Manual (Section 40.3.1.1) provides the following examples of easily readable fonts: Arial, Arial Narrow, Times Roman, Courier.

- The patient's full name should be included on the form in blank (B), including a middle initial if known. An ABN is not considered invalid if there is a misspelling or missing initial, as long as the beneficiary or representative would recognize the name listed as being that of the beneficiary.

- The patient's identification number, blank (C), represents an identification number that can help link the notice with a related claim. This may include a medical record number. The beneficiary's Social Security number may never appear on the form. This section is optional.

- The noncovered service is noted in blank (D). Multiple services may be listed and bundled under one cost. The service should not be written in technical language but, rather, in lay language that is easily understood. Services described only by a CPT/HCPCS code are not acceptable.

- There must be at least one reason listed in blank (E) that describes the reason why Medicare may not pay. Stating only "noncovered" is not appropriate. Medicare lists three possible reasons for noncoverage on the ABN:

  - "Medicare does not pay for this test for your condition."

  - "Medicare does not pay for this test as often as this (denied as too frequent)."

  - "Medicare does not pay for experimental or research use tests."

- Providers must enter a cost estimate under the blank (F) section for any services listed as noncovered. Medicare assumes providers will make a "good faith" attempt to estimate cost and recognizes that final costs may vary. The estimate should be within $100 or 25% of the actual costs, whichever is greater. The ABN is considered invalid if this section is not completed.

- The blank (G) options represent three check boxes with choices that the beneficiary or his or her representative may make. The provider may not choose the check box for the patient. The beneficiary or representative must select only one of the check boxes. The patient may decide to receive some or all of the services noted on the form. Those services that the patient chooses not to receive should be crossed out. If necessary a new form should be created.

- Blank (H) is an optional field for additional information that can be inserted by the provider. Possible uses of this space include:

  - "You should notify your doctor who orders these laboratory tests that you did not receive them."

  - Providing additional information on Medicare payment policy for a specific service.

  - Information on coverage specific to the beneficiary's other health insurance policies.

- The patient's signature should be in cursive, with a printed name if needed for legibility.

The patient or an authorized representative of the person may sign the ABN. An authorized representative is defined as a person who is acting on the beneficiary's behalf and in the beneficiary's best interest. The authorized representative may be those individuals authorized under state law to make health care decisions, for example, a legally appointed representative or guardian of the beneficiary. However, the person acting as an authorized representative for purposes of the proper authentication of the ABN is not required to have such a legal definition. The order of priority of authorized representatives is:

- The spouse, unless legally separated

- An adult child

- A parent

- An adult sibling

- A close friend (defined as "an adult who has exhibited special care and concern for the patient, who is familiar with the patient's personal values, and who is reasonably available")

The beneficiary or representative must enter the date he or she signed the ABN form.

A single ABN may be used for subsequent services if the service has not changed. For example one ABN is acceptable for a patient who has a laboratory test performed monthly. As long as the test does not change in any way, the initial ABN may be used for subsequent services. An ABN is valid for one year; treatment or testing periods greater than one year require a new ABN.

An ABN is not acceptable if the notice is unreadable, illegible, or otherwise incomprehensible, or when the individual is incapable of understanding the notice owing to particular circumstances. Patients who are comatose, confused (e.g., experiencing confusion because of senility, dementia, Alzheimer's disease), or otherwise legally incompetent are not able to understand their rights and therefore require the presence of an authorized representative for purposes of notice. Patients who cannot read the language in which the notice is written or who are functionally illiterate, blind or otherwise visually impaired, or deaf or cannot hear the explanation of the notice or ask questions are considered to have not received a notice at all.

The notice is invalid if given during any emergency or when the beneficiary is under great duress. The provider must first "stabilize" the patient before financial responsibility forms or notices are given to an individual.

The following are other reasons an ABN may be considered invalid:

- When the beneficiary is misled or coerced in any way.
- The reason Medicare may not pay is stated only that it is a possibility Medicare may not pay. Stating "medically unnecessary" is not an acceptable reason Medicare will not pay.
- The ABN is presented to the patient after the service has been furnished.
- The ABN is blank when the beneficiary is asked to sign the form. To be effective the ABN must be completed before it is presented to the beneficiary.
- Services or items are added to the ABN form after the patient has signed it.
- It is more than one year since the patient dated/signed the form.
- The estimated costs are not entered.

"Routine" use of ABNs is not appropriate. This includes using an ABN when there is no specific, identifiable reason. An ABN should not be presented to the beneficiary unless the provider is nearly certain that Medicare will not pay for an item or service. ABNs given routinely are considered defective notices and do not protect the provider from liability. There are limited ("exceptional") circumstances, however, when a provider may routinely give an ABN to a beneficiary. These include:

- Services that are always denied by Medicare, for example, acupuncture services, cosmetic procedures, and routine physical exams.
- Experimental items and services. These services are considered not proven safe and effective and are therefore denied by statute. The provider may use the reason "Medicare does not pay for services which it considers to be experimental or for research use."
- Frequency-limited items and services. For example, a screening mammography is allowed once annually for female beneficiaries age 40 or older. When an item or service is listed as being medically necessary based on a frequency limitation, the provider may present all female Medicare beneficiaries with an ABN for the mammography service. The provider cannot know whether the patient had a previous mammogram within the past year.

Giving an ABN for all claims or items or services, or presenting a "blanket" ABN, is not appropriate. The ABN must be specific to the patient and specific to the service or item provided.

An ABN is not required for items or services that are statutorily excluded from Medicare coverage (also referred to as "categorical denials"), such as cosmetic surgery, dental care, and routine physical examinations. See Figure 4-3 for further examples of excluded services. Note, however, that the ABN form may be used to convey to the patient that the service or item is not considered medically necessary.

The ABN is also not required for items or services defined as "technical denials." This type of denial indicates that the item or service was not furnished in a manner that satisfied the applicable condition of coverage. For example, a screening prostate test is a procedure that is covered for men age 50 and older. If a Medicare beneficiary under the age of 50 receives a screening prostate test, the service is not covered by Medicare as defined under Section 1862 of the Social Security Act. (Only people under the age of 65 with certain disabilities and people of all ages with end-stage renal disease are eligible for Medicare.) The claim is considered technically denied, an ABN is not required, and the beneficiary is liable. However, the ABN may be issued voluntarily in these situations.

Categorical Denials
The following are examples of services/items in which Medicare payment cannot be made based upon statutory exclusion (§1862(a)(2–8) and (10)–(21) of the Social Security Act:
• Routine physicals and most tests for screenings.
• Most shots (vaccinations).
• Routine eye care, most eyeglasses and examinations.
• Hearing aids and hearing examinations.
• Cosmetic surgery.
• Orthopedic shoes and foot supports (orthotics).
• Dental care and dentures (in most cases).
• Routine foot care and flat foot care.
• Services under a physician's private contract.
• Services paid for by a government entity that is not Medicare.
• Healthcare received outside of the U.S. not covered by Medicare.
• Services by immediate relatives.
• Services required as a result of war.
• Services for which there is no legal obligation to pay.
• Home health services furnished under a plan of care, if the agency does not submit the claim.
• Items and services excluded under the Assisted Suicide Funding Restriction Act of 1997.
• Items or services furnished in a competitive acquisition area by any entity that does not have a contract with the Department of Health and Human Services (except in a case of urgent need).
• Physicians' services performed by a physician assistant, midwife, psychologist, or nurse anesthetist, when furnished to an inpatient, unless they are furnished under arrangement with the hospital.
• Items and services furnished to an individual who is a resident of a skilled nursing facility or of a part of a facility that includes a skilled nursing facility, unless they are furnished under arrangements by the skilled nursing facility.
• Services of an assistant at surgery without prior approval from the peer review organization.
• Outpatient occupational and physical therapy services furnished incident to a physician's service.

Figure 4-3 Categorical Denials. Example of items not covered by Medicare. *SOURCE: Medicare Claims Processing Manual, Chapter 30–Financial Liability Protections, section 20.2.1–Categorical Denials, available at www.cms.hhs.gov*

The official ABN form is available in English and Spanish. The form cannot be translated into any other language. If necessary, the provider should ensure that the beneficiary has verbal assistance to fully understand the notice. The use of a translator may be noted in the "Additional Information" section of the form.

The beneficiary or representative may refuse to sign a properly executed ABN. In these cases, CMS states that the provider should consider not furnishing the item or service, unless the consequences (health and safety of the patient, or civil liability in case of harm) are such that this is not an option (Medicare Claims Processing Manual, Section 40.3.4.6). The provider may annotate the ABN, noting that the patient refused to sign. If the beneficiary demands the service and refuses to pay or sign the ABN, the provider should have a second person witness the provision of the ABN and the beneficiary's refusal to sign. When a second person is not available, the second witness may be contacted by telephone to witness the beneficiary's refusal to sign the ABN.

As mentioned previously, the beneficiary is held liable when it is determined that he or she had prior knowledge that Medicare payment for the service would be denied, as specified in the ABN. In the case of a properly delivered ABN, the contractor determines that the beneficiary is liable and responsible for expenses incurred. In the case in which a beneficiary received an ABN, and on determination, the claim was paid as covered, the original ABN cannot be used as evidence of knowledge to hold the beneficiary liable in a later case. If Medicare does pay for the service, the beneficiary is liable for any coinsurance or deductible amounts.

ABN Modifiers

The provider must communicate to the Medicare contractor whether an ABN was obtained. This is accomplished by appending a modifier to the service. The following modifiers are used to communicate the presence or absence of an ABN:

Modifier GA	Waiver of liability statement on file
Modifier GY	Item or service statutorily excluded or does not meet the definition of any Medicare benefit
Modifier GZ	Item or service expected to be denied as not reasonable and necessary (no signed ABN on file)

ABN modifier GA is used to indicate that a waiver of liability (ABN) is on file. When this modifier is used, the provider expects that CMS will deny the item or service as not reasonable and necessary. When modifier GA is used, Medicare will deny the service as patient responsibility. Providers use modifier GA when:

- They believe a service or item will be denied because it does not meet Medicare's definition for medical necessity, and the provider has presented the beneficiary with an ABN. This modifier is used for "medical necessity" denials.

- The service falls within Medicare's frequency limitations (e.g., mammography, colon cancer screening tests).

- The patient refuses to sign the notice, but the ABN is properly witnessed.

ABN modifier GY is appended to the service that is statutorily or categorically excluded from Medicare coverage. Although ABNs are not required in these circumstances, the presence of the modifier indicates that the provider believes the service or item is not a covered Medicare benefit. Providers will use modifier GY when:

- A service or item does not meet all the requirements of the definition of a benefit.

- They wish to obtain a Medicare denial for secondary payer purposes.

ABN modifier GZ is used to identify an item or service that CMS will likely deny because it is not reasonable and necessary, and the patient did not sign an ABN. Providers will use modifier GZ when:

- They failed to present an ABN to the beneficiary.

- The ABN was not valid.

- They expect the item or service will be denied based on Medicare's definition of reasonable and necessary (medical necessity denials).

Figure 4-4, Figure 4-5, and Figure 4-6 provide further detail on the use of these modifiers.

"Waiver of liability statement on file."	
Description	Item or service expected to be denied as not reasonable and necessary and an advance beneficiary notice was given to the beneficiary.
	These are so-called "medical necessity" denials.
	The GA modifier also may be used with assigned and unassigned claims for DMEPOS where one of the following Part B "technical denials" may apply:
	• Prohibited telephone solicitation
	• No supplier number
	• Failure to obtain an advance determination of coverage
When to use the GA modifier	When you think a service will be denied because it does not meet the Medicare program standards for medically necessary care and you gave the beneficiary an advance beneficiary notice.
	You are required to include the GA modifier on your claim anytime you obtain a signed ABN, or have a patient's refusal to sign an ABN witnessed properly in an assigned claim situation (except an assigned claim for one of the specified DMEPOS technical denials).
	The GA modifier must be used when physicians, practitioners, hospitals or suppliers want to indicate that they expect Medicare will deny a service as not reasonable and necessary.
	Use a GA modifier on an assigned claim if you gave an ABN to a patient but the patient refused to sign the ABN and you did furnish the services. (In these circumstances, on all unassigned claims, as well as an assigned claim for a specified DMEPOS technical denial, use the GZ modifier.)
Examples of its use	All instances in which you deliver an ABN to a Medicare patient and services are furnished.
	For example, after having a patient sign an ABN, you furnish a service covered by Medicare but likely to be denied as "too frequent" by Medicare.
What happens if you use the GA modifier?	The claim will be reviewed by Medicare like any other claim and may or may not be denied. The carrier will NOT use the presence of the GA modifier to influence its determination of Medicare coverage and payment of the service.
	If Medicare pays the claim, the GA modifier is irrelevant.
	If the claim is denied, the beneficiary will be fully and personally liable to pay you for the service, personally or through other insurance.
	Medicare will not pay you for the service since your giving an ABN to the patient is prima facie evidence that you knew Medicare probably would not pay for the service.
What happens if you don't use the GA modifier?	The claim will be reviewed by Medicare like any other claim and may or may not be denied.
	If the claim is denied, the beneficiary will be held not liable and you will be held liable. Medicare will not pay you nor allow you to collect from the beneficiary. In order to remedy this situation, you will need to appeal Medicare's action limiting the beneficiary's liability.
	The question of an abusive billing pattern could arise. It is possible that fraud and abuse implications may arise out of your omission of the fact of having had an ABN signed by the patient under these circumstances, especially if there is a consistent pattern of such omissions (viz., a pattern of failure to include the GA modifier when it is applicable).

Figure 4-4 GA Modifier.

"Item or service statutorily excluded or does not meet the definition of any Medicare benefit."	
Description	These are the so-called "statutory exclusions" or "categorical exclusions" and the "technical denials."
	ABNs are not an issue for these services.
	There are no advance beneficiary notice (ABN) requirements for statutory exclusions.
	There are no ABN requirements for technical denials (except three types of DMEPOS denials, and they are listed under modifiers GZ & GA).
When to use the GY modifier	When you think a claim will be denied because it is not a Medicare benefit or because Medicare law specifically excludes it.
	When you think a claim will be denied because the service does not meet all the requirements of the definition of a benefit in Medicare law.
	The GY modifier must be used when physicians, practitioners, hospitals, or suppliers want to indicate that the item or service is statutorily non-covered or is not a Medicare benefit.
	When you submit a claim to obtain a Medicare denial for secondary payer purposes.
Examples of its use	Routine physicals, laboratory tests in absence of signs or symptoms, hearing aids, air conditioners, services in a foreign country, services to a family member.
	Surgery performed by a physician not legally authorized to perform surgery in the State.
What happens if you use the GY modifier?	The claim will be denied by Medicare. The carrier may "auto-deny" claims with the GY modifier. This action may be quicker than if you do not use a GY modifier.
	The beneficiary will be liable for all charges, whether personally or through other insurance.
	If Medicare pays the claim, the GY modifier is irrelevant.
What happens if you don't use the GY modifier?	The claim will be reviewed by Medicare and probably will be denied. This action may be slower than if you had used the GY modifier.
	If the claim is denied as an excluded service or for failure to meet the definition of a benefit, the beneficiary will be liable for all charges, whether personally or through other insurance.

Figure 4-5 GY Modifier.

"Item or service expected to be denied as not reasonable and necessary." (No signed ABN on file.)	
Description	Item or service expected to be denied as not reasonable and necessary and an advance beneficiary notice (ABN) was not signed by the beneficiary.
	These are the so-called "medical necessity" denials.
	The GZ modifier also may be used with assigned and unassigned claims for DMEPOS where one of the following Part B "technical denials" may apply:
	• Prohibited telephone solicitation
	• No supplier number
	• Failure to obtain an advance determination of coverage
When to use the GZ modifier	When you think a service will be denied because it does not meet Medicare program standards for medically necessary care and you did not obtain a signed ABN from the beneficiary.
	When you gave an ABN to a patient who refused to sign the ABN and you, nevertheless, did furnish the services, use a GZ modifier on *unassigned* claims for all physicians' services and DMEPOS; and also on *assigned* claims for which one of the DMEPOS technical denials is expected.
	If you wish to indicate to the carrier that one of the above situations exists, in your opinion, then you may elect to include the GZ modifier on your claim.
Examples of its use	When you would have given an ABN to a patient but could not because of an emergency care situation, e.g., in an EMTALA covered situation in an emergency room, or in an ambulance transport.
	When a patient was not personally present at your premises and could not be reached to timely sign an ABN, e.g., before a specimen is tested.
	When you realize too late, only after furnishing a service, that you should have given the patient an ABN.

Figure 4-6 GZ Modifier. *(continues)*

What happens if you use the GZ modifier?	The claim will be reviewed by Medicare like any other claim and may or may not be denied. The carrier will NOT use the presence of the GZ modifier to influence its determination of Medicare coverage and payment of the service.
	If Medicare pays the claim, the GZ modifier is irrelevant.
	If the claim is denied, the beneficiary will not be liable to pay you for the service. However, even though the beneficiary is found not liable, if you are also found not liable with respect to an unassigned claim, or an assigned claim denied for one of the DMEPOS technical denial reasons specified, you may be allowed to collect from the beneficiary.
	Medicare may or may not hold you liable depending whether you knew that payment would be denied when you furnished the service. In cases where you gave an ABN to the patient, or attempted to, but could not obtain a beneficiary signature, most likely Medicare will hold you liable.
What happens if you don't use the GZ modifier?	You never need to use the GZ modifier when you expect Medicare to pay.
	You are always free to elect not to use a GZ modifier.
	The claim will be reviewed by Medicare like any other claim and may or may not be denied.
	NOTE: The GZ modifier is provided for physicians and suppliers that wish to submit a claim to Medicare, that know that an ABN should have been signed but was not, and that do not want *any* risk of allegation of fraud or abuse for claiming services that are not medically necessary. By notifying Medicare by the GZ modifier that you expect Medicare will not cover the service, you can greatly reduce the risk of a mistaken allegation of fraud or abuse.

Figure 4-6 GZ Modifier. *(continued)*

Third-party payers may also require the use of an ABN, but as noted previously, the official Medicare ABN form cannot be used for non-Medicare patients. The provider should develop a different form for these purposes.

Billing for Medical Necessity

When a patient is presented with an ABN, it is believed that some portions of the services provided will be non-covered by Medicare. Even when it is known that some services may not be reimbursed by Medicare, it is necessary to submit the charges to Medicare in order to receive a denial. The non-covered, denied, charges can then be passed on to subsequent payers.

The beneficiary may also request that a claim be filed to Medicare, even if it is anticipated that the service will be denied. Providers may collect payment from beneficiaries in advance of claim submission, but if Medicare decides a service is covered and pays the claim, the provider must return any payment collected from the beneficiary.

UB-04 Billing

When all or some of the services on the claim are associated with an ABN (all are non-covered), occurrence code 32 is used, along with the date the ABN was signed by the beneficiary. Occurrence code 32 is used multiple times if more than one ABN form is tied to a single claim. The charges are submitted as "covered," or in the "total charges" column. See Figure 4-7 and Figure 4-8 for the appropriate occurrence code and date fields for UB-04 billing.

Along with the use of occurrence code 32, the appropriate modifier should be amended to the item. If a signed ABN has been obtained, the GA modifier is appended to the service, and the charges are listed in the "total charges" column. If the service is appended by the GY modifier (service excluded from Medicare coverage) or the GZ modifier (an ABN should have been obtained but was not), the charges are listed in the non-covered charges column. See Figure 4-9 for a GA appended charge on the UB-04.

| 31   OCCURRENCE | 32   OCCURRENCE | 33   OCCURRENCE | 34   OCCURRENCE |
CODE DATE	CODE DATE	CODE DATE	CODE DATE
/ /	/ /	/ /	/ /
/ /	/ /	/ /	/ /

Figure 4-7 Occurrence Code Fields on the UB-04. Example of UB-04 claim showing occurrence code and data fields for ABN notification on the UB-04 claim form.

47 TOTAL CHARGES	48 NON-COVERED CHARGES
72.00	0.00
27.00	0.00
26.00	0.00
25.00	0.00
25.00	0.00
23.00	0.00

Figure 4-8 Covered Charges on the UB-04. Example of UB-04 claim showing proper submission of covered charges.

42 REV.CD.	43 DESCRIPTION	44 HCPCS / RATE / HIPPS CODE	45 SERV. DATE	46 SERV. UNITS	47 TOTAL CHARGES	48 NON-COVERED CHARGES
320	DX X-RAY	77080	07/15/2008	1	365.00	0.00
300	GLUC QUAN BLD	82947GA	07/15/2008	1	24.00	0.00

Figure 4-9 Example of modifier GA appended to a code when an ABN has been properly secured from the patient.

Any non-covered item or service that has one of the ABN modifiers appended must be identified by an HCPCS code. If no other code is appropriate, HCPCS code A9270, "Noncovered item or service," may be used. Note that modifier GA cannot be used with this code, since the GA modifier indicates a potential covered charge.

CMS-1500 Billing

When billing on the CMS-1500 form, providers add the ABN modifier in the modifier column to the right of the CPT/HCPCS code (see Figure 4-10).

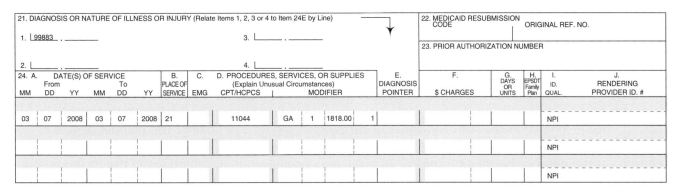

Figure 4-10 Example showing modifier GA appended to procedure code on the CMS-1500 claim form.

Medical Necessity and Coding and Compliance Issues

In the determination of medical necessity, accuracy of ICD-9-CM diagnosis codes and HCPCS procedure codes cannot be overemphasized. Assigning an inaccurate diagnosis code may affect the decision whether to present an ABN to the patient. Assigning diagnosis codes that are not based on supporting documentation can expose the provider to audits, reviews, and potential issues of fraud regarding submission of false claims. Because many of the LCDs are based on CPT and HCPCS codes, accurate determination of these codes prior to performance of the procedure is also essential.

Hospitals and physician offices use various processes for determination of medical necessity. The most effective method of ensuring compliance is to review whether the service or item is covered on the "front end," that is, prior to performance of the service. The best time to perform medical necessity determination is prior to or at registration. Problems with this process include registration staff that may not be trained in ICD-9-CM and CPT/HCPCS coding, limited medical documentation, and lack of access to coverage determinations and cost information. Determining medical necessity can also be time-consuming. The registration area may not be the ideal place to determine medical necessity, present the patient with an ABN, discuss treatment options, and provide payment information.

To ensure that both the hospital and physician are compliant with medical necessity determination, communication and sharing of information is imperative. The physician should be aware of medical necessity issues so treatment options can be discussed with the patient. Likewise the hospital must have access to the provider's patient health information to determine medical necessity and accurate cost information. Coders skilled in applying ICD-9-CM diagnostic code and CPT/HCPCS procedure codes should be employed to review orders, relative documentation, and coverage determinations.

As mentioned previously, one of the most challenging areas for determining medical necessity in the hospital is for outpatient services, specifically, the laboratory and radiology departments. Patients may present with only an order for the service with limited or no diagnostic information attached. The *Medicare Claims Processing Manual,* Chapter 23, Section 10.1, ICD-9-CM Coding for Diagnostic Tests, and the ICD-9-CM Official Guidelines for Coding and Reporting provide guidance on diagnosis coding specific to outpatient facilities and physician offices. These instructions should be followed to ensure compliant coding and billing. The following are key elements of the guidelines:

- Use the ICD-9-CM code that describes the patient's diagnosis, symptom, complaint, condition, or problem. Do not code suspected diagnoses.

- Use the ICD-9-CM code that is chiefly responsible for the item or service provided.

- Assign codes to the highest level of specificity. Use fourth and fifth digits where applicable.

- Code a chronic condition as often as applicable to the patient's treatment.

- Code all documented conditions that coexist at the time of the visit that require or affect patient care or treatment. Do not code conditions that no longer exist.

As noted in previous chapters, CMS requires following the ICD-9-CM Official Guidelines for Coding and Reporting for outpatient services, including hospital outpatient and physician office services. These guidelines instruct physicians to report diagnoses based on test results, if the results are known and available at the time of coding. A basic coding principle according to the *AHA Coding Clinic for ICD-9CM* (1995) is to code at the highest degree of certainty at the time of coding. The highest degree of certainty or specificity means assigning the most precise ICD-9-CM code that most fully explains the narrative description in the medical record. This includes coding signs or symptoms in the absence of a definitive diagnosis. Note that this principle differs from coding guidelines used by hospitals for coding diagnoses of hospital inpatients.

The *Medicare Claims Processing Manual,* Chapter 23, Section 10.1.1, provides these coding examples:

EXAMPLE 1: A surgical specimen is sent to a pathologist with a diagnosis of "mole." The pathologist personally reviews the slides made from the specimen and makes a diagnosis of "malignant melanoma." The pathologist should report a diagnosis of "malignant melanoma" as the primary diagnosis.

EXAMPLE 2: A patient is referred to a radiologist for an abdominal CT scan with a diagnosis of abdominal pain. The CT scan reveals the presence of an abscess. The radiologist should report a diagnosis of "intra-abdominal abscess."

EXAMPLE 3: A patient is referred to a radiologist for a chest X-ray with a diagnosis of "cough." The study confirms the presence of a pulmonary module. The radiologist should report a diagnosis of "pulmonary nodule" and may sequence "cough" as an additional diagnosis.

When the diagnostic test does not provide a diagnosis, or is otherwise "normal," codes for the sign(s) or symptom(s) that prompted the reason for the study should be assigned. Consider the following example:

EXAMPLE: A patient is seen in the emergency room for chest pain. An EKG is ncrmal, and the final diagnosis is chest pain due to suspected gastroesophageal reflux disease (GERD). The patient is told to follow up with his primary care physician for further evaluation of the suspected GERD. The primary diagnosis code for the EKG should be chest pain. Although the EKG was normal, a definitive cause for the chest pain was not determined, and the reason for the test was the chest pain.

In the absence of any presenting symptoms, the appropriate V code for screening tests should be appended as the first-listed diagnosis. Any findings resulting from the diagnostic test should be listed secondarily.

The outpatient guidelines state that terms such as "consistent with," "compatible with," "indicative of," "suggestive of," and "comparable with" are considered unconfirmed and should not be reported. The condition(s) should be coded to the highest degree of certainty for that encounter or visit, such as symptoms, signs, or abnormal test results.

It is the responsibility of the ordering physician to provide the necessary diagnostic information to the testing entity or hospital at the time the test is being ordered. CMS defines an order as a "communication from the treating physician/practitioner requesting that a diagnostic test be performed for a beneficiary" (CMS Transmittal 94, Pub 100-02 Medicare Benefit Policy, Change Request 6100, August 29, 2008 http://www.cms.hhs.gov/transmittals/downloads/R94BP.pdf). The order may be written (hand-delivered, mailed, or faxed), verbal (telephone call from the treating physician/practitioner), or by electronic mail. If the order is verbal, both the ordering/treating physician and the testing physician/hospital must document the telephone call in their respective medical records. The verbal contact must be followed up with a mailed or hand-delivered notice. If the diagnostic information is missing from the order, the treating/ordering physician should be contacted to obtain the necessary information. In the rare instance that this information cannot be obtained, Medicare allows the information to be obtained directly from the patient or the patient's medical record.

At the time an order is written or received, the determination for medical necessity should be initiated. The diagnostic information as well as the CPT/HCPCS code describing the item or service should be reviewed. The information should then be assessed to determine if the service or item is covered under an NCD or LCD. As noted previously, this can be a time-consuming process. Some providers use software products to help determine medical necessity.

Relying on a software product alone to determine medical necessity, however, is not advised. Many policies, especially NCDs, do not provide a list of covered ICD-9-CM diagnosis codes but may provide a list of covered "conditions" in narrative form. The medical record documentation should still be reviewed to determine whether medical necessity is supported based on the patient's condition. Additionally, the provider is dependent on the vendor to update the software based on current policies, which can change frequently. The software product will also not be able to discern the applicability of the policy in reference to the service being provided. For example, an LCD that includes CPT code 20550, "Injection(s): single tendon sheath, or ligament, aponeurosis" (e.g., plantar "fascia"), may apply only to patients with Morton's neuroma. If the patient does not have a diagnosis of Morton's neuroma, then the policy will not apply. The software product will provide edits on any patient that does not have the applicable diagnosis, regardless of whether the policy actually applies.

Some software products that providers use to assist in determining medical necessity may produce a list of covered diagnoses when an item or service is ordered and deemed not covered. This type of software is often used for online ordering systems, whereby a physician completes a computerized order. When a diagnosis is entered that does not meet medical necessity, a listing of covered diagnoses may be provided. Relying on this process to determine medical necessity should be used cautiously, and frequent audits should be performed to ensure that the provider's documentation supports the diagnosis on the order.

Compliance Activities

A number of auditing activities can be performed to ensure compliance with medical necessity determination, such as the following:

- Review the use of modifiers GA, GY, and GZ to determine whether ABNs have been obtained and if the modifiers have been appended accurately.

- Perform coding validation audits on those services most affected by NCDs and LCDs, including outpatient ancillary services and other high-dollar services.

- Monitor the types of denials, identifying patterns and trends. Determine if the denials were made appropriately.

- Compare the diagnosis(es) submitted on the claim and included on an order with documentation in the medical record.

- Review compliance medical necessity risk areas, such as one-day or short-stay inpatient stays and diagnosis-related groups (DRGs) with a symptom as the principal diagnosis.

- Include the appropriate staff in the medical necessity determination process, including the physician.

- Review signed ABN forms for accuracy and completeness, paying particular attention to required fields and proper terminology.

Follow-up compliance activities may include providing the necessary education to physicians regarding documentation, educating physicians on guidelines for determining medical necessity, identifying the impact of lost revenue, providing education to coders, and ensuring that staff involved in the determination of medical necessity have the proper resources. Multidisciplinary staff participation, especially physicians, should be encouraged in the review of draft policies. Draft policies should be reviewed from a "coding perspective" to ensure that coding information is accurate and follows the official coding guidelines.

The process for determining medical necessary, securing ABNs, and ensuring coding accuracy should be regularly reviewed auditing activities. The entire patient experience, from scheduling to billing completion, should be considered when evaluating an efficient method to achieve compliance. An environment of open communication among the provider, patient financial services, health information management (HIM) department, and registration staff is critical.

In hospitals and large specialty clinics where services are distributed across several different departments, the process for determination of medical necessity may include a centralized process. This may be a single site that all patients encounter where billing and health care information are reviewed and medical necessity determinations are confirmed. In some facilities, a decentralized process is used. Medical necessity determinations are reviewed in the department where the service is to be performed, for example, the radiology or laboratory departments.

Reviewing medical necessity determination at the time of coding and billing alone is not an efficient process. At this point it is too late to obtain an ABN from the patient. Working on the "back end" may help prevent some unnecessary denials but can also prove costly, as many services are written off and assumed by the provider.

Establishing a process to determine medical necessity is important for the patient and the health care provider. The patient should not be held liable for services that are considered medically necessary under the payer's coverage guidelines. Improper determination of medical necessity can result in lost revenue and allegations of fraudulent billing for providers.

Chapter Review

Determine whether the following statements are true or false.

_____ 1.   Services with an ABN on file should be billed with modifier GA.

_____ 2.   The CMS official ABN form is used for Medicare beneficiaries only.

_____ 3.   An ABN is necessary if the service is never covered or is considered non-covered under Medicare statute.

_____ 4.   The GY modifier tells Medicare that an ABN was not obtained, and the patient will not be billed for the service.

_____ 5.   An ABN does not need to be signed on every occurrence of a testing series, as long as the testing has not changed.

_____ 6.   Signed blank ABNs are considered defective notices.

_____ 7.   The GY modifier should be used when physicians, practitioners, or suppliers want to indicate that the item or service is statutorily non-covered or is not a Medicare benefit.

_____ 8.   A Medicare beneficiary who lives in California and undergoes a trigger point injection may require a different diagnosis (a diagnosis that is considered covered) than a patient from New York who undergoes the same trigger point injection procedure.

_____ 9.   Medicare will cover investigational items as long as they meet the requirements of the clinical trials NCDs.

_____10.   It is appropriate to present every Medicare beneficiary who undergoes a Pap smear screening with an ABN.

_____11.   An LCD takes precedence over an NCD.

Case Studies

Case Study 1

A patient presents to the hospital radiology department for a CT scan. The physician's order states, "renal mass." The coder notes that the LCD does not include the code for renal mass (ICD-9-CM diagnosis code 593.9) but does include the code 789.30, "Abdominal/pelvic/mass/lump, unspecified site." The results of the radiology test are unavailable at the time of coding.

1. What code should the coder assign?

_____

_____

_____

2. Does the CT scan meet medical necessity according to the LCD?

_____

_____

_____

Case Study 2

A cardiology practice that sees a large number of Medicare patients offers an ABN to every patient receiving diagnostic services. The clinic administrator offers the explanation that many of the services the clinic provides, including stress testing and computed tomography angiography, have LCDs. In addition, he notes that many commercial payers are following Medicare's coverage indications, so therefore he sees no problem with issuing the same ABN for all patients.

1. Discuss the compliance issues and risks associated with the clinic administrator's decision.

_____

_____

_____

Case Study 3

A local coverage determination for a chemotherapeutic drug includes a section termed "Coding Guidelines." The instructions state that the provider should place the covered ICD-9-CM code in the first-listed position. For example, if metastatic carcinoma is the covered indication for the drug, that code should be sequenced first. If the primary site of the carcinoma meets coverage guidelines, that code should be sequenced first. The instructions also indicate that code V58.11, "Encounter for chemotherapy," should be sequenced secondarily.

1. Discuss the accuracy of the coding instruction and any recourse the provider may have.

_____

_____

_____

Case Study 4

A hospital's ancillary departments, which include laboratory/pathology and radiology services, employ a coder at the point of registration to review physician orders and assess the services for medical necessity. When a patient presents an order with a diagnosis that does not meet medical necessity, the coder telephones the physician's clinic office and queries the receptionist at the office as to whether the patient has any other diagnosis that can be added to the order. The receptionist offers a diagnosis that is covered. The coder writes a note in the patient's medical record stating that the additional diagnosis was received by the physician's office, noting the date and the person spoken to.

1. Is this practice appropriate?

_____

_____

_____

2. Would services provided under this scenario be considered covered?

_____

_____

_____

3. Discuss any potential compliance issues.

_____

_____

_____

Case Study 5

A local coverage determination on trigger point injections includes the following information. The ICD-9-CM codes listed below as covered should only be used for purposes of this policy when a trigger point is injected. The ICD-9-CM codes listed should be correlated to the muscles as listed below:

720.1	Serratus anterior; Serratus posterior; Quadratus lumborum; Longissimus thoracis; Lower thoracic iliocostalis; Upper & lower rectus abdominus; Upper lumbar iliocostalis; Multifidus; external oblique; McBurney's point
723.9	Trapezius (upper & lower); Sternocleidomastoid (cervical & sternal); Masseter; Temporalis; Lateral pterygoid; Splenii; Posterior cervical; Suboccipital
726.19	Scaleni; Subscapularis; Levator scapulae; Brachialis; Deltoid (anterior & posterior); Middle finger extensor; Rhomboid, Infraspinatus/Supraspinatus; First dorsal interosseous; Pectoralis major and minor; Supinator; Latissimus dorsi
726.39	Triceps; Extensor carpi radialis; Middle finger flexor
726.5	Glutei; Piriformis; Adductor longus & brevis
726.71	Soleus; Gastrocnemius
726.72	Tibialis anterior
726.79	Peroneus longus & brevis; Extensor digitorum & Hallucis longus; Third dorsal interosseous
726.90	Rectus femoris; Vastus intermedius; Vastus medialis; Vastus lateralis (anterior & posterior); Biceps femoral

The physician has documented that the patient has chronic low back pain, sacral pain, myofascial back pain, and neuropathic pain. The physician performs trigger point injections into the trapezius, rhomboids, paraspinal, and gluteus muscles.

1. What ICD-9-CM codes should be assigned in this case?

_____

_____

_____

2. Has medical necessity been met?

_____

_____

_____

3. Are the injections considered covered according to the LCD?

_____

_____

_____

4. Do the coding instructions in the LCD follow official coding guidelines?

_____

_____

_____

Case Study 6

A hospital uses an online ordering system on which physicians order all laboratory and radiology services electronically. When the physician orders a test on this system, he or she must include a diagnosis (either an ICD-9-CM diagnosis numerical code or diagnostic phrase/statement). At the time of ordering, the online system automatically provides a listing of diagnoses from which the physician may choose. The physician also has the option of choosing a code that is not on the list, "free-texting" in another diagnosis. The diagnosis list includes codes that are taken from the NCDs and lists only those diagnoses that are considered covered.

1. Discuss compliance issues associated with this process.

_____

_____

_____

Case Study 7

During a clinic encounter at a physician's office, a patient is presented an ABN for some lab services. At the time of billing (after the services have been performed) it is noted that the section on estimated cost was left blank.

1. Can modifier GA be appended to the lab services on the claim?

_____

_____

_____

2. Is this a valid ABN?

_____

_____

_____

Case Study 8

A patient presents to the office with a chronic cough. The physician orders a chest X-ray. The diagnosis on the order is cough, ICD-9-CM diagnosis code 786.2. This diagnosis is considered covered under the LCD. The patient presents the order at the local hospital's radiology department. The chest X-ray is completed, and the radiologist's impression is "Normal chest."

1. What diagnosis will the hospital radiology department report?

    _____

    _____

    _____

2. What diagnosis will the radiologist report on the professional claim?

    _____

    _____

    _____

3. Are the claims considered covered under the LCD?

    _____

    _____

    _____

Case Study 9

A hospital coder reviews an order for an abdominal ultrasound. The order has a diagnosis of 789. The coder reviews the abdominal ultrasound report and the radiologist notes under the impression: "cholecystolithiasis, no evidence of acute cholecystitis." The LCD for abdominal ultrasound includes the diagnosis code 574.20, "Calculus of gallbladder without cholecystitis," and includes the code range 789.01–789.09 for abdominal pain. An ABN was not presented to the patient.

1. What diagnosis should the coder assign for the radiology service?

    _____

    _____

    _____

2. Is this service considered covered under the LCD?

_____

_____

_____

Case Study 10

A patient presents to the outpatient surgical center for surgery. The patient is prepped for surgery and an IV is placed. Light sedation is administered. A front office staff member reviews the patient's insurance information and signed consent forms. She notes that the patient's presenting diagnosis is not considered covered under the local coverage policy, and no ABN was presented to the patient. She presents the ABN to the patient's spouse and asks for a signature. The spouse signs the form.

1. Is this a valid ABN?

_____

_____

_____

2. Is this service considered covered?

_____

_____

_____

References

American Hospital Association. (1995). *AHA coding clinic for ICD-9CM.* (Fourth quarter, pp. 45–46).

California Medical Association. *HealthNet Settlement overview.* Retrieved July 17, 2008, from http://www.hmosettlements.com/pages/healthnet.html

Connecticut State Medical Society. *Press release on the HealthNet Settlement.* Retrieved from http://www.hmosettlements.com/settlements/healthnet/ConnecticutStateMedicalSocietyHealthNet.pdf

Department of Health and Human Services, Centers for Medicare & Medicaid Services. *Beneficiary notices initiatives (BNI)* (various articles and forms). Retrieved from http://www.cms.hhs.gov/bni/

Department of Health and Human Services, Centers for Medicare and Medicaid Services. Fee schedule administration and coding requirements. In *Medicare claims processing manual* (chap. 23). Retrieved from http://www.cms.hhs.gov/MedicalReviewProcess/Downloads/mrfactsheet.pdf

Department of Health and Human Services, Centers for Medicare & Medicaid Services. *Medicare medical review program.* Retrieved from http://www.cms.hhs.gov/MedicalReviewProcess/Downloads/mrfactsheet.pdf

Department of Health and Human Services, Centers for Medicare and Medicaid Services. *Medicare medical review program factsheet.* Retrieved from http://www.cms.hhs.gov/MedicalReviewProcess/Downloads/mrfactsheet.pdf

Department of Health and Human Services (DHHS), Centers for Medicare & Medicaid Services, *Medicare program integrity manual* (chaps. 1, 3, and 13).

Department of Health and Human Services, Centers for Medicare & Medicaid Services. *Medicare claims processing manual* (chap. 1, secs. 1.1–1.5).

Department of Health and Human Services, Centers for *Medicare & Medicaid Services. Medicare claims processing manual* (chap. 1, secs. 60.3–60.4.5).

Department of Health and Human Services, Centers for M*edicare & Medicaid Services. Medicare claims processing manual* (chap. 30).

Department of Health and Human Services, Centers for Medicare & Medicaid Services. (2003, September 26). Medicare program; revised process for making Medicare national coverage determinations. *Federal Register, 68*(187), 55634–55641.

Department of Health and Human Services. (2002, October 4). Pro*gram memorandum: Intermediaries/carriers.* Transmittal AB-02-134. Change request 2383. Retrieved from http://www.cms.hhs.gov/Transmittals/downloads/AB02134.pdf

NHIC, Corp. Provider education, Medicare part B. Retrieved from http://www.medicarenhic.com/ne_prov/index.shtml

Developing a Coding Compliance Program

Objectives

At the completion of this chapter, the learner should be able to:

- Identify the seven key components of a corporate compliance program.
- Describe the importance of a corporate compliance program and the purpose of a coding compliance program.
- Discuss the purpose of the Office of Inspector General's compliance guidance for health care entities and identify key elements.
- Describe the difference between "mandatory" and "permissive" offenses.
- Discuss the roles of the coding compliance manager and the coding compliance committee.
- Identify areas that should be defined within coding compliance policies.
- Discuss the importance of coding compliance education.
- Recognize the importance of coding accuracy and distinguish between coding and documentation errors.
- Explain differences in coding certification and professional coding organizations.
- Identify the coding resources that must be kept up to date.

Key Terms

chargemaster
code of conduct
coding certification
coding compliance
coding compliance education
Coding Compliance Manager

coding resources
compliance officer
compliance program
Comprehensive Error Rate Testing (CERT) program
corporate compliance program

mandatory exclusions
OIG Compliance Guidance
outcomes
outcome indicators
permissive exclusions
process

Recovery Audit Contractors (RACs)
structure

Integrating Coding and Corporate Compliance

Corporate businesses and health care organizations alike may be subject to criminal and civil actions under a variety of federal and state laws, including the False Claims Act, the Wire and Mail Fraud Act, securities and employment laws, and a number of others. In today's business market, many organizations have adopted **corporate compliance programs** to educate everyone from top executives to line-staff employees on the laws and regulations that affect their operations. A corporate compliance program can prevent both intentional and accidental wrongdoing and can be viewed positively by investigators and the courts, often reducing civil or criminal penalties. The mere existence of a compliance program, however, does not excuse any corporation of wrongdoing. In fact, a poorly planned and executed compliance program can be viewed worse than having no compliance program at all.

Health care providers need to address many of the same compliance concerns as their corporate counterparts. In addition to the laws and regulations already in existence, health care providers face continuing enforcement initiatives from the Centers for Medicare & Medicaid Services (CMS), the Office of Inspector General (OIG), the United States Department of Justice (DOJ), and various national and state accreditation bodies. In addition to conducting federal and state payer oversight, private payers are also engaged in reviewing and auditing health care services for quality, medical necessity, and health care financial waste. Health care organizations today must have a comprehensive corporate compliance program that embodies accountability, responsibility, investigation, and education.

A health care provider's **compliance program** will consist of various policies and standards and will vary depending on the specific entity. Generally, corporate compliance programs include policies and procedures designed to define and identify laws and regulations, correct identified problems, and put controls in place to prevent future problems. Policies may address a variety of compliance issues including:

- Fraud and abuse awareness
- Whistle-blower protections
- HIPAA privacy rules
- Referral guidelines
- Teaching physician rules
- Coding and documentation
- Billing and reimbursement
- Misuse of funds and property
- Antidumping regulations
- Conflicts of interest
- Labor laws
- Researching compliance issues
- Marketing
- Medical records creation/retention
- Patient risk identification (e.g., medical error reduction, medication safety, patient safety)
- Business associates agreements
- Security of health information

Coding compliance is inherently linked to a number of the preceding compliance risk areas including proper documentation, accurate billing, medical records creation and retention, referral guidelines, and teaching physician rules. Acknowledging that one of the biggest areas of risk for health care providers is the accurate submission of claims and reimbursement to Medicare, an effective health care corporate compliance plan will also include an effective coding compliance plan.

OIG Compliance Guidelines

There is **OIG compliance guidance** for several specific health care areas including hospitals, physicians, nursing facilities, pharmaceutical manufacturers, ambulance suppliers, hospices, durable medical equipment manufacturers, and home health agencies. The OIG also publishes an annual work plan that outlines activities that the OIG will be reviewing. These resources, along with the results and summaries of audits that the OIG has performed, are located on the OIG Web site at www.oig.hhs.gov. Although there may be subtle differences in the compliance guidance publications, there is a common theme that the OIG outlines in seven basic compliance elements. These elements stem from the federal sentencing guidelines, which are detailed policies and practices that the federal criminal justice systems use to prescribe appropriate sanctions for offenders convicted of federal crimes. The seven elements include the following:

1. Establishing compliance standards through the development of a **code of conduct** and written policies and procedures

   a. The code of conduct is a general organizational statement of ethical and compliance principles that guide the entity's operations.

   b. The code is similar to a constitution, in that it details the fundamental principles, values, and framework for action within an organization.

   c. The code of conduct articulates a commitment to compliancy by management, employees, and contractors and summarizes the broad ethical and legal principles under which the organization operates.

   d. The code of conduct should include a requirement that professionals follow the ethical standards dictated by their respective professional organizations.

   e. The code of conduct should be brief, easily readable, and cover general principles applicable to all members of an organization.

Compliance policies and procedures should be developed to assist employees in carrying out their job responsibilities as well as the mission and objectives of the organization. Policies need to be consistent with applicable federal and state regulations. According to the OIG Program Guidance for Hospitals, policies and procedures should be:

- Clearly written, with relevant day-to-day responsibilities

- Readily available to individuals who need them

- Monitored and reevaluated on a regular basis

- Distributed to all directors, officers, managers, employees, contractors, and medical and clinical staff members

Compliance policies and procedures should include risk assessment tools that assist an organization in identifying its weaknesses and areas of risk. The risk assessment tool should reflect federal and state regulations, the OIG work plan, internally identified risk areas, and areas of risk and liability identified through the CMS Conditions of Participation (CoPs) and associations such as The Joint Commission.

2. Assigning compliance monitoring efforts to a designated **compliance officer** or contact

   a. The compliance program/department should be led by a qualified compliance officer, who is supported by a compliance committee. According to the OIG, the individual leading the compliance program should be "trustworthy." Furthermore, "The organization must have used due care not to delegate substantial discretionary authority to individuals who the organization knew, or should have known through the exercise of due diligence, had a propensity to engage in illegal activities" (www.oig.hhs.gov).

   b. The purpose of the compliance department is to ensure compliance with federal and state regulations and to monitor the organization's compliance program.

   c. The compliance committee is minimally composed of senior leadership, legal representatives, physicians, and the compliance officer.

3. Conducting comprehensive training and education on practice ethics and policies and procedures

   Organizations that fail to provide adequate training and education for their staff risk liability for violation of health care fraud and abuse laws. Each individual employee or contractor of an organization requires the skills necessary to perform his or her job responsibilities. This may include required annual compliance training for staff in specific areas, or general education provided to all staff. According to the OIG, "The organization must have taken steps to communicate effectively its standards and procedures to all employees and other agents, by requiring participation in training programs or by disseminating publications that explain in a practical manner what is required." The training and education needs to be routinely reviewed to ensure it is up-to-date and reflects the objectives outlined in the compliance program. Training should be based on trends identified internally as well as those identified by outside sources such as the OIG, CMS, and health care accrediting bodies. Training should be well documented, identifying the specific session, length, date the education took place, and the individuals who attended.

4. Conducting internal monitoring and auditing focusing on high-risk billing and coding issues through performance of periodic audits

   Audits should be regularly conducted to ensure that the organization is correctly submitting claims and accurately assigning codes. The compliance plan should include specific details about how issues are identified, audited, corrected, and continuously monitored. Components of a coding compliance program are discussed later in this chapter.

5. Developing accessible and open lines of communication

   Open communication is vital to the identification of potential areas of compliance risk. There should be internal processes in place for reporting instances of potential fraud and abuse. The OIG encourages an organizational culture of open communication without fear of retaliation. Many organizations have established hotlines or other similar mechanisms such as comment boxes so that issues can be reported anonymously. All staff, outside contractors, patients, visitors, and vendors should have the ability to report potential compliance issues.

All issues identified through these lines of communication need to be investigated and resolved. The results of internal investigations should be shared with administration and relevant departments on a regular basis. Policies and procedures should be updated to ensure that issues do not recur.

A compliance program that contains internal reporting processes and procedures will enable employees to freely report issues or concerns. An effective reporting mechanism can reduce the possibility of whistle-blower suits that often occur in organizations that limit or prohibit the communication of potential problems.

6. Enforcing disciplinary standards through well-publicized guidelines

Including enforcement and disciplinary methodologies in the compliance program will assist in creating a culture that encourages appropriate ethical behavior. These actions also add credibility and integrity to compliance programs. Disciplinary policies and procedures should be readily available to all staff and included in orientation and training packages. The following are components of appropriate disciplinary actions:

- Methods of disciplinary action may include warnings (oral), reprimands (written), probation, demotion, temporary suspension, termination, restitution of damages, and referral for criminal prosecution.

- Violations should be consistently applied, with provisions given for extraordinary circumstances. Grievous violations may include termination.

- Violations should be thoroughly investigated and documented, including the date of the incident, names of responsible parties, and follow-up actions.

- Policies should include disciplinary actions for those who were aware of violations but failed to report them.

- Potential employees should be checked against government sanctions lists, including the OIG's List of Excluded Individuals/Entities and the General Services Administration's (GSA's) Excluded Parties Listing System. Current employees should be routinely checked to ensure they have not been excluded from the Medicare program.

Individuals or entities may be excluded from Medicare and other health care programs, such as state Medicaid programs, for a number of violations. During fiscal year 2006, three thousand four hundred twenty-two (3422) individuals and entities were barred from participating in Medicare and other state and federal health care programs. Exclusions vary from a few years to permanent exclusion and are based on the nature and seriousness of the offense. Federal guidelines outline minimum exclusionary periods. Offenses are considered either "mandatory" or "permissive." **Mandatory exclusions** must be applied on conviction of violation of certain state or federal health care fraud and abuse laws. **Permissive exclusions** are partly discretionary and may be imposed by a court of law, licensing board, or other agency.

The minimum period of exclusion for a mandatory exclusion offense is five years. If there is one prior conviction, the exclusion will be for ten years. If there are two prior convictions, the exclusion will be permanent. The following are examples of mandatory exclusion offenses:

- A criminal offense related to the delivery of an item or service under Medicare or Medicaid

- A conviction under federal or state law of a criminal offense relating to the neglect or abuse of a patient

- A conviction under federal or state law of a felony relating to fraud, theft, embezzlement, breach of fiduciary responsibility, or other financial misconduct against a health care program financed by any federal, state, or local government agency

- A conviction under federal or state law of a felony relating to the unlawful manufacture, distribution, prescription, or dispensing of a controlled substance

Under a permissive exclusion, individuals or entities may be excluded for a minimum of three years on conviction of the following offenses, for example:

- Interference with, or obstruction of, any investigation into certain criminal offenses

- Submission of claims for excessive charges, unnecessary services, or services that were of a quality that fails to meet professionally recognized standards of health care

- Failure to disclose information required by law

- Failure to supply claims payment information

- Defaulting on health educations loans or scholarship obligations

7. Responding appropriately to detected violations through the investigation of allegations and the disclosure of incidents to appropriate governmental entities

Once a potential compliance issue has been suspected or identified, appropriate steps must be in place to thoroughly and promptly investigate the matter. Investigations should try to identify the root cause of the problem and then promptly initiate corrective measures. If the potential problem is a billing or coding error, for example, measures should be taken to immediately reduce the possibility of further errors. If the discovery identifies that an overpayment occurred, the overpayment should promptly be reported and repaid. As appropriate, referrals to the appropriate law enforcement agency should be made.

As noted earlier, an effective compliance program that works to prevent and detect violations can be viewed positively during an investigation. This is especially true for considerations in permissive exclusionary offenses. An effective compliance program can demonstrate the trustworthiness of the provider. Other considerations include the provider's past history of misconduct, response to allegations, willingness to modify practices, repayments, and acknowledgment of wrongdoing. The following factors may be considered:

- Was there any voluntary disclosure by the provider?

- Were overpayments repaid?

- What changes were made in response to identified problems?

- How long had the compliance program been in effect?

- What problems did the compliance program detect?

- What measures were taken to reduce the possibility of further violations?

- Are staff sufficiently trained in policies and procedures pertaining to Medicare and other state and federal health regulations?

- What are the qualifications of the compliance officer and others involved in the compliance program?

The Coding Compliance Program: Developing Policies and Procedures

An effective coding compliance program should be an integral part of a health care organization's corporate compliance program. A coding compliance program is a valuable asset to the health care entity, because it assists the organization in meeting its obligations to payers, employees, shareholders, and the community. Whereas corporate compliance programs probably do not include the detailed policies and procedures that specifically address complex coding and billing issues, a coding compliance program can provide these necessary guidelines. The coding compliance program should complement the overall organization's corporate compliance program, and should include the support of administration. It is important to note that a single model coding compliance program will not fit every organization's needs. The size and type of the facility, as well as the framework of the coding processes, will affect the structure of the coding compliance program.

An effective coding compliance program will be continually evaluated and reevaluated. It is understood that rules will change, new reimbursement methodologies will be adopted, codes will change, new laws will be enacted, and there will be employee turnover. One method used to assess the effectiveness of the compliance plan is a compliance scorecard. The scorecard can measure specific processes and serve as a motivational tool for employees and managers. Scorecard items should be reviewed and approved by staff and administration. Some scorecard items for a coding compliance department may include the following:

- Coding accuracy goal of 95%

- Reduction in billing/claim errors (measured as a percent of total claims billed)

- 100% participation in coding and documentation educational programs

- Turnaround time to complete audits (measured in days, weeks, months, etc.)

- Attainment by all coding staff of the necessary continuing education units (CEUs) to maintain coding certification

The effectiveness of the coding compliance program should not be based solely on performance in a single area. For example, the coding accuracy of ancillary services cannot be compared with the coding accuracy of inpatient hospital coding. Similarly, poor audit results in one particular area do not mean that the coding compliance program is poor. Identifying problems and addressing them are indicative of an effective coding compliance program.

The results of a well-developed and well-executed coding compliance program, along with dedicated educational efforts, will be that coding will improve over time, documentation will support the medical necessity of charges, denial rates and physician queries will decline, and all employees will have received the training they need to perform their job responsibilities in a compliant manner. However, to reach this goal the program must be effectively managed with operational policies and procedures that are owned and adopted by all employees.

The OIG has recommended that to be effective, both coding compliance programs and corporate compliance programs be continually assessed and monitored. The effectiveness of a program is the measurement of various **outcome indicators** and may include billing and coding error rates, identified overpayments and underpayments, and audit results. The focus on examination of the compliance program is a crucial activity that examines the underlying **structure**, **process**, and **outcomes** of the program. *Structure* measures refer to the capacity of the program to prevent and detect violations

Table 5-1 Structure, Process, and Outcome of an Effective Coding Compliance Program.

Structure	Process	Outcome
Does the coding compliance department have a code of conduct?	Include the code of conduct within the coding compliance policy. Staff sign attestation that they have reviewed the policy annually.	Coding staff observe the code of conduct.
Does the coding compliance department regularly report auditing results? Have results been effectively communicated to coding, billing, and clinical departments?	Audits results are presented at quarterly Compliance Advisory Committee meetings. Results are shared with responsible departments promptly.	Audit findings are reported and education is initiated.
Is the necessary education performed to address compliance issues?	Following reporting of auditing results, training sessions are scheduled.	Education is conducted; errors are reduced.
Have auditing and education improved the results? Have processes changed as a result of audit findings?	Perform follow-up audits to access the effectiveness of retraining.	Additional training is performed as needed; errors are reduced.
Is the coding compliance department properly organized? Do employees have the necessary qualifications to accurately assess coding?	Coding compliance staff maintain coding certification. Review staff credential maintenance on an annual basis.	Coding staff receive timely updates on coding and regulatory changes, reducing the potential for coding errors.
Does the coding compliance department have sufficient resources (staff, budget), training, authority, and autonomy to carry out its mission?	Budget will contain sufficient resources for accurate coding including resources, training, continuing education opportunities, computer software, auditing, and consultation services. The department will assist with coding services as applicable.	The coding compliance department will be the health care facility's expert resource for coding advice. Adequate resources reduce the potential for coding errors.
Are coding compliance issues thoroughly investigated, researched, and documented?	Reviews are based on pre-identified risk areas such as the OIG work plan. Issues are identified internally and externally. Coding and regulatory guidelines are thoroughly researched.	A thoroughly investigated review demonstrates accuracy and competence. Proper education can be conducted.
Does a relationship exist between the corporate compliance program, the coding compliance committee, and the coding compliance department?	Committee structures will be multi-disciplinary including coding, business management services, administration, and providers as appropriate.	Communication among the various departments helps to ensure effective working relationships and follow through on compliance issues.

of law. *Process* measures refer to the manner in which the program seeks to prevent and detect violations of the law. *Outcomes* measures refer to the observable, measurable results related to preventing and detecting violations of law and creating a compliant culture.

Table 5-1 displays the structure, process, and outcome measures as they relate to a coding compliance program.

Fraud and abuse violations, Medicare review programs, and most recently, the development of the Medicare **Recovery Audit Contractor (RAC) program** have brought to the forefront the importance of good coding and documentation. In 2003, Medicare instituted the **Comprehensive Error Rate Testing (CERT) program**. The CERT program measures the error rate for claims submitted to Medicare Carriers, Durable Medical Equipment Regional Carriers (DMERCs), and Fiscal Intermediaries (FIs). Another program that monitors the accuracy of Medicare payments is the Hospital Payment

Monitoring Program (HPMP). This program measures the error rate for the Quality Improvement Organizations (QIOs).

The CERT program reduced the errors in Medicare reimbursement from 9.8% in 2003 to 3.9% in 2007. Although the reduction in the error rate was significant, Medicare determined that the 3.9% equated to $10.8 billion in Medicare overpayments and underpayments.

Also in 2003, under section 305 of the Medicare Prescription Drug Improvement and Modernization Act, Congress directed the Department of Health and Human Services (HHS) to conduct a three-year demonstration program using **Recovery Audit Contractors (RACs)**. The demonstration program operated in New York, Massachusetts, Florida, South Carolina, and California and ended in 2008. The RAC reviewers found more than $1 billion in improper payments to the Medicare program. In 2006, Congress passed legislation to make the RAC program permanent and required expansion to all 50 states by no later than 2010.

The RAC program identified a number of sources for the errors including excessive units of service billed, incorrect discharge disposition, medical necessity, and coding. Although the largest percentage of errors was medical necessity (62% based on the audit findings through March 27, 2008), coding contributed to greater than 25% of all errors found. Incorrect assignment of the principal diagnosis contributed to 14% of the errors, and incorrect procedure codes contributed to 12% of the errors. Some coding errors identified included respiratory system diagnoses with ventilator support, excisional debridement, pneumonia, sepsis, and circulatory system diagnoses.

Programs such as CERT and RAC demonstrate the need to establish coding policies that address internal and external auditing and accuracy. Policies should address coding processes when auditing is performed "prebilling," such as for assessing individual coder accuracy or addressing specific problem areas. Policies should also include measures to be taken when a "postpayment" review occurs, such as in the case of CERT or RAC reviews.

It is important that the coding compliance program include policies that help ensure accurate coding and billing as well as stress the importance of good documentation. Policies should incorporate documentation requirements, payer policies, and coding guidelines. The policy will generally include an overall policy statement regarding the organization's commitment to compliant coding and a direction that coders observe official coding guidelines. The following checklist can be used to address specific policy issues and serve as a basis for reviews:

- Is the importance of provider documentation emphasized? The provider's documentation must support every code assigned. In the ICD-9-CM Official Guidelines for Coding and Reporting, "provider" means physician or any qualified health care practitioner who is legally accountable for establishing the patient's diagnosis.

- When and how should a coder query the physician? Review the physician query process, addressing related issues such as correcting errors and amending the medical record.

- What is the process for ensuring that codes assigned through the **chargemaster** are accurate? Review the developmental process for charges including the chargemaster description of the service, code assignment, and applicable dosage units and other units of service.

- Do policies address resources and instructions for ICD-9-CM, CPT-4, and HCPCS coding? Develop and frequently review facility-specific coding guidelines and policies, ensuring consistency with official guidelines and federal regulations.

- Are there specific coding areas that represent a compliance risk, and are instructions provided that address them?

- Does the policy emphasize that coding guidelines must be applied to all record types?

- Do policies address new-hire training and continuing education? Are coding resources adequate, and is there support and education for coding professionals?

- How are coding errors identified? The policy should address how internal coding audits are conducted, reported, and followed up. Discuss the process for addressing coding errors identified through prepayment or postpayment reviews.

- What documentation should be utilized to assign codes? How should documentation that is incomplete, unsigned, or missing be considered? The entire medical record should be reviewed to determine the specific reason for the encounter and the conditions treated.

- Are all staff educated on the importance of quality documentation, risk identification, and accurate coding and billing?

- How are issues related to denials or rejected claims relayed to coding?

- What is the process for making coding changes or corrections?

- Are issues such as upcoding, medical necessity, and DRG optimization addressed in policy?

- Does the policy address abstracting issues that may affect reimbursement such as admission and discharge status, present on admission (POA) criteria, and accurate demographic data?

- Are claims submitted to billing before coding review or before all appropriate codes have been added?

- Does the policy address the appropriate utilization of modifiers and variances in payer billing requirements? What is the process for addressing variances in official coding guidelines and coding advice from payers?

- Does the organization code directly off superbills and encounter forms? How does the facility ensure that the documentation supports the services billed?

As mentioned earlier in this chapter, within the corporate compliance program the code of conduct serves to guide employees in making ethical and compliant choices. Similarly, within a coding compliance program, a code of conduct should be developed that addresses compliance with coding guidelines and the responsibility to report coding compliance violations. The practice of upcoding or downcoding and the selection of codes that affect reimbursement such as complications and comorbidities should be addressed. For physician coding, guidelines should be established for selecting the appropriate evaluation and management code (for example, 1995 or 1997 CMS guidelines). For hospital coding, the importance of accurately reporting POA indicators should be included. The code of conduct can be incorporated with professional coding associations' codes of ethical behavior, such as the AHIMA's *Code of Ethics* and *Standards of Ethical Coding*, the American College of Medical Coding Specialists' (ACMCS) *Code of Ethics,* and the AAPC's *Medical Coding Code of Ethics.*

A coding compliance program may be an integral part of a broader health information management compliance program, which may include privacy and security issues of health records. As mentioned previously, the specific makeup of the coding compliance program will depend on the type and size of the organization. Regardless of whether an organization has a corporate compliance program or a health information management compliance program, a coding compliance program can be developed to address regulatory issues, coding policies, and coding integrity. Whether the health care organization consists of a single physician in private practice, a 25-bed critical access hospital, a 1000-bed teaching hospital, or a multiorganizational health care network, a coding compliance program can demonstrate the provider's commitment to compliant coding and billing.

Coding Compliance Education

Policies and procedures are only one part of the coding compliance program. **Coding compliance education** is a key element. Without it, the efforts of the coding compliance program are reduced to being only as good as the paper it is printed on. The purposes of an aggressive and thorough coding educational program include:

- Promoting an understanding of coding guidelines and federal regulations

- Implementing the policies and procedures developed and ensuring that employees understand their role in the compliance process

- Demonstrating the organization's commitment to compliance to employees, outside reviewers, and regulatory agencies.

Compliance education will vary based on the needs of the institution and will vary for new and existing employees. Educational needs should be assessed at least annually. In a large facility, regularly scheduled classes can be held on topics that are typically complex or areas of high risk. Smaller offices or facilities may wish to combine resources to bring educational opportunities to their coders. Offering convenient classes during work hours helps ensure that coders will obtain necessary education. Such classes can also provide opportunities for certified coders to obtain CEUs. Establishing regular educational classes also provides evidence of the organization's commitment to compliant coding. Some examples of fundamental coding classes that could be offered include:

- Evaluation and management coding

- Modifier usage

- CPT-4/ICD-9-CM coding

- Global period coding and billing (general or specific topics of interest)

- High-risk coding areas such as debridement (excisional and nonexcisional), interventional radiology, sepsis and urosepsis, preventive medicine

- Regulatory issues such as the proper use of the advance beneficiary notice (ABN) and local and national coverage decisions

- Payment methodologies including Medicare Severity Diagnosis-Related Groups (MS-DRGs), Ambulatory Payent Classifications (APCs), Ambulatory Patient Groups (APGs), and physician fee schedules

- Consultations and shared visits

- Midlevel provider coding

- Using the proper coding resources, including using the Internet to research regulatory or coding issues

The list and type of educational opportunities that can be offered are limitless. Offering opportunities for coders to gather in a coding "roundtable" format provides valuable opportunities for coders to discuss real-life coding examples with their peers. Educational sessions on clinical topics can be especially helpful for specialty coders who wish to gain insight into complex procedures. Anatomy classes can be especially helpful for coding orthopedics, obstetrics and gynecology, cardiac procedures, and interventional radiology. Topics should also include issues identified through coding reviews and audits.

Some organizations offer extended educational programs to coders designed to enhance coding education and to prepare individuals for coding certification exams. These programs bring the classroom to the workplace. Many offer semester-length courses in medical terminology, ICD-9-CM, CPT-4, pharmacotherapy, anatomy and physiology, and reimbursement methodologies. Numerous outside educational resources can be utilized for these classes, or the organization may choose to employ its own coding instructors.

Educational opportunities for employees should be flexible, allowing for *just in time* training for immediate educational needs. Just in time training can address the constantly changing regulatory requirements or coding errors that have been identified. Utilizing just in time training for new employees can help prevent unintentional coding errors. All education provided should be well documented, noting the date, topic, length, and names of attendees. Figure 5-1 shows a schedule of classes that could be ongoing. Figure 5-2 shows an organizational in-house coding curriculum. Offering on-site continuing education units to coding staff provides an opportunity for coding professionals to maintain coding certification conveniently and cost effectively.

Most professional coding associations that provide certification or accreditation to their members require continuing educational hours. The number of hours will vary with the association's requirements. The associations will also vary as to what they accept as an approved CEU. Some associations require a preapproval process before continuing educational hours can be accepted. Maintenance of certification should be required of coding staff to demonstrate that they are receiving updates on coding and regulatory changes.

Coding Accuracy

Along with providing coders continuing education and training updates, their accuracy rates should be periodically evaluated. Not only is coding accuracy critical for compliant claims submission, but it also affects the provider's complication rates, mortality rates, severity of illness computations, health care policy, and other administrative databases. Coding accuracy can also affect future rate setting figures and prospective payment system payment weights.

In some organizations coding accuracy is a goal measured in employee performance evaluations. Coding accuracy rates can also be used to determine salary and annual raises.

In determining coding accuracy it is important to distinguish coding errors that result from inaccurate code assignment verses errors that result from poor documentation. Documentation errors should not be counted as coding errors. Consider the following documentation errors that could result in coding errors:

- The physician documents that the patient has pneumonia. Documentation elsewhere in the medical record indicates that the patient may have a bacterial pneumonia. The physician fails to respond to repeated query attempts. The coder assigns ICD-9-CM code 486, "Unspecified pneumonia."

- The physician documents that the patient suffered "both bone fracture" in the right lower arm. An open reduction with internal fixation is performed. The coder is unable to assign an accurate code because the documentation does not indicate the specific site, for example, proximal end, distal end, or shaft.

- Under the "review of systems" in an evaluation and management (E/M) note, the physician documents, "Pertinent to headache addressed in HPI, others negative." The physician should indicate the specific systems reviewed and *all* others negative. The phrase "others negative" should not be used to indicate a complete review of systems.

General Hospital's Coding Compliance Course Offerings
USING THE TRICKS OF THE TRADE: This class will provide instruction on using the 3-M Encoder, Code-Correct and the CMS website, including finding the Medicare fee schedule. (1 CEU)
THE BASICS OF MEDICARE: This class will focus on the basics of Part A and Part B Medicare services, including beneficiary benefits, contractors, local and national coverage decisions and fee schedules. (2 CEUs)
EVALUATION AND MANAGEMENT (E/M) DOCUMENTATION AND CODING: This class will provide a review of documentation requirements for E/M services using the 1995 and 1997 guidelines. The use of E/M codes will be discussed, including definitions, E/M components and medical necessity. Participants will learn to apply codes from medical documentation. (2 CEUs)
THE OFFICE OF INSPECTOR GENERAL (OIG): Learn about the regulatory authority, regulations, audits, inspections and mission of the OIG in this class. A review of OIG targets for the current year will also be discussed. (1 CEU)
DOCUMENTATION GUIDELINES FOR TEACHING RULES AND MIDLEVEL PROVIDERS: This class will provide a review of documentation requirements, focusing on the teaching physician and midlevel provider requirements. Participants will discuss compliance issues and will review medical documentation. (2 CEUs)
The **PHYSICIAN QUALITY REPORTING INITIATIVE:** This class will provide a background on the Physician Quality Reporting Initiative (PQRI) measures and provide helpful information on appropriate coding and modifier usage. (1.5 CEUs)
THE CORRECT USE OF MODIFIERS FOR PHYSICIAN AND FACILITY: This class will provide an overview of the correct use of modifiers for physician and facility (hospital) services. Participants will discuss the use of modifiers and "CCI Edits" as they pertain to professional and facility services and will apply CPT/HCPCS modifiers in exercises. (2 CEUs)
CONSULTATIONS AND SHARED VISITS: This class will focus on the CMS guidelines for consultations and shared visits. Appropriate billing for these services will also be discussed. (1 CEU)
NEW! **RECOVERY AUDIT CONTRACTORS (RACs):** Learn what all the fuss is about with the RAC ATTACKS! This class will discuss CMS' efforts to identify improper payments to providers through the use of RACs, the experiences of providers who have had RAC audits and the scheduled roll-out for our State. (1.5 CEUs)
NEW! **PREGNANCY AND GYNECOLOGICAL CODING:** Chapter 11 of ICD-9-CM contains codes for normal pregnancy and delivery, miscarriage, abortion and various obstetrical complications. If you don't regularly code obstetrical cases, you may find this chapter a challenge. In this class, participants will review ICD-9-CM coding guidelines for pregnancy and gynecological conditions, along with pertinent HCPCS coding. A review of common payer payment guidelines will also be included. Send us your toughest coding questions before the class! (1.5 CEUs)
SKIN LESIONS AND LACERATION REPAIR: Don't get burned coding common skin procedures. These seemingly easy procedures can be some of the most complicated services to code. This class will guide the participant through the coding guidelines and present clinical examples. (1 CEU)
GI ENDOSCOPY CODING: This class will focus on gastrointestinal coding, specifically coding upper and lower endoscopies. Participants will discuss CPT and Medicare guidelines for coding colonoscopies, including reviewing screening versus diagnostic procedures. Correct use of modifiers and local coverage decisions (LCDs) will also be discussed. (2 CEUs)
WORKING DENIALS/THE APPEAL PROCESS – REVISED: One of the most important elements of accurate coding and billing is eliminating as many billing problems as possible *before* they occur. But working denials can be the coder's worst nightmare. This class will focus on methods to help you work denials and prevent them in the future. (1 CEU) **NEW ADDITION!** This class will also include a review of Medicare's denial and appeal process. (2 CEUs)
NEW! **PREVENTIVE MEDICINE:** This class will assist the participant in determining whether the visit is a preventive medicine visit or an office visit. Documentation requirements will be discussed, as well as the definitions of the comprehensive history and physical examination, anticipatory guidance, ordering of tests, and management of other medical problems. Medicare and commercial payment policies will also be discussed. (1.5 CEUs)
NEW! **RESEARCH CODING AND BILLING:** This class will guide participants in the proper assignment of V70.7, Examination of participant in clinical trial, and will discuss CMS' current requirements for coding and billing for patients involved in clinical trials/research. (1.0 CEU)

Figure 5-1 Coding Compliance Course Offerings. Example of listing of coding courses that could be offered regularly as part of a coding compliance program. Offering continuing education units to coding staff on site provides an opportunity for coding professionals to maintain coding certification conveniently and cost effectively. Coding courses may be tailored to address specific coding areas of concern.

General Hospital's Coding Curriculum			
Course	**Date/Time**	**Course Description**	**Notes**
Medical Terminology Start date: September 9 End date: December 5 Room: HIM Education Suite	Tuesday: 1:30–3:30 p.m. Friday: 8:30–10:30 a.m.	Students will learn medical terminology through a combination of anatomy and physiology and word building principles, focusing on the component parts of medical terms: prefixes, suffixes and word roots. Students practice formation, analysis and reconstruction of terms. Introduction to operative, diagnostic, therapeutic and symptomatic terminology of all body systems, as well as systemic and surgical terminology, is included.	24 class periods (Recommended before taking coding courses)
Pharmacotherapy December 9 and 12 Room: HIM Education Suite	Tuesday: 1:30–3:30 p.m. Friday: 8:30–10:30 a.m.	This course places an emphasis on the understanding of the action of drugs such as absorption, distribution, metabolism and excretion of drugs by the body. Included are drug classifications, most commonly prescribed drugs for each body system, and pharmacotherapy references including the formulary and PDR.	2 class periods
CPT Start date: September 8 End date: October 30 Room: HIM Education Suite	Monday: 2:00–4:00 p.m. Thursday: 2:00–4:00 p.m.	This class covers theories, concepts and applications of Current Procedural Terminology (CPT) coding. Included will be an introduction to basic coding principles, and conventions of CPT coding for each of the CPT manual sections.	16 class periods
ICD-9-CM Start date: January 12 End date: March 9 Room: HIM Education Suite	Monday: 10:00 a.m.–12 p.m. (no class 2/16) Thursday: 3:00–5:00 p.m.	This class discusses theories, concepts and applications in ICD-9-CM diagnostic coding. This in-depth advanced ICD-9-CM course includes practical exercises and discussion of official coding guidelines.	16 class periods
Certification Review September 15 Room: HIM Education Suite OR November 5 Room: HIM Education Suite OR March 12 Room: HIM Education Suite	September 15: 1:30–4:30 p.m. November 5: 9:00 a.m. to 12 p.m. March 12: 9:00 a.m.–12 p.m.	This class provides a review of certification exams, including a breakdown of exam sections, time allotments, as well as other important information. Class also includes study tips and a sample study schedule, and recommended resources. A brief review of coding competencies will also be discussed. Mock exam will be given and reviewed during class.	1 class period
Regulatory Issues March 18 Room: HIM Education Suite	March 18: 8:00 a.m.–12 p.m.	This class discusses various reimbursement methodologies including ambulatory surgical center payment rates (APCs), clinical laboratory fee schedule, hospital inpatient prospective payment system, hospital outpatient prospective payment system, inpatient psychiatric facility prospective payment system, Medicare physician fee schedule, the UB-04 and CMS 1500 claims. A review of the hospital and physician chargemaster development and maintenance will be presented.	

Figure 5-2 General Coding Curriculum. Example of an in-house coding curriculum offered as part of a coding compliance program. These classes may be eligible for continuing education units (CEUs).

- A patient has a diabetic ulcer of the left ankle that requires debridement. The documentation of the debridement does not indicate the deepest level debrided or the method of debridement (excisional or nonexcisional). The documentation does not indicate whether the patient has Type 1 or Type 2 diabetes. The coder is unable to correctly identify the type of diabetes, the extent of the debridement, and whether the debridement was excisional or nonexcisional.

- The physician documents the removal of a 2.0-cm benign lesion of the upper arm. The physician documents that "adequate margins" were taken to ensure complete removal. The coder assigns the code for a 2.0-cm lesion removal, as the physician failed to document the specific excised diameter.

As documentation errors should not be counted as coding errors, neither should billing errors or chargemaster errors be counted as coding errors. For example, codes that are entered into a coding or abstracting system but do not cross over accurately to the claim should not be counted as a coding error. An error in the chargemaster that incorrectly cross-walks a charge code to a CPT-4 or HCPCS code is not a coding error. When billing denials occur because payers do not follow coding guidelines, these are also not coding errors.

Accuracy standards should be consistent among all coding areas, such as hospital inpatient, outpatient, ancillary services, and physician coding. Nationally, the recognized best-practice standards indicate that a minimum of 95% accuracy is desirable. Some organizations may introduce incentive pay for accuracy rates that are higher. Coding reviews on individual accuracy rates should be performed at least biannually. An individual's accuracy rate can indicate the frequency of the review. For example, for a coder who is maintaining 95% accuracy, reviews can be performed only twice a year. For a coder failing to maintain the accuracy rate, reviews can be quarterly or even monthly. If coding accuracy is linked to salary and performance expectations, human resource policies should clearly outline the necessary disciplinary steps to assist the employee in achieving the performance goals. This may include additional training, a formal educational plan, or 100% coding review. Performance expectations in regard to coding accuracy should be clearly communicated to new staff at the time of hiring.

The Coding Compliance Manager and Coding Compliance Committee

Many health care organizations create a position of **coding compliance manager**, but this will vary depending on the individual needs of the facility. In smaller settings, the coding compliance manager may have other responsibilities such as coding manager or health information management (HIM) director. The coding compliance "department" may consist of one individual who has multiple responsibilities or an entirely separate department with multiple employees. The coding compliance department may be part of a facility's overall compliance area. The coding compliance manager may be responsible for monitoring and conducting audits as well as identifying risk areas. Other responsibilities include conducting educational and training programs, reporting issues, monitoring changes in federal and state guidelines, and ensuring that coding vendors (billing vendors, coding consultants) understand the institution's coding compliance guidelines. This individual will likely have an extensive coding background applicable to the organization's setting (e.g., hospital inpatient and outpatient, physician services, long-term care, teaching rules). An understanding of federal and state regulations is also important. Other desirable skills and knowledge sets include:

- Familiarity with fraud and abuse regulations

- Chargemaster or charge creation experience

- Claims and billing experience

Coding Compliance Manager Job Description
Purpose: To maintain the Corporate Compliance Program for ABC Hospital in accordance with ABC's Hospital Corporate Compliance Manual and the Office of Inspector General's Compliance Program Guidance.
Description: The Coding Compliance Manager manages, oversees, and monitors the audit process for the coding and billing operations. Responsible for: • Overseeing the Recovery Audit Contractors (RAC) audits and other outside payer audits, responding to denials, and ensuring timely responses. • Developing and implementing audit plans. • Preparing correspondence, reports, and presentation materials. • Serving as a subject matter expert in coding, billing, MS-DRG coordination, reimbursement, and compliance, as well as specific laws and regulations imposed on health care systems. • Managing and developing in-service educational programs and informational materials. • Assisting the VP, Health Information Manager, and Chief Compliance Officer in the development and implementation of RAC and other audit appeal strategies. • Managing and directing the operations of the compliance review program, including supervising Coding Compliance Analysts. • Keeping pace with the latest developments, advancements, and trends in coding, billing, reimbursement, laws, and regulations imposed on health care.
Minimum Qualifications: *Education*: Bachelor's degree in Health Information Management (HIM), Business Administration or related field or an equivalent combination of education and experience. *Experience*: 5–10 years experience in healthcare business practices relative to coding, billing, auditing, utilization, third-party payer regulations, risk assessment, reimbursement and contractual agreements, management and supervision. Expert knowledge of ICD-9-CM, CPT-4, and HCPCS classification systems, as well as MS-DRG, APC and other reimbursement methodologies. *Licensure/Certification*: RHIA, RHIT, CCS, or CPC-H *Other*: High moral and ethical character with a sense of honesty, integrity and caring. Independent, objective, detail-oriented, and analytical. Must possess excellent verbal presentation and education skills.
Contacts: *Reports to*: Executive Vice President, CFO, CRO. *Relationship with*: All levels of management and administration, department directors, physicians, nurses, ancillary staff, practice managers, coding and billing staff, registration staff. Reporting liaison with CRO, local board, ABC's Hospital Compliance Program Committee.

Figure 5-3 Coding Compliance Manager Job Description.

- An understanding of the relationship between coding and billing
- Familiarity with the local Medicare contractor
- Communication, management, and human relation skills

The coding compliance manager may report to the organization's compliance officer, HIM director, director of finance, or directly to the chief operating officer (COO). The coding compliance manager should have a current coding certification. See Figure 5-3 for a job description for a hospital coding compliance manager.

The coding compliance manager may be supported by staff that perform auditing, education, and other compliance activities. Titles of these individuals will vary but may include coding compliance auditors or reviewers, coding auditors, medical auditors, or compliance specialists. To gain the respect

Coding Compliance Analyst Job Description
Purpose: To perform audits in accordance with ABC's Health System's annual Compliance Work Plan and prepare written and oral communications to the Coding Compliance Manager and/or Corporate Compliance Officer.
Description: The Coding Compliance Analyst supports the organization's corporate integrity program through the identification and assessment of coding compliance risk and maintains a current understanding of regulatory trends and changes in coding policy and reimbursement methods. • Serves as a resource for coding and clinical staff on issues related to compliant coding and billing • Applies knowledge of medical terminology, abbreviations, anatomy and physiology, diseases, and procedures to accurately review coding assignments • Applies knowledge of ICD-9-CM, CPT-4 and HCPCS nomenclature, coding rules, guidelines and proper sequencing to analyze medical record documentation and coding assignments • Applies knowledge of ethical coding principles and revenue cycle activities to evaluate coding compliance through coding audits • Works with departments and physicians to monitor compliance to coding standards and provide guidance to help them meet the requirements • Assists departments and physicians in development of corrective action plans involving coding issues when areas of opportunity are identified • Receives, develops, coordinates and/or oversees internal and external coding audits for the purpose of monitoring and detecting any misconduct or noncompliance to final resolution. • Assist in the development of coding education plans, materials, and resources to educate employees with respect to overall objectives of the corporate compliance program • Carries out all duties and responsibilities as assigned by the Coding Compliance Manager, Chief Compliance Officer and/or the Compliance Committee.
Minimum Qualifications: *Education:* Associates Degree in Health Information Management or related field preferred. *Experience:* Minimum three years of diagnostic and procedure coding. Experience with Microsoft Word and Excel, encoder products, auditing software preferred. *Licensure/Certification:* RHIA, RHIT, CCS, CPC-H *Other:* Detail-oriented and analytical. Strong customer service and communication skills. Ability to operate various computerized medical coding and information processing systems. Exceptional organization skills. Ability to analyze medical records and create audit reports that assist physicians, management and hospital staff in understanding coding compliance issues.
Contacts: *Reports to:* Coding Compliance Manager.

Figure 5-4 Coding Compliance Analyst Job Description.

of the coding staff whose work is being reviewed, the auditors must be highly experienced in the area they are auditing. Utilizing individuals who are not responsible for the actual coding and billing processes within the organization will help demonstrate objectivity of the coding review and credibility of the auditing process. Figure 5-4 is a typical job description for the position of coding compliance analyst.

Many organizations utilize outside consultants or companies to perform coding audits. This can provide a valuable educational experience, as good consultants will be able to share best practices of several organizations. Consultants can also be utilized when the structure of the organization is small, and individual or independent reviews within the coding department are not possible. Prior to an outside audit, consultants should be provided with the coding policies and procedures that are used within the organization. Consultants should also be aware of local Medicare policies or state regulations that directly affect the organization's coding. Even if an organization has its own coding compliance department, consultants can be utilized periodically to assess the accuracy of the coding compliance auditing.

The coding compliance department and manager should be viewed as a valuable resource for other departments in the organization for answering coding and billing questions as well as for reporting potential compliance issues. The coding compliance program that runs like a police state will not provide a means for employees to seek advice or to report potential problems. Employees within the coding and billing areas, as well as other departments, should be encouraged to report potential compliance issues to the coding compliance manager.

A coding compliance committee should be part of the coding compliance program and have representatives from finance and accounting, administration, business office services, clinical staff, utilization management, and coding services. In some organizations, the coding compliance committee may function in cooperation with other committees, such as the chargemaster or medical record committee. The committee can discuss issues related to claims management, documentation, coding, duplicate billing, and issues relating to medical necessity. The committee can also share resources related to coding updates and regulatory changes.

The compliance committee structure should help foster communication among the various departments. The importance of communication among coding, billing, and patient accounts departments cannot be overstressed. In many organizations denial information is not shared with the individuals who are responsible for coding. As a result, coders may not be aware of coding errors that led to payment denials or delays. Communication among departments can result in immediate cost benefits owing to decreased denials, fewer delays in payment, and improved coding accuracy.

The activities of the coding compliance program must be carefully documented and may include:

- Summaries of compliance committee minutes, including approvals of the compliance plan or calendar and any policies/procedures

- Employee background, including résumés demonstrating coding qualifications, certifications, and ongoing continuing education

- Training and education agendas, handouts, and attendance rosters

- Hotline reports and investigations

- Corrective action including employee education, discipline, self-disclosures, rebilling, and policy/procedure revisions

- Monitoring and auditing activities

Staffing Coding Professionals and Coding Certification

Coding staff should be required to obtain the necessary training and education needed to accurately assign diagnosis and procedure codes. Hiring unqualified individuals to perform coding duties can lead to fraudulent coding and billing and be viewed as lack of commitment to compliant coding and billing. Along with a thorough understanding of coding systems, it is preferable that coders have course work in medical terminology, anatomy and physiology, pathology, and reimbursement systems.

When hiring certified coding individuals, it is important to recognize that there are several associations and organizations that provide **coding certification**, and the individual requirements for obtaining certification will vary. For example, the fact that a coder is "certified" may demonstrate that the individual has met only the minimum necessary standards of the professional association and has passed a certification exam. Other associations provide certification to individuals who pass an exam that reflect a "mastery" skill in a particular coding area.

It is important to understand the association's educational requirements, certification maintenance policy, and underlying philosophy. For example, some businesses and associations grant a coding certification after attendance at a day-long coding seminar. Others may provide coding seminars in a 40-hour "boot camp" format and then certify individuals after they have successfully passed an examination. Still other certifications are associated with approved programs in technical schools and universities. The educational requirements for coding certification vary from none required to high school diploma to associate and bachelor degrees. The phrase "truth in advertising" is important for both the organization that is hiring the certified coder and the coder who seeks certification. There are numerous examples of coders who spent hundreds of dollars on a coding certification course and exam only to learn later that the credential is not recognized by the majority of health care providers. There are an equal number of examples of employers who have hired individuals with letters after their name and a coding certificate in hand, but the individual could not perform entry-level coding. Certification alone does not indicate coding competence. The ideal candidate will likely have a combination of education, training, certification, and experience.

Several professional coding associations offer specialty coding certifications. For instance, there are coding certifications that emphasize hospital (facility) coding, professional (physician) coding, and specialty coding (e.g., dermatology, interventional radiology, emergency department). There are also certifications that represent apprenticeship or associate status, indicating that the individual has passed an entry-level coding exam but may be lacking in experience.

A coding exam should be administered to all potential employees. The exam should include questions replicating actual coding scenarios reflective of the facility and the specific position. Questions on regulatory requirements, coding guidelines, basic anatomy and physiology, and medical terminology can help gauge an individual's knowledge of the entire coding process. Including general compliance questions that assess how an individual might respond to a specific situation can provide valuable insight into the applicant's ethical behavior and understanding of compliance guidelines. Consider these examples of questions that appear on a hiring coding test:

1. The physician has marked the diagnoses and services performed for a patient on a superbill. You notice that the dictated documentation from that visit includes different diagnoses. You should:

    a. Select the code(s) noted by the physician on the superbill.

    b. Determine the code(s) yourself from the physician's documentation.

    c. Use a combination of both sets of codes.

    d. Query the physician.

2. You are the hospital coder responsible for coding ancillary visits, specifically, radiology and laboratory services. You notice that orders originating from a local physician's office always has the same diagnosis code noted, specifically "Pneumonia," ICD-9-CM diagnosis code 486. This occurs regardless of the specific tests that were ordered. You should:

    a. Assign the diagnosis listed on the order.

    b. Assign diagnosis codes based on the results of the tests.

    c. Inform the coding supervisor of the questionable diagnosis.

    d. Telephone the physician's office receptionist.

Questions such as these can help assess the employee's possible response to difficult problems and potential conflicts.

Coding Performed by Physicians

Sometimes, physicians may feel they should assign their own codes. Just as the coder should be skilled in correct coding assignment, the physician should be trained in ICD-9-CM and CPT-4 coding, the official coding guidelines, and state and federal regulations. But often, physicians are not able to spend the time necessary to be fully informed about the complex coding guidelines, frequent changes, payer billing requirements, and regulatory updates. Consequently, the physician's practice can be placed at risk for fraudulent coding and billing. Many coding auditors can attest that coding performed entirely by the physician who is not familiar with coding guidelines is often less accurate than coding performed by experienced coders.

The physician should not be entirely excluded from the coding process, however. The importance of their documentation and requirements needed to accurately assign codes should be stressed with physicians, and such discussion can close the communication gap that often exists between physicians and coders. As mentioned elsewhere in this book, the coding can be only as good as the documentation.

Coding Compliance Resources

Within the coding compliance program should be a commitment to utilizing the appropriate **coding resources**. Using outdated coding resources can result in coding and billing errors and pose a compliance risk for the organization. It is often surprising the number of denials that can be immediately traced back to using an outdated code book or superbill. Coding resources that must be kept up-to-date include:

- *International Classification of Diseases, 9th Revision, Clinical Modification (ICD-9-CM)* code book

- *Current Procedural Terminology (CPT-4)* code book

- *Health Care Common Procedure Coding System (HCPCS) Level II Coding Procedures* code book

- National Correct Coding Initiative (NCCI) manual or electronic file

- Computerized encoding systems

- The most recent update to the *ICD-9-CM Official Guidelines for Coding and Reporting*

- AHA's *Coding Clinic for ICD-9-CM*

- AMA's *CPT Assistant*

- Encounter forms, billing sheets, superbills

Coders should also have access to the numerous online resources that can assist coding accuracy and reduce the possibility of future denials. These include access to local and national payer coverage decisions, local contractor Web sites, the CMS Web site, and regulations published in the *Federal Register*. Other valuable resources available online include medical terminology aids, medication and pharmacy information, resources on specific diseases, anatomy plates, and details on surgeries and procedures. A detailed listing of Web sites can be maintained and should be regularly updated.

The development of a coding compliance program does not need to be onerous. Many facilities already have policies on coding, billing, and documentation. The OIG Web site contains many publications helpful in developing compliance programs. Professional associations also have examples of coding compliance structure and policies that provide assistance in the development of a coding compliance program. It is important that the coding compliance program is not "left on the shelf." A program that is on paper only will not protect an organization from fraud and abuse risk and liability.

Chapter Review

1. List the seven components of a corporate compliance program and briefly describe each.

_____

_____

_____

2. If a health care facility has an overall compliance program, why is it necessary that the facility also have a coding compliance program? How are the two programs different?

_____

_____

_____

3. The OIG's Compliance Program Guidance for Hospitals states, "Because incorrect procedure coding may lead to overpayments and subject a hospital to liability for the submission of false claims, hospitals need to pay close attention to coder training and qualifications." What measures can health care facilities take to ensure that coders are properly trained and are qualified?

_____

_____

_____

4. Review one of the areas that should be included within a coding compliance policy, for example, coding from incomplete records, making coding changes, or documentation that should be reviewed for coding purposes. Write the policy statement(s).

_____

_____

_____

5. Define the purpose of the code of conduct, and identify some of the issues that should be addressed in the code.

_____

_____

_____

6. Explain why documentation errors are not necessarily coding errors.

    _____

    _____

    _____

7. Define the characteristics, responsibilities, and qualifications of the coding compliance manager.

    _____

    _____

    _____

8. Write a coding question for a hiring test that assesses the potential applicant's understanding of the official coding guidelines.

    _____

    _____

    _____

9. What factors can demonstrate the trustworthiness of the health care provider?

    _____

    _____

    _____

10. Structure, process, and outcome are components of effective assessment of a coding compliance program. If the *structure* question is: Are coding compliance policies reviewed regularly? what would be the *process* and the *outcome?*

    _____

    _____

    _____

Case Studies

Case Study 1

The coding compliance manager has completed a review of inpatient hospital coding. In a few records she determines that the coder should have queried the physician to resolve conflicting information in the medical record. There is an organizational policy on physician queries that discusses the proper format of a query, but it does not address whether the physician should be queried as a result of findings on audits or postpayment.

1. What should a coding compliance program policy include regarding physician queries?

_____

_____

_____

Case Study 2

Within a surgical practice, a few physicians document the CPT-4 procedure code on their operative reports. Sometimes the coding is correct, but the surgeons are not generally considering coding guidelines and bundling rules. In a coding audit it is determined that some coders are assigning the codes as the surgeons have noted on their surgical reports, whereas others appear to be coding from the documentation within the operative note.

1. What should a coding compliance program policy state regarding codes within dictated reports and use of those codes by coders for billing?

_____

_____

_____

Case Study 3

A patient is seen for multiple plantar warts. The physician states in the documentation that "multiple plantar warts were removed with laser." The coder assigns CPT-4 codes 17000 and 17003.

1. Has the coder assigned the codes accurately?

_____

_____

_____

2. What instruction, if any, should be given to the coder and/or the physician?

_____

_____

_____

Case Study 4

A local Medicare contractor's Part B policy states: "Codes V67.00, V67.09, V67.1, V67.2, and V71.1 are non-specific ICD-9-CM codes that require an additional ICD-9-CM code to specify the disease entity treated. When a metastasis of the primary neoplasm is suspected, report V71.1 with a secondary neoplasm ICD-9-CM code (e.g., 196.0–198.89) or personal history of neoplasm ICD-9-CM code (e.g., V10.00–V10.9)."

1. Determine the accuracy of the coding information provided by the contractor.

_____

_____

_____

2. Provide guidance in the form of a policy statement that would assist the coder in determining how to accurately assign codes in situations when a primary neoplasm is suspected.

_____

_____

_____

Case Study 5

An outside consulting firm has been hired to perform a coding audit of inpatient and outpatient records at a hospital. The audit shows the following:

- Inconsistent application of HCPCS modifiers. For example, some coders apply the modifier RT/LT only to Medicare claims, whereas other coders apply them to all payers.

- Inconsistent coding of excisional debridement for inpatients. Some coders are assigning ICD-9-CM procedure code 86.22 when the physician notes "the wound was sharply debrided." Other coders appear to be assigning 86.22 only when the physician notes "excisional debridement."

1. Create an educational plan that could be used to address the issues identified in the audit.

_____

_____

_____

2. Write coding compliance policy statements that could address each of the issues identified.

    _____

    _____

    _____

3. Are the problems that were identified coding or documentation errors?

    _____

    _____

    _____

References

American Health Information Management Association. (2008, July 24). *Benchmarking coding quality.* Audio seminar/webinar. Available for order at https://imis.ahima.org//orders/productDetail.cfm?pc=AU DMC072408&bURL=%2Forders%2FproductByCategory%5FAUD%2Ecfm%3Ft%3D7

American Hospital Association. (2008, July 16). Regulatory advisory; Medicare recovery audit contractors (RACS): Coding and documentation strategies. Retrieved from http://web.mhanet.com/ userdocs/articles/RAC/AHA_RAC_CodingAdvisory_071608.pdf

Department of Health and Human Services, Office of Inspector General. (2005, January 31). OIG supplemental compliance program guidance for hospitals. *Federal Register, 70*(19), 4858–4875.

Department of Health and Human Services, Office of Inspector General. Work plan for fiscal year 2009 Retrieved from http://oig.hhs.gov/publications/docs/workplan/2009/WorkPlanFY2009.pdf

Hapner, Peggy. (2001, May). Covering the bases of coding compliance [Electronic version]. *Journal of AHIMA, 72*(5), 69–71.

TMF Health Quality Institute, the Quality Improvement Organization Support Center for the Hospital Payment Monitoring Program. 2006, January; rev. 2008, March. *Hospital Payment Monitoring Program (HPMP) compliance workbook.* Retrieved from http://hpmp.tmfhqi.net/LinkClick.aspx?fileticket=nory3jyb h2U=&tabid=522&mid=1248

Wiggin and Dana, LLC. (2000, March 16). Compliance programs for nursing facilities: Ten steps towards making a "good faith & meaningful commitment" towards compliance. Retrieved from http://www .wiggin.com/pubs/alerts_template.asp?ID=737167212000

Auditing and Prevention

Objectives

At the completion of this chapter, the learner should be able to:

- Identify coding and billing risk areas.
- Differentiate between high-risk and high-volume target areas.
- List resources that can be utilized to determine potential issues that should be reviewed in a coding compliance program.
- Discuss the importance of performing coding and claims reviews.
- Explain basic sampling methods and identify tools required to perform coding and billing auditing.
- Discuss the differences between retrospective and prospective reviews, identifying pros and cons of each.
- Design an audit tool, time line, and criteria, including key elements based on the nature of the audit.
- Discuss important auditing follow-up processes including reporting, education, and re-assessments.
- Explain the impact of outside auditing, particularly Recovery Audit Contractors (RACs).
- Discuss the role of the coordinator who handles coding or payer audits.

Key Terms

areas of risk	degree of confidence	high-risk and high-volume areas	RAT-STATS
assessment	extrapolation	prospective reviews	retrospective reviews
audit objective	follow-up		sample size
audit response team			time period for review

Assessing Areas of Risk

Identifying the numerous coding compliance areas that can be audited is probably very easy to most coding compliance managers. They are probably very aware of the issues that coders struggle with, potential billing problems, and areas that need documentation improvement. Limiting the number of audits into a manageable amount is much more difficult.

The Office of Inspector General (OIG) identifies many targeted areas for coding and billing in its compliance program guidance publications. The OIG also publish the findings of audits that it has performed on its Web site. Local Medicare contractors also regularly have articles on their Web sites on common billing and coding errors that they have identified in claims processing. High-risk coding and billing errors that should regularly be audited include:

- Duplicate billing: submitting claims or charges for more than the actual number of units supplied

- Incorrect coding: submitting claims with incorrect CPT-4, HCPCS, or diagnosis codes, including misapplication of modifiers

- Unbundling: submitting charges separately for services that are generally combined

- Services not performed: submitting charges for services or procedures that were not performed or supported in documentation

- Upcoding: submitting CPT-4 or ICD-9-CM codes with a higher reimbursement than what was actually performed

- Billing for medically unnecessary services: billing as covered, services that the Medicare program has defined as noncovered

- Inaccurate/incomplete documentation: billing for services based on incomplete information, information that does not accurately reflect the patient's true condition, or providing falsified information

High-risk and high-volume areas are typically frequent targets for review. High-risk areas include the CMS and OIG targeted areas noted in the preceding list, present on admission (POA) coding, recovery audit contracting (RAC) initiatives, hospital-acquired conditions (HACs), consultation services, nonphysician provider payments, and billing during global periods. Services that are high volume may not necessarily be high cost, but the mere volume of the services can create financial risk if problems exist. Other high-risk areas can be identified internally, such as reviewing newly hired or cross-trained coders. High-cost services such as cardiology procedures and certain pharmaceuticals should also be reviewed.

There are a number of resources that can be used to identify potential coding **areas of risk** for hospital inpatients. The Centers for Medicare & Medicaid Services (CMS) use the Medicare inpatient discharge data for each hospital within a state and compare them with the data of all other hospitals within that state, within the regional area, or within the nation. These data identify unusual coding patterns. For example, the data may show that one particular hospital may have a higher-than-average number of discharges with MS-DRGs relating to septicemia or one-day stays (such as chest pain). These are areas that coding compliance departments should be regularly reviewing. Table 6-1 lists MS-DRGs that are frequently targeted for review. Aside from these examples, other MS-DRGs include simple pneumonia (MS-DRG 193), heart failure and shock (MS-DRGs 193 and 194), chest pain (MS-DRG 313), esophagitis and gastroenteritis (MS-DRGs 391 and 392), back pain

Table 6-1 MS-DRGs Frequently Targeted for Review

CMS DRG	MS-DRG	Possible Coding Scenario (Codes effective 10/1/08)
• 014 (cranial hemorrhage or cerebral infarction) and 559 (acute ischemic stroke with use of thrombolytic agent)	• 064 (intracranial hemorrhage or cerebral infarction with major complication or comorbidity [MCC])	434.91 410.91
	• 065 (intracranial hemorrhage or cerebral infarction with complication or comorbidity [CC])	434.91 585.6 403.91
	• 066 (intracranial hemorrhage or cerebral infarction without CC/MCC)	434.91 401.9 250.00
	• 061 (acute ischemic stroke with use of thrombolytic agent with MCC)	434.91 410.91 99.10
	• 062 (acute ischemic stroke with use of thrombolytic agent with CC)	434.91 478.34 99.10
	• 063 (acute ischemic stroke with use of thrombolytic agent without CC/MCC)	434.91 345.10 99.10
• 079 (respiratory infections and inflammations age >16 with CC)	• 177 (respiratory infections and inflammations with MCC)	507.8 428.31
	• 178 (respiratory infections and inflammations with CC)	507.8 511.9

(MS-DRGs 551 and 552), nutritional disorders (MS-DRGs 640 and 641), and septicemia (MS-DRGs 871 and 872).

Other potential risk areas in hospital inpatient coding are discharge status codes. For certain MS-DRGs a hospital will receive a per diem transfer payment rather than the full MS-DRG payment if the patient is discharged to certain postacute care settings. These settings include other acute hospitals or distinct-part hospital units, a skilled nursing facility, or to home under the provision of home health services when those services begin within three days after the date of discharge. CMS policy on postacute transfers has frequently been cited as confusing and difficult to comply with. Nonetheless, CMS holds the hospital responsible for properly reporting the patient's discharge disposition, even though the hospital may not be aware of changes post patient discharge, such as home health services. Because this is a focused area of risk identified by the CMS, OIG, and RACs, discharge disposition should regularly be reviewed with an emphasis placed on the specific MS-DRGs that are affected. Some compliance programs perform a 100% review of the discharge disposition of these affected MS-DRGs. It is critical that coders are supplied with the current listing of patient status codes if they are responsible for appending the discharge disposition to the claim. These listings periodically change.

Aside from identifying potential areas of compliance risks, Medicare uses hospital and physician claims data for a number of other purposes, including rate setting, detecting improper payments, and identifying potential areas of fraud and abuse. Data analysis can compare claims information among various provider groups. The data can be analyzed for volume of business, types of providers, volume of Medicare/Medicaid patients, prevalence of services, and administrative costs. Data may come from national or local contractor claims. Other sources of data may come from the OIG, U.S. Government Accountability Office (GAO) reports, fraud alerts, beneficiary and provider complaints, referrals from medical licensing boards, and referrals from other Medicare contractors. CMS instructs its local contractors to perform an analysis of the data and determine:

- Areas of potential errors (noncovered procedures or not correctly coded)
- Unusual trends, changes in utilization over time, or other schemes to inappropriately maximize reimbursement
- Whether there is a need for a local coverage decision (LCD)
- Strategies that will efficiently prevent or address potential errors (e.g., prepayment edits)
- Billing patterns that illuminate potential errors
- High-volume or high-cost services that are widely being overutilized
- Problem areas and/or specific providers for possible fraud investigations

In addition to coding that has been manually assigned by coders (sometimes referred to as "soft coded"), auditing should include any coding that is "hard coded." Hard coding generally refers to coding features that are built into the hardware or software of a billing system. Many hospital charges are hard coded into the chargemaster billing system. The entire charge capture process should be reviewed and updated annually.

An organization's internal billing system may hold a wealth of information for auditing purposes. Data mining can include pulling all claims with a specific modifier-CPT code combination; by specific provider, specialty, or department; by MS-DRG groupings; and by payer types. There are many more possibilities. Additionally, data from the billing system may help identify potential problem areas such as excessive charges or reimbursement for a particular service. Because it is known that payers utilize the billing data, providers should also utilize the data to identify potential problem areas.

If a provider utilizes an outside billing company or coding consultants, it is important that their services be reviewed as well. It is ultimately the responsibility of the provider rendering the medical services to ensure that coding and billing are accurate. The contracted billing company should have an effective compliance program, and it should be willing to provide results of internal coding audits. The company should also provide figures on payment denials or delays if it is handling the denials as well. It is important to determine that employees of the contracted company or the consultants are adequately trained individuals, as hiring untrained or poorly trained individuals may be a method that the billing company utilizes to reduce costs.

Claims Review

One area that is often missed when conducting coding reviews is claims review. A review of the hospital or provider claim should also coincide with a coding review. A review of claims alongside the coding will help ensure that the codes that were intended to be applied to the claim actually show up on the claim. Many providers have different coding and billing systems, which can result in computer interfacing issues. Modifiers may be missing, or numbers of units or charges may be incorrectly calculated. The following are a number of errors that may occur on claims submission:

- Incorrect provider number/assignment
- Incorrect dates of service

- Incorrect place of service

- Duplicate billing

- Inaccurate units of service billing

- Codes that have not appropriately crossed over from the coding system to the billing system, including the application of modifiers

Assessing claims alongside the coding may help identify claim edits that the provider may include prior to submission of billing. For example, if a review determined that modifier 25 was inadvertently being applied to surgical CPT codes, an edit could be built into the system to allow modifier 25 to be included only with evaluation and management (E/M) services.

Sampling and Audit Methods and Design

A common mistake that first-time coding auditors often make is to take on more auditing than they can possibly review. It is easy to become quickly overwhelmed when conducting several audits simultaneously and reviewing volumes of records. Auditing is a time-consuming process, but it can be managed properly if some basic steps are considered.

Most audits require an initial audit that identifies a baseline or starting point. This sample audit provides a snapshot of the targeted area and helps determine the size of future auditing samples or whether continued audits need to performed at all. There is no definitive figure for the number of records that should be reviewed in the sample audit. The actual number will depend on the total volume of claims and the area being reviewed.

One question frequently asked is whether coding audits should focus solely on government claims, such as Medicare and Medicaid, or include all payer types. There should always be a strong focus on CMS and OIG target areas, but all payer types should be reviewed. This will ensure that patient populations not routinely affected by governmental payers will be audited, for example, pediatrics, and obstetrics and gynecology.

One does not need to be a statistician to determine the proper **sample size** or what should be reviewed; however, there are some basic sampling strategies that should be considered. A *sample* is a subset of units (claims or medical records) selected from a larger set of the same units (claims or medical records). Whether one chooses to perform a small random audit or an audit of the entire number of units (sometimes referred to as the *universe*) will depend on a number of factors but most importantly, on the specific topic that is being audited. Another consideration is the percentage of accuracy or precision that is desired. Obviously, reviewing 100% of the total number possible will result in a higher degree of accuracy and precision, but a complete review of all records may not be necessary. For example, a four-physician neurology office practice sees a total of approximately 75 consultations per week, which equates to approximately 3900 consultations per year. If a review of all 3900 cases is performed, there will be 100% confidence in the findings. If fewer than the entire number of claims are reviewed, the confidence level will be less, but this may still be an acceptable sample size. The goal should not necessarily be a 100% review but, rather, a comfortable confidence level in the findings. In the preceding example, if 10 consultations for each physician are reviewed, or 40 medical records, and the result is that consultation codes were accurately reported 100% of the time, a more comprehensive review may not be necessary. However, if the review reflects a 50% or greater error rate, a more comprehensive review should be considered.

When an audit reflects 100% accuracy or no issues are identified, that does not necessarily mean that the subject area does not need to be audited again in the future. Codes, guidelines, and coding personnel change, often requiring reauditing of areas that historically have shown no problems.

Table 6-2 Standard Guide to Minimum Sample Size

Population Size	Sample Size	Population Size	Sample Size
10	10	550	226
20	19	600	234
40	36	700	248
50	44	800	260
75	63	900	269
100	80	1,000	278
150	108	1,200	291
200	132	1,300	297
250	152	1,500	306
300	169	3,000	341
350	184	6,000	361
400	196	9,000	368
450	207	50,000	381
500	217	100,000+	385

If a compliance issue is identified during a preliminary review, it will be necessary to determine how far back the problem may have occurred. This may require that an "open" review, or a review of unbilled claims, also become a retrospective review. Retrospective and prospective reviews are discussed later in this chapter.

A standard guide to minimum sample size has been utilized for a number of years. This guide is generally considered when performing research studies but can be used as a gauge for other audits as well. Table 6-2 is a guide to minimum sample size that represents at least a 95% **degree of confidence.**

The determination of the appropriate sample size is generally determined by the nature of the population to be sampled, the type of investigation, and the degree of precision desired. In 1970 R.V. Krejcie and D.W. Morgan developed a formula for estimating the sample size and created a table for determining the sample size based on confidence level. The table continues to be used to determine sample size for a variety of research and auditing studies.

The higher the degree of confidence in the audit size, the more accurate an **extrapolation** figure will be. Extrapolation refers to making an inference about the whole (the universe) based on a smaller subset, or what is known. For example, a coding review of consultation services determined that Dr. Jones billed an office consultation CPT code 500 times in the past year. A random sample of 30 records indicated that Dr. Jones assigned the wrong CPT E/M code level in 15 records. An inference can be made that Dr. Jones miscoded 250 records in the past year.

Extrapolation is also helpful in determining financial vulnerability. For example, a review of CPT code 20552, "Injection(s); single or multiple trigger point(s), one or two muscle(s)," is conducted. It is determined that a group practice billed 2000 claims with CPT code 20552 during the past year. In a randomly selected sample of 100 records, it is determined that in 50 records the coder should have selected CPT code 20550, "Injection(s); single tendon sheath, or ligament." This resulted in an underpayment of approximately $5 per erroneous claim. Because the sample audit reflected a 50% error rate that resulted in lost revenue of $5 per claim, an inference can be made that 1000 claims were coded incorrectly, resulting in $5000 in lost revenue.

CMS and commercial payers use extrapolation methods to determine overpayment amounts. However, the Medicare Prescription Drug Improvement and Modernization Act of 2003 (MMA) limits the use of extrapolation to "a sustained or high level of payment error, *or* documented educational intervention has failed to correct the payment error . . ." (http://www.cms.hhs.gov). CMS uses statistical sampling in determining the amount of overpayments. This includes having the sampling methodology reviewed and approved by a statistician or a person with equivalent expertise.

The OIG uses a statistical software package developed by the Regional Advanced Techniques Staff (RATS) in San Francisco The software was later renamed **RAT-STATS.** Its purpose is to assist the user in performing random samples and evaluating the result and is designed to run on personal computers using Microsoft Windows (Windows 95 and later versions). A data file such as an Excel spreadsheet or Access data file can be uploaded, and statistical computations can be generated that determine sample size and confidence level. The software is a free download at www.oig.hhs.gov.

Regardless of the method used to determine the sample size, the records selected in the sample audit should be selected randomly, for example, every 5th or 10th record. If the targeted area is relatively small in number, the entire number may be audited.

When Medicare or the OIG determines the time period for a review, a number of factors are considered. The *Medicare Carriers* and *Medicare Intermediary Manuals* state that any claims within the past four years may be "reopened." However if the review determines that fraud and abuse occurred, the review can extend to "anytime." The actual period of time for the review may be based on:

- How long the pattern of sustained or high level of payment error is believed to have existed;

- The volume of claims that are involved;

- The length of time that a national coverage decision (NCD) or regional or local coverage policy has been in effect;

- The extent of any other prepayment review that may already have been conducted; and

- The dollar value of the claims involved.

Understanding the importance of claims data and how payers utilize those data is helpful in determine potential auditing areas. Note that an audit may consist of reviewing a single code, a line item, or the entire claim. For instance, an audit may focus only on the number of billed units for a particular pharmaceutical. In addition, several target areas may be addressed in a single audit. For example, a review of procedures performed bilaterally may review accurate CPT code assignment, modifier 50 use, and number of units on the claim.

Prospective and Retrospective Reviews

In most coding audits, reviews are conducted on "open," or unbilled, medical records; that is, they are **prospective reviews.** If **retrospective reviews** are performed, that is, on claims that have already been paid, and coding errors exist, the organization must correct the claims and rebill the governmental payer. For example, If the audit results show that medical necessity was not met, payment occurred for services not performed, or services were coded at a higher level than supported in medical record documentation, the claim will need to be corrected and monies refunded. This is true even for a single claim and is an important consideration when determining sample size. Coding must be supported by the medical record documentation at the time the claim is submitted. In other words, the code assignment should be made to the highest degree of certainty at the time of coding. If billing is completed before documentation is completed, any discrepancies between the final medical documentation and coding must be corrected, and if necessary, the coding and the claim should be corrected. This is true whether the detected error shows an overpayment or an underpayment.

Whether audits are conducted prospectively or retrospectively, coding compliance policies should address the process for any amendments that may be made in the medical record. For example, if a retrospective review indicates that the documentation could have better supported medical necessity, should an amendment be made to the documentation? This can be very dangerous territory. If documentation is changed only for the purposes of supporting the code assignment, this could be viewed as a fraudulent activity, with the integrity of the documentation called into question. It would be unreasonable to believe that a physician could remember specific details of a physical examination 30, 60, or 90 days after the patient was seen. It would probably be inappropriate to add to the review of systems or physical exam documentation in these cases. However, if the physician failed to document the patient's diagnoses, this information could reasonably be added in an amendment. It is important to recall the guidelines or changes to the medical record. Only the physician who originated the document should amend it. As mentioned in a previous chapter, changes in the medical record are never blackened out or deleted.

In the majority of situations, an audit should not be so large that it becomes impossible to manage, resulting in a large number of held or unbilled claims. However, in some cases it may be necessary that all claims of a certain type be held for review prior to submission. In one case, an internal audit identified a documentation and coding issue regarding CPT code 76937, "Ultrasound guidance for vascular access." The audit found that 95% of the time the documentation did not adequately support billing 76937. The facility may decide to hold all claims with the 76937 code and review the documentation prior to claim submission to ensure accuracy. As staff are educated, and the documentation improves, the error percentage should decrease to a point where a 100% review is no longer required.

Some reviews, frequently initiated by payers, are performed only on billed claims. These may include claims that may have been denied, incorrectly processed, or reviewed for medical necessity.

Auditing Tools

An important first step in auditing is determining the purpose the audit. This may be in the form of a written statement or an objective or objectives that describe the question to be answered, the reason for the evaluation, or a description of the targeted area. The following is an example of a coding **audit objective**:

"The purpose of the coding audit is to ensure compliant coding and billing at Helping Hands Hospital, and specifically to identify appropriate coding of modifier 59, "Distinct procedural service," based on nationally accepted coding guidelines."

Following development of the purpose of the audit, the sample size of the baseline audit should be determined. As noted previously, the sample size is dependent on a number of factors. At this time, creating a time line or a time management chart can be helpful in determining the scope of the project. Items on the chart include development of the purpose of the audit, creation of auditing tools (setup), collection of auditing information, analysis of the information, generation of reports, meetings with appropriate staff, education and training, **assessment, follow-up,** and any future auditing.

There are a number of tools available to assist in the auditing process, including manual and computerized audit forms. The design of the audit form can either facilitate collection of good data or create an onerous process. The following are a number of standard elements that are included in the auditing process:

- Date of the audit
- Patient demographic information, including encounter and/or medical record number, date(s) of service, discharge status (if appropriate), and payer
- Coder
- Provider (physician, consultant, surgeon, radiologist, etc.)
- Original code(s) assigned
- Audited code(s)
- Original MS-DRG or relative value unite (RVU)
- Audited MS-DRG or RVU
- Auditor identification

The audit tool may also include specific auditing criteria based on the nature of the audit. For example, if an audit is being conducted on the use of modifier 57 "Decision for surgery," specific audit criteria may include questions such as:

1. Did the patient have an E/M service performed on the day of, or the day before surgery?
2. Does documentation support the decision for surgery?
3. Does the surgery performed have a 90-day global period?

Once the audit form has been designed, the form should be used to "walk through" an initial review of a small number of records to assess usability and flow of the form. Any adjustments in the form should be made at this time. It is generally desirable to design the audit form following the flow of the medical record. For example, if diagnosis information is typically located before surgical information in the medical record, the diagnosis criteria should be listed before the surgical criteria on the form. The form should be kept as simple as possible, with ample space and standard terminology. The audit form may be revised several times before a final version is used for auditing purposes.

It is always desirable to have an area on the audit tool for general comments. This can be helpful in identifying notes such as where supporting documentation exists in the medical record or that the code change is based on official coding guidelines.

There are a number of ways to create the audit form, including standard word processing, spreadsheets, computer databases, or purchased software. In recent years software development specifically targeted for auditing has improved significantly. Auditing software may have the ability to calculate levels of services, provide payment information, create reports, develop time management charts, and send findings via e-mail. Software may be specifically designed for hospital or physician use, for small or large group practices, and for teaching facilities. Although there are many commercial products on the market that can be used to assist with coding auditing, it is important to note that such products will probably not meet all auditing needs. A coding compliance program is a process, not a product. It should be designed and tailored to fit an organization's needs.

Reporting the Results

As critical as the audit process is itself, the reporting process is equally important. The results need to be clear, accurate, and timely. Results reported to specific individuals may be different from the results of the entire review. For instance, if a review is conducted on physician coding in a large group practice, individual physicians may have only their results reported to them. This may be desirable in situations when a review is focused on a single physician or only on a few physicians. However, if the entire group is reviewed, physicians may be interested in aggregate audit findings, such as the number of claims overcoded, undercoded, or otherwise incorrect. Generally speaking, auditing results are kept confidential and not shared with the public. The facility may wish to seek the opinion of legal counsel before releasing any information to the public.

Within the organization the audit results should be shared with the compliance committee and administration, as appropriate. Along with the actual results of the audit it is important to report what actions will take place in response to the audit findings. For example, what education will be provided to prevent errors in risk areas? Do policies or procedures need to be updated? What follow-up actions, including future audits, will be conducted and when?

Assessing the Appropriate Preventive Measures

As noted earlier, if auditing indicates that coding errors have occurred, the errors must be corrected and, if applicable, the claim resubmitted. Coding errors or variances are generally attributed to a number of factors including:

- Ambiguous coding policies and procedures
- Poor medical record documentation
- Lack of necessary coding resources
- Inexperienced or untrained coders
- Coding of the medical record prior to completion of medical record documentation
- Lack of understanding of coding rules and guidelines
- Failure to review the entire medical record

Addressing the root cause of the issue is an important step in determining what follow-up education or additional training is required.

Following up on the outcomes of any audit is as important as conducting the audit itself. Assessing the outcome may involve improving guidelines, changing policies, and developing new strategies. Recommendations may include education, retraining, or process changes. Failure to follow up on the outcomes can result in serious compliance risks for the health care facility and the provider.

Accountability and responsibility should be assigned to address any issues identified during the auditing process. For example, if an audit discovered that nursing documentation was insufficient to correctly assign codes for infusion services, the director of nursing and the coding supervisor may be assigned to address the issue. Follow-up auditing may be necessary to validate that appropriate education had been conducted, and accuracy has improved.

Handling Outside Audits

Although most of this chapter thus far has been devoted to conducting internal coding audits, all providers at one time or another will be audited by an external reviewer. CMS established two programs to monitor the accuracy of payments, specifically, the Comprehensive Error Rate Testing (CERT) program and the Hospital Payment Monitoring Program (HPMP). In addition, Section 302 of the Tax Relief and Health Care Act of 2006 requires that RACs identify overpayments and underpayments on Medicare claims. The RAC program began with a three-year demonstration period, targeting services in a few states, initially California, Florida, New York and later Massachusetts, South Carolina, and Arizona. The RAC program will be permanent for all states by January 2010. Unlike with CMSs' other review programs, the RACs are paid a contingency fee on all errors they discover. Consequently, some providers have voiced concern that RACs target only high-dollar hospital services and ignore efforts to review claims when the provider was underpaid. (It is estimated that 96% of reviewed claims resulted in overpayment determinations, whereas only 4% of the claims reviewed reflected an underpayment.) Although acute-care inpatient hospitals have been the primary target, other providers including skilled nursing facilities, inpatient rehabilitation facilities, outpatient hospitals, physicians, ambulance companies, and durable medical equipment companies have seen overpayments collected from them.

The success of the RACs in returning overpayments to the Medicare program (currently at more than $1 billion) will ensure that the auditing program will be around for some time to come. Additionally, commercial payers are following suit, performing extensive coding and medical necessity reviews on hospital and physician services. Provider claims, coding, and documentation are being scrutinized more carefully than ever before.

In light of the increased outside auditing activities, many facilities have created an **audit response team** to address the various time lines, medical necessity and coding issues, and appeals. The team may be composed of the following individuals:

- Coding manager
- Coding compliance manager
- Compliance officer

- Hospital/provider practice administration
- Business office services
- Utilization review/management
- Director of health information management services
- Finance and accounting
- Physician/clinical advisor

In some organizations, an audit coordinator or RAC coordinator may be employed. Because of the aggressive auditing by the RACs and mandatory reporting deadlines, the role of the audit coordinator is critical for coordinating the audit responses, claims review, and appeals processes. The audit or RAC coordinator may be responsible for:

- Sending and receiving correspondence related to outside auditing activities
- Entering required data into a tracking tool and ensuring accurate record keeping
- Coordinating deadlines with various departments, such as medical records, coding, utilization management, and financial
- Identifying trends related to medical necessity, coding, and documentation

Outside auditors usually request copies of the medical record. These requests should be submitted promptly, however, not before a thorough review of the medical record has been conducted. (Only photocopies, never the original medical record, should be provided.) The outside auditor should indicate the reason for the audit and the record to be reviewed prior to submittal of documentation, to determine any vulnerability. Depending on the exact nature of the audit, the request may involve the entire medical record or only portions of it related to a specific encounter. It is generally considered desirable to provide only the records that are requested; however, in the Medicare appeals process, no new documentation may be entered for review after the second appeal level. Therefore it is imperative that staff who prepare the medical record copy are skilled in choosing the appropriate documentation that will support the services in question. HIPAA privacy regulations also need to be considered. In addition to medical record documentation, guidelines such as those in official coding guidelines or LCDs or NCDs may be submitted as supporting evidence.

Policies and procedures should be in place to address the outside auditing process, including whether outside auditors are permitted to come in-house for medical review. This issue is often addressed in payer-provider contracts. When outside auditors are permitted to do on-site reviews, an employee of the facility should be available to assist the auditor during the review to answer any questions regarding medical record documentation. The auditor's identification and credentials should be verified prior to having access to patient information.

During the appeals process it is recommended that a physician advisor be utilized to assist with medical necessity issues. The physician can provide valuable input in appeal communications and can speak directly with the payer's medical director.

Although no audit is ever welcomed, it is important to cooperate with the outside auditor and respond to questions and issues promptly. This does not mean, however, that the outside auditor is always correct. Providers should utilize all resources available to support the services they provided.

The provider may find it helpful to speak with other providers to determine whether they have addressed similar issues and what the results were of any previous audits. It is also important to utilize familiar contacts that the provider has established with payers.

Having a central individual who is responsible for handling all outside auditing activities will help ensure coordination and organization of the response process, develop experience in handling appeal processes, and provide a central location for all auditing correspondence. All too often an outside audit request arrives at a facility but does not get delivered to the correct contact person. As a result, the deadline for responding to any appeal may have passed.

Chapter Review

1. Identify at least five common coding risk areas.

   _____

   _____

   _____

2. Provide examples of high-risk and high-volume target areas for a five-physician family practice office.

   _____

   _____

   _____

3. What types of errors will a review of actual claims data along with the coding provided identify?

   _____

   _____

   _____

4. A retrospective coding review of orthopedic cases identifies coding errors and documentation issues of shoulder procedures. How should the errors be addressed? What reimbursement factors need to be considered?

   _____

   _____

   _____

5. If an RAC contractor has identified a consistent coding error among several providers, such as coding of excisional debridement, should the provider also conduct a review of the same issue? Why or why not?

   _____

   _____

   _____

6. When would a 100% review be desirable or required?

_____

_____

_____

7. What governmental resources are available to providers to identify potential coding compliance risk areas?

_____

_____

_____

8. What factors should be considered when determining the appropriate sample size of an audit?

_____

_____

_____

9. Why is coding based on incomplete documentation a risk area?

_____

_____

_____

10. Identify common components of an audit tool.

_____

_____

_____

Case Studies

Case Study 1

A coding compliance manager at a five-physician group practice is conducting an audit of the use of CPT modifier 25. Modifier 25 is appended to an E/M code when a separately identifiable E/M service occurred on the same day as a significant procedure/surgery. This is the first time this area has been audited.

1. Determine the considerations for selecting an adequate sample audit size. Identify the materials required (e.g., medical record, claim information).

   _____

   _____

   _____

2. Develop the criteria needed to conduct the audit.

   _____

   _____

   _____

3. Create an audit tool to facilitate the data collection.

   _____

   _____

   _____

Case Study 2

A data inquiry of claims information at a hospital indicates that modifiers GA, GY, or GZ were not appended to any code within the past year. The hospital utilizes Advance Beneficiary Notices (ABNs), particularly for patients seen in the radiology and laboratory departments. The coding compliance manager has determined that coders in these two departments are appending the appropriate ABN modifier in the hospital's coding and abstracting system.

1. What are some potential causes of the discrepancy between the coding and billing systems?

   _____

   _____

   _____

2. What type of audit should be conducted to investigate the issue?

   _____

   _____

   _____

3. What criteria should be developed?

   _____

   _____

   _____

Case Study 3

A patient has contacted the compliance office indicating that she was charged for services she never received. The patient states that she saw the orthopedist in the clinic for back pain. The physician and patient discussed treatment options including medicinal therapy and epidural injections. The patient decided to try medication prior to proceeding with the injection. When the patient received her bill, she noticed that she was charged for the epidural injection. She telephones the physician's business office, and the charges are removed and an adjusted claim is sent out.

1. Does this case require further investigation?

    _____

    _____

    _____

2. What processes, if any, should be reviewed?

    _____

    _____

    _____

Case Study 4

A baseline coding audit of debridement services performed in a hospital was conducted on 25 claims. The review indicated that in roughly half the medical records reviewed, the documentation did not support the code assignment. The auditor believes that coders may not fully understand the coding guidelines for coding excisional verses non-excisional debridement. She also believes that the physicians are not informed on the documentation requirements necessary for coding debridement services.

1. Should more auditing be performed on debridement services?

    _____

    _____

    _____

2. What are the considerations for looking at a larger sample size?

    _____

    _____

    _____

3. If further review is indicated, should the review be performed retrospectively or prospectively?

_____

_____

_____

4. What immediate measures can be taken to ensure accurate coding of debridement services?

_____

_____

_____

5. What are the training and educational needs?

_____

_____

_____

Case Study 5

In circumstances when a patient is declared clinically brain dead, a hospital requires that certain procedures be conducted and that a Brain Death Assessment form be completed. The compliance manager wants to assess the compliance rate for completion of the form.

1. What factors should be considered in conducting the assessment?

_____

_____

_____

2. What criteria should be included on an audit tool for this assessment?

_____

_____

_____

References

Centers for Medicare & Medicaid Services. (2005, June 10). CMS manual system. Publication 100-08, Medicare program integrity. Transmittal 114. Change request 3734. Retrieved from http://www.cms.hhs.gov/transmittals/downloads/R114PI.pdf

Centers for Medicare & Medicaid Services. Data analysis. In *Medicare program integrity manual*, chap. 2. Retrieved from http://www.cms.hhs.gov/manuals/downloads/pim83c05.pdf

Centers for Medicare & Medicaid Services. *Medicare carriers manual*, pt. 3, chap. XII, sec. 12100. Retrieved from http://www.cms.hhs.gov/manuals/downloads/pim83c03.pdf

Centers for Medicare & Medicaid Services. *Medicare intermediary manual,* pt. 3, chap. VIII, sec. 3799. Retrieved from http://www.cms.hhs.gov/manuals/downloads/pim83c03.pdf

Centers for Medicare & Medicaid Services. Data analysis. In *Medicare program integrity manual*, chap. 2. Retrieved from http://www.cms.hhs.gov/manuals/downloads/pim83c05.pdf

Centers for Medicare & Medicaid Services. (2008, July). The Medicare recovery audit contractor (RAC) program: An evaluation of the 3-year demonstration. Retrieved from http://www.cms.hhs.gov/RAC/Downloads/RAC%20Evaluation%20Report.pdf

Wiggin and Dana, LLC. (2000, March 16). *Compliance programs for nursing facilities.* Retrieved from http://www.wiggin.com/pubs/alerts_template.asp?ID=737167212000

Emerging Technologies

Objectives

At the completion of this chapter, the learner should be able to:

- Discuss the motivation for development of electronic coding systems.
- Describe the basic types of encoders.
- Define automated coding and computer-assisted coding.
- Identify advantages and disadvantages of automated coding.
- Discuss the impact of automated coding systems on coding professionals.
- Discuss the challenges of compliant coding using automated coding systems.
- List compliance auditing activities that identify potential risk areas associated with automated coding.

Key Terms

analyzer	book-based encoders	grouper
automated coding system	computer-assisted coding (CAC)	logic-based encoders

Changes in Coding Tools

For several years the coding tools of the trade consisted of ICD-9-CM and CPT coding books and perhaps a medical dictionary. As technology is altering the health care landscape, so is it also changing the coding process. Although some coders still use coding books, either by choice or lack of availability of other products, electronic coding systems that include encoders, groupers, analyzers, and other software applications are quickly becoming the norm. Automated coding systems, or systems that assign codes based on documentation or the spoken voice, are increasingly being sought as a way to combat the shortage of qualified coding professionals and to speed up the coding and billing process.

Whether coding is performed manually or with electronic assistance, qualified coding personnel are needed to assign and verify coding accuracy. Coding accuracy is largely dependent on the accuracy and completeness of the documentation, and the coder's education and experience. The coder's job of interpreting medical data, applying coding guidelines, and understanding the complexity of payer regulations requires a wide range of skills. Demands for accuracy and expedited financial transactions put additional pressures on coders and business managers.

Encoders: Friend or Foe?

Since the advent of encoders in the 1980s the technology and accuracy of encoding software have increased dramatically. There are basically two types of encoders, knowledge- or **book-based encoders** and **logic-based encoders.** The knowledge- or book-based encoder is essentially a computerized code book. The coder enters a word or phrase and is directed to various screens that are similar to the coding book's index or tabular section. In some systems, the phrase that is entered pulls up a series of codes that may be appropriate. For example, if the term "cataract" is entered, the encoder will list all cataract conditions, including diseases associated with cataracts (e.g., diabetes) and commonly performed procedures or tests associated with cataracts, such as cataract extraction and ultrasound of the eyes. In a logic-based encoder, the coder enters a term and then is guided through a series of questions to arrive at an appropriate code. Thus, when the term "cataract" is entered, a series of questions appear that lead the coder to specific diagnosis code(s) and procedure code(s), if applicable. Some encoder systems provide a combination of knowledge- and logic-based methodology.

Most encoder systems rely heavily on the user's understanding of medical terminology and coding guidelines. For example, experienced coders often relate that an encoder product can lead a coder to the wrong code if the user does not understand the proper assignment of neoplasm codes or fifth digits. An encoder cannot substitute for education and experience. Individuals who use encoders should receive the same training and education as someone who uses the standard coding manuals.

Encoders can improve coding accuracy and compliance with coding guidelines. For example, an encoder should be able to alert the coder when an incomplete or obsolete code has been entered, when certain coding pairs are inappropriate, and when some essential codes may be missing. Many also incorporate National Correct Coding Initiative (NCCI) edits, which can reduce claim errors and reduce the time needed to work claim errors and denials. In this way, encoders can help improve coding accuracy and reduce coding compliance risks.

Encoders are often equipped with other software products such as coding references, medical dictionaries, anatomy references, medical abbreviations, lab and pathology references, and other helpful tools. In some systems, users can add their own coding notes such as specific payer instructions.

The encoder's accuracy will depend largely on the software content and frequency of the coding updates. All coding software systems need to be updated frequently as coding and regulations change. Some encoders include medical necessity software that alerts the user when a diagnosis is missing that would support medical necessity for services that have been performed. Constant changes to policies and regulations generally require more than annual updates.

An encoder will not be able to apply all coding guidelines. For example, the encoder will not be able to apply the outpatient coding guidelines for "possible," "probable," and "questionable" diagnoses. Although some encoders do assist in the sequencing of diagnoses (for example, sequencing diagnoses identified as complications or comorbidities before other diagnoses), they cannot choose the "principal" or first-listed diagnosis.

Many encoders are accompanied by other coding software products such as groupers and optimization software. A **grouper** is a software program that assigns similar patients to a payment group or classification. The grouping may be based on diagnoses or procedures, or both. Other factors may be considered including discharge disposition and the status indicator of the procedure. Two common groupers are diagnosis-related groups (DRGs) for inpatients and ambulatory payment classifications (APCs) for outpatients. Other groupers exist for ambulatory surgery centers (ASCs), physician reimbursement, and long-term care.

An **analyzer** software product can perform advanced analysis of the coding, incorporating patient attributes such as gender, age, and discharge disposition. In the hospital setting, it can assist in determining the most appropriate Medicare Severity Diagnosis-Related Group (MS-DRG), provide severity of illness (SOI) indicators, and supply estimated reimbursement and risks of mortality. For the physician, analyzer software can provide Resource-Based Relative Value Scale (RBRVS) calculations and global fee indicators.

Automated Coding Systems and Computer-Assisted Coding (CAC)

An **automated coding system** or a **computer-assisted coding (CAC)** system automatically assigns codes based on medical information that is electronically stored. Although the terms are often used interchangeably, an automated coding system is commonly inferred to be a completely automated system that requires no human intervention. Computer-assisted coding sometimes refers to software systems that assist in the coding assignment, such as encoders. The American Health Information Management Association (AHIMA) defines computer-assisted coding as "the use of computer software that automatically generates a set of medical codes for review and validation and/or use based upon clinical documentation provided by healthcare practitioners" (www.ahima.org). Both systems require human intervention and validation of final code assignment. Automated coding systems and CAC are often associated with electronic health records. Other terms have also been associated with these systems, including *automated documentation, autocoding,* and *computer-generated coding.* For purposes of this chapter, we will discuss automated coding systems in terms of coding that is generated automatically from medical record documentation.

Similar to an encoder, an automated coding system may apply a numeric code to a phrase or term that has been entered into the electronic health record. For example, a physician may place an electronic lab order (sometimes referred to as an "online order") and may enter "hypertension" as the diagnosis or reason for the test. A single or multiple set of codes may appear from which the physician may select a specific ICD-9-CM code. In another example of automated coding, codes are extracted from terms in medical documentation or from the spoken word. Thus, based on key indicators in a physician's note, the system may automatically assign an evaluation and management (E/M) code and pertinent diagnoses. Some systems allow for codes to be selected automatically from documentation and forwarded directly into the billing system, and there may be no human intervention or review of the codes. However, this is not recommended, as there is a potential for improper billing if the coding and documentation are not reviewed prior to billing.

Table 7-1 Advantages and Disadvantages of Automated Coding Systems

Advantages of Automated Coding Systems	
The coding process may be more efficient, so that coding staff can spend more time reviewing and auditing. The cost of coding services may decrease when coders are used more efficiently as coding reviewers rather than front-line coding assigners.	
Automated coding systems can increase coding consistency and improve coding productivity. Automated coding systems are usually very consistent in the assignment of codes, but although they can be consistently accurate, they can also be consistently inaccurate.	
Automated coding systems are usually integrated with other electronic systems that include coding tools, references, and auditing capabilities.	
Antifraud software can be used in combination with automated coding systems to limit coding compliance risks. However, systems without this feature may actually increase the risk of fraudulent coding.	
Drawbacks to Automated Coding Systems	
Documentation	If the documentation is poor or lacking critical detail, the code selections will reflect the documentation. Although this is true for both human coding and automated coding, the user's knowledge may be helpful in providing clarification or seeking other documentation sources.
Overcoding	Automated coding systems may gravitate to a higher evaluation and management (E/M) level than was medically necessary. For example, if the coding system counts "bullets" or items of services performed in a checklist to arrive at an E/M level, it may consistently arrive at a complex/comprehensive service (a level 4 or 5 E/M code). This may be inappropriate for the nature of the problem and not medically necessary. Unless the automated coding system includes antifraud software, the system may inappropriately bundle services. This can cause payment denials and place the provider at risk for fraud.
Undercoding	Undercoding can also be a problem in the automated coding system. For example, the system may not be considering time as a key factor in the selection of an E/M code. The wrong code category may be selected, such as new or established patient. The system may not arrive at a code that reflects severity, such as bacterial pneumonia or systolic or diastolic congestive heart failure.
Complexity of surgical procedures	Automated coding systems may not arrive at the correct coding assignment for surgical procedures owing to the complex nature of the operation or the multiple terms used to describe the service. For example, to accurately code a "closed fracture of the distal radius" that has been treated with an "open reduction, internal fixation" the code assignment needs to be based on documentation that describes the fracture as "intra-articular" or "extra-articular." Additionally, the number of bone fragments reduced needs to be known. Other factors, such as proper application of modifiers, may not be considered in the automated coding assignment.
Point of entry	In some automated coding systems, codes are assigned when someone enters the clinical information into the system. If this occurs before the procedure is actually performed, for example during the registration process, the coding assignment may not be accurate based on the actual procedure that is performed. The system is dependent on the accuracy and detail of the information entered. Staff need to be aware of the terminology required to arrive at the proper code assignment.
Application of coding guidelines	As mentioned previously, neither an encoder product nor an automated coding system will necessarily be able to apply all the coding guidelines accurately. In an automated coding system, for instance, the phrase "family history of colon cancer" may be misinterpreted as the patient has a history of colon cancer or a current colon cancer. In another example, the system may not be able to discern symptoms that are integral to a disease, which may result in overcoding.
Application of the correct model	An automated coding system may not be able to apply the correct coding model in the appropriate setting. Thus, a coding system that automatically applies codes for physician services may not have the capability to apply the correct set of guidelines for coding for a hospital. In another example, the coding system may not be able to apply either or both the 1995 and 1997 E/M guidelines. This could result in the reporting of a lower E/M service than is supported by the documentation.
Lack of standardization	Although many automated coding systems promise to be "HIPAA compliant," there is currently no standardization of automated coding systems. For example, in a large physician practice, the orthopedic physicians may be using a different type of software than the family practice physicians. The assignment of E/M codes may vary based on the software design. The lack of standardization is also evident when documentation is reviewed or audited by an outside entity. The reviewer may not use an automated coding system or understand how the system arrives at codes. The provider must know how the system assigns codes to support coding assignment in auditing cases.

Most automated coding systems use natural language processing software or a system that assigns codes based on structured texts or templates. Some systems use complex algorithms to generate codes, whereas others use a rules-based approach (e.g., "if this and this is present, then..."). Although these systems can be highly sophisticated, automated coding systems will not be able to assign an accurate code in every case. For example, the software system may not be able to correctly provide the diagnosis codes for a complicated medical condition or rare disorder. Likewise the system may not be able to assign correct procedure codes in complex surgical cases.

Automated coding systems can be specific to the medical specialty. For example, there are automated coding systems developed specifically for emergency departments, interventional radiology, and tumor registries. The systems are usually developed for either physician use or hospital (facility) use. Because physician and facility coding guidelines may differ, this is an important determining factor before purchasing a system. An automated coding system functions less accurately when there are multiple documents to review, such as during an inpatient hospital stay. Currently, there is no automated coding system on the market that can serve all providers in every instance. Table 7–1 outlines the advantages and disadvantages of automated coding systems.

As noted previously, consistent coding assignment by an automated software system can be an advantage, but it can also be a disadvantage if the assigned coding is upcoded or otherwise fraudulent. If the cause of the coding inaccuracy is poor documentation, physicians should be educated so the quality of documentation and the coding can be improved.

The Impact of Automated Coding Systems on Coding Professionals, and Other Considerations

Automated coding systems dramatically change the coder's role, from "code assigner" to "code reviewer." In quality assessment, coders review the code assignment for accuracy, sequencing, and optimization.

Any automated coding system requires proper training and testing to ensure coding compliance. Regular coding reviews should be conducted to ensure coding appropriateness and compliance. Automated coding systems should include the necessary tools to assist in the coding and review process, including coding references and auditing software. Coding policies that exist for manual coding processes need to be incorporated into automated coding processes. An automated coding or CAC system does not replace the need for a coding professional.

In the purchasing process, consideration of either an encoder product or automated coding system should include software updating schedules and costs associated with updates. Just as it is important that coding manuals be updated annually, automated coding systems should also be updated regularly. If the software includes editing capabilities such as the NCCI edits, updates should occur at least quarterly. As with all computerized coding systems, information systems staff should be involved in the selection process and should understand the importance of timely updates.

Any coding system should be user-friendly, as this may affect coding quality, productivity, and user acceptance. Coding professionals should be involved in the selection process and testing of encoders or an automated coding system. They may have a strong preference for either the logic-based or book-based encoder.

In an automated coding system, regular audits should be performed to review the accuracy of coding to ensure compliance and to ensure that codes are accurately transferring to the billing system. Audits should also include a review of the financial impact on employee staffing and the cost-benefit ratio associated with redirection of coding responsibilities.

Coding professionals should develop an understanding of the technology affecting health systems today, including the electronic health record, encoders, and automated coding systems. Some skills may need to be upgraded as coders move from being code assigners to code reviewers. Whether automated systems can improve coding accuracy and compliance still depends on the human element of knowledge of coding guidelines and regulations, as well as good documentation.

Chapter Review

1. What are seen as the advantages and disadvantages of CAC?

   _____

   _____

   _____

2. Perform an Internet search on encoders and select one product. Is the encoder logic-based or book-based? What factors were considered to arrive at this determination?

   _____

   _____

   _____

3. Name at least three advantages and disadvantages of encoders.

   _____

   _____

   _____

4. Explain the purposes of coding groupers and analyzers.

   _____

   _____

   _____

5. Discuss how the coder's role has changed with the development of automated coding systems.

   _____

   _____

   _____

6. Discuss the importance of documentation in an automated coding system.

   _____

   _____

   _____

7. Discuss why human intervention is still important when utilizing automated coding or CAC.

_____

_____

_____

8. When automated coding systems calculate E/M services, they can overcode the service. Why can this occur, and what processes can be implemented to reduce the coding compliance risk?

_____

_____

_____

Case Studies

Case Study 1

A hospital purchases an encoder product for inpatient and outpatient coding use. Some coders are hesitant to use the software, stating that they prefer to use the coding manuals. Other coders quickly adapt to the new encoder and use it exclusively.

1. Is it critical that all coders in the institution utilize the same process for coding?

   _____

   _____

   _____

2. What type of review would be helpful to show coding differences?

   _____

   _____

   _____

3. Would there be a point at which all coders should be required to use an encoder product?

   _____

   _____

   _____

Case Study 2

An advertisement for an automated coding product designed specifically for physician offices includes the following statements:

- Correct diagnosis and procedures codes are automatically selected based on the clinical record and the patient's insurer requirements and fee schedule, instantly creating accurate bills for both insurers and patients.

- The appropriate visit level is based on the documentation during the visit and is displayed for physician approval, preventing undercoding.

- The selected code(s) are printed to a superbill for the patient and automatically sent to the electronic data interchange for reimbursement. Just one click accomplishes these tasks instantly!

1. Discuss any coding compliance risks that the automated coding product may produce.

   _____

   _____

   _____

2. If you were considering purchasing this product, what questions might you ask of the vendor?

   _____

   _____

   _____

3. What type of auditing can be performed prior to purchasing this product that would measure coding reliability?

   _____

   _____

   _____

4. What types of audits should be performed postpurchase to ensure coding accuracy and compliance?

   _____

   _____

   _____

Case Study 3

For each of the following scenarios, discuss whether the coding tasks would best be performed by a coding professional or by an automated coding product. Identify which tasks could be accomplished by both.

1. Identification and determination of whether a patient's medical condition was present on admission.

   _____

   _____

   _____

2. The application of modifiers on a patient who underwent hammer toe repair on three toes of the right foot.

   _____

   _____

   _____

3. The application of NCCI edits on a patient who had an interventional radiology procedure.

   _____

   _____

   _____

4. Determination of whether "postoperative anemia" was a postoperative complication.

   _____

   _____

   _____

5. Determination of a physician's E/M code on the day of discharge that is time-based.

   _____

   _____

   _____

6. Determination of whether chest pain was due to coronary artery disease, esophageal reflux, or rib contusion.

_____

_____

_____

7. Selection of an appropriate consultation E/M code, including the documentation requirements for a consultation (e.g., the name of the individual requesting the consultation, the question to be answered, evidence that the report has been shared with the requesting provider, and the intent of the service).

_____

_____

_____

8. Determination of CPT coding for multiple infusions, including chemotherapy, hydration, and other therapeutic infusions based on time.

_____

_____

_____

Case Study 4

A physician orders a chest X-ray on an electronic ordering system. The physician indicates that the ordering diagnosis is "chest pain." A series of descriptors and codes appear (see Figure 7-1).

1. Has the automated coding system provided a valid listing of codes? If not, what codes are not accurate?

_____

_____

_____

2. What compliance risks are associated with utilizing codes from this list?

_____

_____

_____

Record Selection for: Chest Pain

Name	Code
Chest wall pain following surgery	338.12
Anginal chest pain at rest	413.0
Chest pain with normal coronary angiography	413.9
Chest pain with normal angiography	413.9
Chest pain	786.5
Acute chest pain	780.50
Chest pain at rest	786.50
Resting chest pain	786.50
Chest pain	786.50
Radiating chest pain	786.50
Crushing chest pain	786.50
Cardiac chest pain	786.50
Chest wall pain	786.52
Pleuritic chest pain	786.52
Other chest pain	786.59
Atypical chest pain	786.59
Burning chest pain	786.59
Musculoskeletal chest pain	786.59

Figure 7-1 Example of ICD-9-CM Codes Associated with the Diagnosis "chest pain" in an Electronic Health Record Automated Coding System.

References

AHIMA e-HIM™ Work Group on Computer-Assisted Coding. (2004, November–December). Delving into computer-assisted coding (AHIMA practice brief). *Journal of AHIMA, 75,*(10), 48A–H (with Web extras). Retrieved from http://library.ahima.org/xpedio/groups/public/documents/ahima/bok1_025099. hcsp?dDocName=bok1_025099

American Health Information Management Association. (2005, July 26).Testimony of the American Health Information Management Association to the Standards and Security Subcommittee of the National Committee on Vital and Health Statistics. Retrieved from http://library.ahima.org/xpedio/ groups/public/documents/ahima/bok1_018867.hcsp?dDocName=bok1_018867

American Health Information Management Association, Foundation of Research and Education. Automated coding software: Development and use to enhance antifraud activities. Retrieved from http://library.ahima.org/xpedio/groups/public/documents/ahima/bok1_032014.html

Hagland, Mark. (2002). Revolution in progress: How technology is reshaping the coding world [Electronic version]. *Journal of AHIMA, 73,*(7), 32–35.

Appendix A: Encoder Exercises

Directions: Using the encoder disc included with this book, or another encoder product, assign the appropriate codes for the following exercises. (Answers are found in the *Instructor's Manual*, located on the Instructor Resources CD-ROM.) Try to use only the encoder in the assignment of the codes. *Note: The free trail of EncoderPro included with this book is good for 30 days from date of install. Please consult with your instructor before installing.*

For exercises 1–10, assign the appropriate ICD-9-CM and CPT codes, including evaluation and management (E/M) services if applicable, for the following physician (office) services.

1. An established patient seen in the office today for a history of *Staph aureus* bacteremia and an open infected wound of the left knee. Three weeks ago the patient underwent a simple irrigation and partial skin debridement. Patient returns to clinic today and claims that he is doing very well. He has no problems with his knee and has returned to full activities without limitation. A detailed history and physical examination is performed, with straightforward decision making. Impression: Cellulitis of the left knee with history of *Staph aureus* bacteremia.

   _____

   _____

   _____

2. Patient seen in the emergency department after having fallen and landing directly on his chin. He sustained a laceration inferior to the submandibular area and has come in for repair. He had no loss of consciousness. A detailed history and physical exam, with moderate complexity, was performed. Impression: 1-cm full-thickness laceration of the submandibular area, simple repair.

   _____

   _____

   _____

3. Established patient seen in the clinic today relating that she continues to have problems with tachycardia. Her symptoms started last year while she was pregnant. She was also seen by an endocrinologist, who decided that she has a mild thyroiditis, but this is not related to her issues with tachycardia. Additionally, she does have migraine headaches. An expanded problem-focused history and physical examination was performed, with low complexity medical decision making. Impression: Tachycardia, migraines, mild thyroiditis.

   _____

   _____

   _____

4. Patient presents here for the first time for a chief complaint of right red eye, itchy, and mattery. The patient states that she woke up this morning with her right eye red, itchy, and mattery. She has had increased tearing today, and the eye has been bothersome throughout the day. No change in vision; no purulent eye drainage. A detailed history and physical examination with straightforward medical decision making was performed. Impression: Acute conjunctivitis.

_____

_____

_____

5. The patient is seen in consultation today for constant right upper quadrant pain associated with frequent loose yellow stools in a patient who is diabetic. Previous laboratory workup included serum liver chemistries remarkable for an AST minimally elevated several points above normal. Amylase minimally elevated several points above normal. Previous workup included CT scans, ultrasound, and HIDA scan all normal. Upper endoscopy and colonoscopy were also unrevealing. A comprehensive history and physical exam was performed, with moderate complexity. Impression: Constant right upper quadrant pain associated with loose stools and abnormal labs. Possible biliary microlithiasis or a variant of diabetic intestinal dysmotility. Insulin dependent diabetes.

_____

_____

_____

6. Patient seen today for postoperative check. Patient underwent laparoscopic-assisted vaginal hysterectomy for menorrhagia and dysmenorrhea three weeks ago. She reports that she is feeling well today. She still has some left lower quadrant pain near her left laparoscopic incision site, but this is improving daily. An expanded problem-focused history and exam was performed, with straightforward decision making. Impression: Patient is status post laparoscopic-assisted vaginal hysterectomy for menorrhagia and dysmenorrheal, recovering well.

_____

_____

_____

7. New patient seen today for multiple issues including numbness in the left hand, interstitial cystitis (managed by urology), hypothyroidism, heart murmur, and GERD. Patient was recently seen by neurology for workup of her numbness for possible stroke, but results were negative. Apparently, there was some concern that the patient's symptoms were due to anxiety. She is currently

being managed for interstitial cystitis. On exam she has a regular heart rhythm with a very faint systolic murmur. A comprehensive history, detailed physical exam, with moderate complexity was performed. Impression: Complaints of numbness in the left hand with recent negative workup by neurology. Interstitial cystitis. Hypothyroidism on recent labs. Heart murmur.

_____

_____

_____

8. Patient is a 30-month-old female with trisomy 21 admitted into the hospital for rash and fever of five days' duration. Patient has a recent history of otitis media, currently finishing up a course of antibiotics. Five days ago, Mom reports hearing her making grunting noses and after a minute noticing that she was shaking her arms and legs, with head extended, and eyes crossed. The mother called 911 and reported the seizure. She was seen in the local emergency department and given the diagnosis of febrile seizure. Mom reports a rash started yesterday and spread to where it covers her entire body today. The child continues to have fevers. A comprehensive history and physical exam was performed, with medical decision making of moderate complexity. Impression: 30-month-old with trisomy 21 and recent history of otitis media and febrile seizures. Consistent vomiting, diarrhea, rash, fever, and fussiness. Probable vaginal candidiasis.

_____

_____

_____

9. Established 33-year-old patient is here for follow up of leg pain and requesting a flu shot. The patient continues to have bilateral leg pain with no apparent cause. I told the patient that I really had nothing further to offer in the way of her leg pain and she understands that. I will refer the patient to the Pain Clinic. We did give her a flu shot today. A problem-focused history with straightforward decision making was performed today. There was no physical exam performed. Impression: Continuing leg pain of unknown etiology. Influenza vaccine, split virus, administered today.

_____

_____

_____

10. This 52-year-old male patient is being discharged from observation today. The patient was admitted yesterday with symptoms of left-hand clumsiness and difficulty writing. He states these symptoms lasted approximately five minutes. He denies any previous episodes. He noted at the time that he

was sweating, anxious, and felt nauseous. He also felt that he had trouble finding the right words. He states that his numbness was from the shoulder down and that it did not "feel right." The patient was admitted as an observation patient to the stroke unit. He had no additional symptoms overnight. An MRI was negative for infarction, and MRA of the head did not show significant vascular abnormalities. Carotid dopplers did not show significant stenosis. Lower extremity dopplers were negative for DVT. He was started on Plavix as antiplatelet therapy for secondary prevention given that he was already taking an 81-mg aspirin when these events occurred. His LDL was 77; therefore, a cholesterol lowering agent was not started. Additionally, HbA1C was 5.2%; therefore, no underlying undiagnosed diabetes was present. Impression: TIA, acute stroke ruled out. The patient will follow up in our clinic in six weeks.

Directions: For exercises 11–15, assign the appropriate ICD-9-CM diagnosis and CPT procedure codes for the following ancillary services performed in the hospital (outpatient) setting.

11.

FINAL RADIOLOGY REPORT

CLINICAL INDICATION: Leg pain.

EXAM PERFORMED: AP lateral views of the left hip were obtained.

FINDINGS: Decreased coverage of the lateral aspect of the femoral head due to acetabular dysplastic changes. Small sclerotic lesion is seen in the intertrochanteric region likely representing bone island.

IMPRESSION: Dysplastic changes of the acetabulum. Sclerotic lesion of the intertrochanteric region.

Diagnosis code(s): _____

Procedure code(s): _____

12.

FINAL RADIOLOGY REPORT

CLINICAL INDICATION: Thyroid nodule.

EXAM PERFORMED: Ultrasound-guided fine-needle aspiration biopsy of the thyroid.

FINDINGS: The thyroid gland has normal size, shape, and echogenicity. The right lobe measures $1.7 \times 5.6 \times 1.7$ cm, and the left lobe $2.6 \times 6.4 \times 2.4$ cm in their three dimensions. The isthmus measures 3 mm in thickness. Multiple thyroid nodules are noted as follows: right inferior nodule measuring $7 \times 8 \times 4$ mm and left inferior predominantly solid nodule with cystic components measuring approximately $3.8 \times 2.3 \times 2.3$ cm.

PROCEDURE: Following written, informed consent and explanation of the procedure, the entry site was localized under ultrasound guidance. A "timeout" was performed. The skin was then prepared and draped in the standard sterile fashion. 3 cc of 1% Lidocaine was used to infiltrate the overlying skin and muscles. Three passes were made with a 25-gauge spinal needle. After confirming adequacy of the specimens, the patient was reexamined by ultrasound. The patient tolerated the procedure well.

COMPLICATIONS: None

IMPRESSION: Bilateral thyroid nodules. Successful ultrasound-guided thyroid biopsy of the left thyroid nodule without complications.

Diagnosis code(s): _____

Procedure code(s): _____

13.

FINAL PATHOLOGY REPORT

SPECIMEN SUBMITTED: Left thyroid aspiration.

INDICATION: Left thyroid mass.

INTERPRETATION: Benign thyroid nodule with cystic changes.

Diagnosis code(s): _____

Procedure code(s): _____

14.

FINAL RADIOLOGY REPORT

CLINICAL INDICATION: Head trauma.

EXAM PERFORMED: CT, brain, w/o contrast.

BRIEF HISTORY: The patient is a 30-year-old male who was involved in a cyclist–motor vehicle collision. The patient was riding his bicycle on the street when he was apparently struck from behind and flipped over the bicycle, landing head first on the pavement. The patient does not recall if he lost consciousness. He presently complains only of severe facial pain.

FINDINGS: There is left periorbital and alar soft tissue swelling with pockets of subcutaneous emphysema. There are comminuted fractures of the left orbit lateral, inferior, and medial walls. A depressed fragment lies against the lateral rectus muscle. There is intraorbital, extraconal air. The globes, extraocular muscles, optic nerves, and intraconal fat are intact. There are comminuted fractures with depressed fragments of the left maxillary sinus anterior, medial, and posterior walls. The left maxillary sinus is filled with fluid. There are minimally displaced fractures of the medial wall of the right maxillary sinus. There is an air–fluid level in that sinus. The nasal bone and nasal processes are fractured bilaterally with angulation toward the right. The nasal septum is deviated toward the right. The majority of ethmoid air cells are filled with fluid. The nasal cavity is filled with fluid. There is mucosal thickening in the sphenoid sinuses. Frontal sinuses and mastoid air cells are clear. There are mid and posterior minimally displaced left zygomatic arch fractures.

Brain parenchyma and the brainstem appear normal. Ventricles and sulci are normal shape and size. There is a small ossification along the anterior falx. There is streak artifact in the skull base. No intracranial hemorrhage is identified.

IMPRESSION: Multiple facial fractures as described above. The findings were immediately discussed with the emergency department physician.

Diagnosis code(s): _____

Procedure code(s): _____

15.

FINAL RADIOLOGY REPORT

CLINICAL INDICATION: Diarrhea and dehydration. Evaluate for interval disease progression and/or obstruction.

EXAM PERFORMED: CT of the abdomen, with contrast.

BRIEF HISTORY: The patient is a 71-year-old female with metastatic serous ovarian carcinoma. Status post ileal–colonic resection. Admitted for diarrhea and dehydration.

FINDINGS: The small right pleural effusion that was evident on the previous exam has disappeared. Lung bases are otherwise clear.

Compared with the prior CT scan, there is a stable or slightly decreased cystic lesion in the liver measuring 1.6 × 1.5 cm, compared with 1.8 × 1.5 on the previous exam.

There is interval decrease of ascites in the perihepatic space, and of the peritoneal thickening along the right lobe of the liver. However, peritoneal thickening along the ascending colon with nodular lesion is still visualized. There is no definite solid metastatic lesion in the liver. Gallbladder is decompressed. No biliary ductal dilation. Although several peritoneal nodules are seen in the perisplenic region, these lesions are less prominent compared with the prior CT findings. Spleen and pancreas are normal. Right adrenal is normal, and left adrenal gland shows mild thickening. Several enlarged mesenteric lymph nodes are seen in the right ileocolic vessels.

Multiple, stable renal cysts are noted bilaterally. Kidneys and bladder otherwise unremarkable.

Changes of post hysterectomy are seen. In addition, the peritoneal mass lesion near the vaginal cuff shows interval decrease in size. There is interval decrease in thickening of the sigmoid colon as well as tethering of the sigmoid colon and small bowel in this area. Diffuse thickening of the ileal loops is seen in the pelvis. Small bowel is not grossly distended. Overall there is improvement in peritoneal carcinomatosis. No free air. No hydronephrosis or hydroureter.

The aorta shows athererosclerotic changes without caliber changes. No definitely enlarged retroperitoneal adenopathy. No inguinal adenopathy. No definite osteolytic lesions in the skeleton.

IMPRESSION:

1. Interval improvement of peritoneal carcinomatosis. However there are still considerable peritoneal wall thickening and peritoneal nodules.

2. Interval decrease of soft tissue mass near the vaginal cuff and sigmoid colon narrowing.

3. Multiple renal cysts.

4. Diffuse thickening of the ileum, with a differential diagnosis of inflammation versus serosal implants.

Diagnosis code(s): _____

Procedure code(s): _____

Directions: For exercises 16–20, assign the appropriate ICD-9-CM diagnosis and procedure codes for these inpatient facility cases.

16.

DISCHARGE SUMMARY

ADMISSION DIAGNOSIS: Elevated blood pressure with trace protein in UA. Past due date.

DISCHARGE DIAGNOSIS: Post dates with elevated blood pressure and trace protein. Marginal placenta previa. Poor prenatal care.

BRIEF HISTORY AND SUMMARY: The patient is a 33-year-old G3 P2 at 42 2/7 weeks gestational age by last menstrual period and confirmed with 20-week ultrasound. The patient presented to the clinic two days ago for prenatal visit and was found to have elevated blood pressures at 146/66, and repeat was similar. She did have trace protein in her urine. This was her first prenatal visit since her 24th week. She noted good fetal movement. She did note occasional irregular nonpainful contractions. Due to the concern of a postdate pregnancy with elevated pressures and trace proteins, she was admitted to the hospital for delivery.

Medical induction of labor was initiated. Her membranes were artificially ruptured and she quickly progressed to complete. A vaginal delivery with second-degree perineal laceration and repair ensued. No infant abnormalities were noted. Her postpartum course was unremarkable.

The patient was given home instructions with follow-up in the clinic in six weeks.

Diagnosis code(s): _____

Procedure code(s): _____

17.

DISCHARGE SUMMARY

ADMISSION DIAGNOSIS: Limb pain and right-sided hypesthesias.

DISCHARGE DIAGNOSIS: Cervical ependymoma. Acute postoperative pain.

PROCEDURES PERFORMED: Spinal cord stimulator implantation.

BRIEF HISTORY AND SUMMARY: The patient is a 60-year-old right-handed woman who presented with fourth and fifth digit pain and has experienced some right-sided hypesthesias as well. She underwent a trial of a spinal cord stimulator, which gave her excellent pain relief. She was admitted for implantation of spinal cord stimulator.

On day one of hospitalization the patient underwent a T-10 laminotomy and implantation of spinal cord stimulator from T-7 to T-9 with intraoperative fluoroscopy. She tolerated the procedure well. She did have some significant postoperative pain in her thoracic spine that required some adjustment of her narcotic pain regimen. Her spinal cord stimulator functioned well. By day three of hospitalization she was having significant improvement in her pain control and was able to be discharged home. Her incision is clean, dry, and intact.

Patient is instructed to keep her incision clean and dry and to avoid any strenuous activity of heavy lifting greater than 5–10 pounds. The patient may resume previous diet. Patient is to follow up in the clinic in six to eight weeks.

Diagnosis code(s): _____

Procedure code(s): _____

18.

DISCHARGE SUMMARY

ADMISSION DIAGNOSIS: Postoperative fever.

DISCHARGE DIAGNOSIS: Pyelonephritis. Morbid obesity (BMI 42). Cholelithiasis. Postoperative day 8, status post abdominal hysterectomy, bilateral salpingo-oophorectomy for grade 1 endometrial cancer.

BRIEF HISTORY AND SUMMARY: The patient is a 55-year-old morbidly obese woman who presented at our emergency department with abdominal pain, back pain, and fever. The patient was postoperative day 8 following a total abdominal hysterectomy, bilateral salpingo-oophorectomy for grade 1 endometrial carcinoma, performed at another hospital. On admission she was noted to have leukocyte esterase and nitrates in her urine. She was also found to have tenderness and rebound in her abdomen. She was started on Levaquin for presumed pyelonephritis and IV Flagyl was added due to her peritoneal signs. A CT scan was obtained that revealed essentially normal postoperative changes with some edematous changes around the external iliacs bilaterally with likely seroma forming although phlegmon could not be excluded. On hospital days 1 and 2, the patient continued to be febrile. By day 3 she was feeling much better, her pain had significantly improved, and she denied abdominal pain. Her urine culture and blood cultures have been negative to date.

The patient was given home instructions and will follow up with her oncologist in one week.

Diagnosis code(s): _____

Procedure code(s): _____

19.

DISCHARGE SUMMARY

ADMISSION DIAGNOSIS: Carbon monoxide poisoning.

DISCHARGE DIAGNOSIS: Carbon monoxide poisoning. Possible cognitive deficits.

PROCEDURES PERFORMED: Hyperbaric oxygenation on hospital days one and three.

BRIEF HISTORY AND SUMMARY: The patient is a 35-year-old female who was in her usual state of health until three days ago when she started feeling lightheaded and like she was going to pass out. Her husband was experiencing similar symptoms. For the past few days, they have been running a generator in the garage to heat the home because they were out of heating fuel. Prior to admission, the husband went into the garage, which was "foggy" with smoke. Within 45 minutes the two adults started feeling lightheaded and like they were going to pass out. There was no actual loss of consciousness, chest pain, or nausea. The patient does report a remote history of thyroid cancer, migraines, and asthma. The patient reports she quit smoking six months ago.

The patient and her spouse were admitted to the hospital for hyperbaric oxygen treatments on day one and day three of their hospital stays. Neurocognitive testing was performed on the patient, which showed mild memory impairment. Unclear if this is just baseline.

The patient was instructed to resume her previous diet. Discharge instructions were provided. She is to follow up with neuropsychology in six weeks.

Diagnosis code(s): _____

Procedure code(s): _____

20.

DISCHARGE SUMMARY

ADMISSION DIAGNOSIS: Burn to anterior neck and right hand.

DISCHARGE DIAGNOSIS: Two percent third-degree body surface burn to anterior neck. Second-degree burn to the right hand. Diabetes mellitus Type 2, uncontrolled. Hypertension.

PROCEDURES PERFORMED: Excisional debridement of anterior neck. Split-thickness skin graft from left scalp to neck wound.

BRIEF HISTORY AND SUMMARY: The patient is a 51-year-old male who sustained a third-degree burn while washing his face. He is a known diabetic since age 28. He admits that he does not measure his glucose frequently. On the day of admission, per his usual routine, he took his insulin around noon. Approximately one hour later he gave his dog a treat and is unclear of subsequent events. He passed out, and when he came to he noticed blood everywhere. He then remembers putting water on his face and believes the water was too hot. He admits he has experienced previous hypoglycemic episodes in the past.

The patient was admitted to the burn unit. On hospital day three the patient went to the operative room for an excision of the neck wound with split-thickness skin grafting to the area. The donor site was from the left scalp. The patient's second-degree burn to the hand was kept clean and dry and required no further treatment. The patient was also started on an insulin gtt the day of surgery. Throughout the hospitalization, the patient's blood sugars were extremely difficult to control. He had several hypoglycemic episodes in the hospital. By hospital day seven his neck wound was healing well. He was ambulating well and tolerating intake well. His blood sugars were better controlled. The patient was highly encouraged to monitor his blood sugars closely while at home.

Home instructions were provided. The patient is to resume activities as tolerated. No shaving to graft site. Wear soft collar until next appointment except for showers. Follow up in the burn center and endocrinology in one week.

Diagnosis code(s): _____

Procedure code(s): _____

Discussion Points

1. Discuss the difficulty or ease of using the encoder to assign codes to these exercises.

    _____

    _____

    _____

2. Which coding areas were especially difficult or especially easy to code using the encoder?

    _____

    _____

    _____

3. Were accurate code(s) arrived at using the encoder?

    _____

    _____

    _____

4. What other resources, aside from the coding product itself, were utilized to arrive at the codes?

    _____

    _____

    _____

5. What potential compliance risks should be considered when using the encoder?

    _____

    _____

    _____

6. What were the advantages and disadvantages of using the encoder?

    _____

    _____

    _____

Appendix B: Web Sites of Interest

Advance Beneficiary Notice (ABN)	*www.cms.hhs.gov/BNI*
American Medical Association	*www.ama-assn.org*
Centers for Medicare & Medicaid Services	*www.cms.hhs.gov*
CMS Correct Coding Initiative	*www.cms.hhs.gov/NationalCorrectCodInitEd/*
Evaluation and Management Documentation Guidelines	*www.cms.hhs.gov/MLNEdWebGuide/ 24_EMDOC.asp*
Federal Register	*www.gpoaccess.gov/federal-register*
HIPAA	*www.cms.hhs.gov/HIPAAGenInfo/*
U.S. Government Printing Office	*www.gpoaccess.gov/index.html*
American Health Information Management Association	*www.ahima.org*
American Academy of Professional Coders	*www.aapc.com*
American Hospital Association	*www.aha.org*
National Center for Health Statistics	*www.cdc.gov/nchs*
American Medical Billing Association	*www.ambanet.net/AMBA.htm*
American College of Medical Coding Specialists	*www.acmcs.org*

Appendix C: Abbreviations

AAMC   American Association of Medical Colleges

AAPC   American Academy of Professional Coders

ADR   Additional Development Request (also, Additional Documentation Request)

AFDC   Aid to Families with Dependent Children

AHA   American Hospital Association

AHIMA   American Health Information Management Association

AHRQ   Agency for Healthcare Research and Quality

AMA   American Medical Association

AMBA   American Medical Billing Association

APG   Ambulatory Patient Group

APC   Ambulatory Payment Classification

ARNP   Advanced Registered Nurse Practitioner

ASC   Ambulatory Surgery Center

BENE   Beneficiary

CAH   Critical Access Hospital

CCA   Certified Coding Associate

CCI   Correct Coding Initiative

CCS   An AHIMA credential awarded to individuals who have demonstrated coding skills in the hospital setting.

CCS-P   An AHIMA credential awarded to individuals who have demonstrated coding skills in the physician office setting.

CDC   Centers for Disease Control and Prevention

CHAMPUS   Civilian Health and Medical Program—Uniformed Services

CHAMPVA   Civilian Health and Medical Program—Veterans Administration

CHPS   Certified in Healthcare Privacy and Security

CMI   Case Mix Index

CMRS   Certified Medical Reimbursement Specialist

CMS   Centers for Medicare and Medicaid Services

CPC   Certified Professional Coder

CPC-H   Certified Professional Coder—Hospital

CPC-P   Certified Professional Coder—Payer

CPT	(Physician's) Current Procedural Terminology
CQI	Continuous Quality Improvement
CY	Calendar Year
DME	Durable Medical Equipment
DRG	Diagnosis Related Group
DX	Diagnosis
E & M	Evaluation and Management
EHR	Electronic Health Record
EMR	Electronic Medical Record
FCS	Facility Coding Specialist
FI	Fiscal Intermediary
FY	Fiscal Year
HCFA	Health Care Financing Administration
HCPCS	Healthcare Common Procedure Coding System
HH	Home Health
HHS	Department of Health and Human Services
HIM	Health Information Management
HIPAA	Health Insurance Portability and Accountability Act of 1996
HMO	Health Maintenance Organization
ICD-9-CM	International Classification of Diseases, 9th Edition, Clinical Modification
INPT	Inpatient
IOM	Institute of Medicine
IS	Information Systems
IT	Information Technology
JC	The Joint Commission
LOS	Length of Stay
LP	Licensed Practitioner
MDS	Minimum Data Set
MPI	Master Patient Index
MR	Medical Record (also Medical Review)
NAHQ	National Association of Healthcare Quality
NCHS	National Center for Health Statistics
NCQA	National Committee for Quality Assurance
NDC	National Drug Code
NF	Nursing Facility

NUBC	National Uniform Billing Committee
OBRA	Omnibus Budget Reconciliation Act
OCE	Outpatient Code Editor
OPPS	Outpatient Prospective Payment System
OT	Occupational Therapy
PA	Physician Assistant
PCS	Physician Coding Specialist
PHI	Protected Health Information
PM	Program Memorandum
PPO	Preferred Provider Organization
PPS	Prospective Payment System
PRO	Peer Review Organization
PT	Physical Therapy
PX	Procedure
QA	Quality Assurance
QI	Quality Improvement
RA	Remittance Advice
RBRVS	Resource Based Relative Value Scale
RC	Revenue Cycle (also, Revenue Code)
RFI	Request for Information
RHC	Rural Health Clinic
RHIA	Registered Health Information Administrator
RHIT	Registered Health Information Technician
RM	Risk Management
RN	Registered Nurse
ROI	Release of Information
RUG	Resource Utilization Group
SNF	Skilled Nursing Facility
SNOMED	Systematized Nomenclature of Medicine
SNOMED CT	Systematized Nomenclature of Medicine—Clinical Terminology
SWG	Swingbed
TEFRA	Tax Equity and Fiscal Responsibility Act of 1982
TOB	Type of Bill
UM	Utilization Management

Glossary

A

ABN modifier GA   Waiver of liability on file.

ABN modifier GY   Statutorily excluded.

ABN modifier GZ   Not reasonable and necessary.

Abuse   Payment for items or services that are billed by mistake by providers but should not be paid for by Medicare. Examples of abuse include billing for a noncovered service, misusing codes on a claim, and inappropriately allocating costs on a cost report.

Accreditation   An evaluation process in which a health care organization undergoes an examination of its policies, procedures, and performance by an external organization.

Additional Documentation Request (ADR)   A request by Medicare to submit additional documentation (medical records).

Adjudication   The determination by a payer following a request for payment of health care services (following submission of a claim).

Administrative Simplication   A general term used to describe the development of standard formats that make claim transactions between payers and health care providers simpler, faster, and less confusing. The intent of administrative simplification is to simplify health care billing and other transactions by adopting standards to transmit data electronically.

Admission Date   The date the patient was admitted for inpatient care, outpatient services, or the start of care.

Admitting Diagnosis Code   Code indicating the patient's diagnoses at the time of admission.

Adult   In the Medicare Code Editor, defined as an individual between the ages of 15 and 124 years, inclusive.

Advance Beneficiary Notice   A notice that a physician, supplier, or other provider presents to a patient when payment is expected to be denied.

Age Conflict   In the Medicare Code Editor, the inconsistency between a patient's age and any diagnosis in the patient's medical record.

Allowed Charge   An individual charge determination (approved amount) made by a carrier on a covered Part B medical service or supply.

Ambulatory Payment Classifications (APCs)   Medicare's prospective payment system for outpatient hospital services, including surgical, dialysis, and diagnostic services.

Ambulatory Surgical Center   A freestanding facility, other than a physician's office, where surgical and diagnostic services are provided on an ambulatory basis.

Ambulatory Surgical Center (ASC)   A place other than a hospital that does outpatient surgery.

Analyzer   A coding software product that can perform advanced analysis of the coding by incorporating patient attributes such as gender, age, and discharge disposition.

Anti-Kickback Statute   Statute 42 U.S.C. § 1320a-7b, also known as the Anti-Kickback Statute, makes it illegal to knowingly and willingly solicit or receive anything of value in exchange for referring an individual, purchasing, leasing, ordering or arranging for payment to be made under a federal health care program.

Appeal   A complaint taken on disagreement with any decision about health care services. Examples of appeals include disagreement about payment, coding, demographic information, or medical services provided.

Areas of Risk   Those areas identified either internally or externally that may pose financial risk to a provider. Generally, these include high-volume or high-cost areas.

Assessment   The process of following up on the outcomes of an audit that may result in improving guidelines, changing policies, and developing new strategies.

Assignment   The agreement by a physician to accept the Medicare approved amount as full payment for services.

Attending Physician   The physician who would normally be expected to certify the medical necessity and services provided to a patient's medical care and treatment.

Audit Objective The purpose of the audit, or the statement that describes the question to be answered, the reason for the evaluation, or a description of the targeted area. The audit objective is the basis for the audit.

Audit Response Team A committee that works collaboratively to address payer audits. The team is responsible for ensuring that deadlines are met and that medical necessity and coding are reviewed. The team provides assistance throughout the appeal process if necessary.

Automated Coding System Commonly refers to a computer system that assigns codes without human intervention.

Automated Review Claim review and determination made using system logic (edits). Automated claim reviews never require the intervention of a human to make a claim determination.

B

Bad Faith Bad faith on the part of an insurance company generally refers to unfounded refusal to pay for services allowed under a plan/policy. Such refusals are not always fraudulent; bad judgment or mere negligence is not bad faith.

Beneficiary The name of a person who has health care insurance or coverage through an insurance program.

Benefits Money or services provided by an insurance company or policy.

Bertillon Classification of Causes of Death Created by Jacques Bertillon in 1893, a classification system for describing causes of mortality and morbidity. Commonly considered the forerunner to the International Classification of Diseases (ICD).

Biller An individual assigned to the function of billing.

Billing Using coded data and transferring necessary information to claims for reimbursement. Sometimes referred as "medical billing."

Book-Based Encoders An electronic encoder that most closely resembles an on-line coding book.

C

Capitation A prospective payment method that pays the provider of service a uniform amount for each person served, usually on a monthly basis, rather than on a per-service basis.

Carrier A private company that has a contract with Medicare to pay for Medicare Part B services.

Case Mix The distribution of patients into categories reflecting differences in severity of illness or resource consumption.

Case Mix Index The average MS-DRG relative weight for all Medicare admissions.

Category II Codes Current Procedural Terminology (CPT) codes that describe services or test results, used for performance measurement.

Category III Codes Current Procedural Terminology (CPT) codes that describe new and emerging technology.

Centers for Disease Control and Prevention (CDC) A group of federal agencies that oversee health promotion and disease control and prevention activities in the United States.

Centers for Medicare & Medicaid Services (CMS) A federal agency within the U.S. Department of Health and Human Services. CMS administers the Medicare and Medicaid programs as well as the State Children's Health Insurance Program (SCHIP).

Certificate of Medical Necessity (CMN) A required document attesting to the medical necessity for certain supplies, such as durable medical equipment. For example, CMNs are necessary for the purchase of oxygen, motorized wheelchairs, manual wheelchairs, seat lifts, infusion pumps, and parenteral nutrition.

Charge Master The charge master contains the individual charge items and procedures across a health care facility. The charge master may link charges to individual HCPCS codes and supplies.

Claim A request for payment for services and benefits received.

Classification System A method or system of grouping similar diseases and procedures together.

Clinical Documentation Improvement Program A program in health care organizations that is designed to improve provider documentation. Such programs strive to improve the accuracy and quality of the documentation.

Clinical Documentation Specialist (CDS) An individual who is commonly part of a facility's documentation improvement program. This individual may be responsible for education, monitoring, and assisting physicians in the documentation process. The goal of a clinical documentation improvement program is to ensure that the documentation is accurate and complete for coding and reimbursement purposes.

"Cloning" of Medical Records Used to describe the copying or cutting and pasting of documentation so that medical records have nearly identical documentation. Cloning of medical records can occur from patient to patient, or with patients seen for subsequent visits.

Clustering A practice that can involve both upcoding and downcoding. Involves coding one or two middle levels of services exclusively, under the philosophy that some will be higher and some will be lower, on the belief that the services will average out over time.

CMS Medical Review Program The fulfillment by CMS of a requirement under the Social Security Act to implement measures that ensure payments made by the Medicare program are reasonable and necessary. CMS contracts with Carriers, Fiscal Intermediaries, and Program Safeguard Contractors to perform data analysis of claim data to identify incorrect billing.

Code of Conduct A set of rules that outlines rules of behavior that guide an organization's or individual's decisions and actions.

Coder An individual assigned to the function of coding.

Code Set Any set of codes used for encoding data elements, such as tables of terms, medical concepts, medical diagnostic codes, or medical procedure codes.

Coding Applying a numerical or alphanumeric value to diagnoses, procedures, supplies and other services. Sometimes referred as "medical coding."

Coding and Billing Advice A general term used to describe coding instructions and guidance that may or may not be from official sources.

Coding Certification A process whereby an individual meets established criteria set by a professional organization or company. May involve meeting eligibility requirements, completion of specialized education, and successful passing of an exam. Maintenance of certification may require payment of dues and evidence of continuing education units/hours. Several coding certification processes currently exist.

Coding Compliance A comprehensive process by which health care providers strive to adhere to coding and billing compliance utilizing policies, procedures, standards, processes, and assessments.

Coding Compliance Education Educational programs provided to coding staff, physicians, and others, focusing on ensuring compliance with coding guidelines and payer regulations.

Coding Guidelines Official guidelines for the assignment of codes, including the ICD-9-CM Official Guidelines for Coding and Reporting.

Coding Resources The resources required to accurately assign codes. May include books, software, and access to current federal regulations and payer policies.

Coding System Any one of several coding systems used to apply numeric or alphanumeric codes to health care services, medical diagnoses, and patient encounters. Coding systems include ICD-9-CM, ICD-10-CM, CPT-4, HCPCS, ICD-0-3, CDT, SNOMED-CT, and others.

Companion Guide A detailed guide developed by payers that provides information necessary to submit claims and encounters electronically. Companion guides may detail specifications of each electronic segment or data element submitted as an electronic claim.

Compliance Hotline A telephone hotline dedicated to receiving calls solely on compliance issues. May also include e-mails, written memoranda, newsletters, and other forms of information exchange to maintain open lines of communication. Usually includes an anonymous method of reporting.

Compliance Officer An individual who is generally responsible for managing compliance issues within an organization.

Compliance Program A program in an organization that provides guidance and instructions to staff to promote a high level of ethical and lawful corporate conduct.

Comprehensive Error Rate Testing Program (CERT) A program implemented by CMS to monitor and report the accuracy of Medicare payments. The program utilizes independent reviewers who periodically review random samples of Medicare claims.

Computer-Assisted Coding (CAC) A system that automatically assigns codes based on medical information that is electronically stored. An automated coding system may be defined as a system that requires no human intervention. Computer-assisted coding is sometimes defined as a system that assists the coder in arriving at a code, such as an encoder.

Continuing Education Units (CEUs) Units of education or training that allow an individual to maintain a certain skill set. Often required to maintain certification.

Contractor An entity that has an agreement with CMS or another funding agency to provide a service or perform a project.

Contractor Policy Coverage decisions developed by CMS contractors to describe Medicare policies or provide coverage guidance. Policies are developed by contractors when there is an absence of a national coverage policy for a service, there is a need to provide interpretation of an existing national policy, or guidance on coding and documentation is needed.

Cooperating Parties for ICD-9-CM The group of organizations that collaborate in the development and maintenance of the ICD-9-CM coding system. Includes the American Hospital Association, the Centers for Medicare & Medicaid Services, and the National Center for Health Statistics.

Copayment The amount paid for each medical service, such as a doctor's visit or encounter at a hospital. The copayment amount is usually a set amount.

Corporate Compliance Program A process whereby an organization strives to adhere to compliance with federal and state laws and regulations.

Corporate Integrity Agreement An agreement that is executed as part of a civil settlement between a health care provider and the government to resolve a case based on allegations of health care fraud or abuse. Such agreements are generally in effect for a period of three to five years and require specific measurements to be implemented.

Correction of Errors in Medical Records A method for correcting errors and amending documentation in health records. The method of correction will depend upon the error and the health record medium (e.g., paper or electronic record).

Cost Report The report required from providers on an annual basis to make a proper determination of amounts payable under the Medicare program.

Covered Charge Service or benefit for which a health plan makes either partial or full payment.

CPT Level I Codes Current Procedural Terminology (CPT) codes that make up one level of the HCPCS coding system.

CPT Level II Codes National codes that are developed by the Centers for Medicare & Medicaid Services to describe services and supplies not specifically reported in CPT.

CPT Level III Codes Local codes developed by local Medicare contractors that report services and supplies not specifically reported in CPT or Level II codes. Level III codes were eliminated from use under HIPAA.

Critical Access Hospital A small health care facility that gives limited outpatient and inpatient hospital services to people in rural areas.

Current Dental Terminology (CDT) The medical code set of dental procedures maintained and copyrighted by the American Dental Association (ADA) and adopted under the HIPAA code set requirements.

Current Procedural Terminology, 4th Edition (CPT-4) The medical code set of physician and other health care services maintained and copyrighted by the American Medical Association (AMA) and adopted under the HIPAA code set requirements.

D

Deductible The amount paid for health care before a health insurance plan begins to pay.

Degree of Confidence The measurement, usually expressed as a percentage, that expresses the confidence of the results of a study.

Department of Health and Human Services (DHHS) The agency that administers many social programs at the federal level dealing with the health and welfare of the citizens of the United States. Sometimes referred to as the "parent" of CMS.

Diagnosis-Related Group (DRG) Used in the inpatient prospective payment system. Under this system, each patient case is categorized into a diagnosis-related group. Each group has a payment weight, based on the average resources used to treat Medicare patients in that DRG. An individual facility's payment rate (base payment rate) is multiplied by the DRG weight to arrive at the payment. DRGs were replaced with MS-DRGs (Medicare-Severity Diagnosis-Related Groups) in fiscal year 2008 for prospective payment hospitals.

Diagnostic Code Numeric or alphanumeric codes used to classify and report diseases, conditions, and injuries.

Downcoding Reducing the code or the value of a code when the documentation supports a different service (a higher service) billed by the provider.

DRG Creep   A variety of upcoding schemes that involves the practice of billing using a DRG or MSDRG that provides a higher reimbursement rate than the code that accurately reflects the patient's diagnosis.

Duplicate Billing   Submission of more than one claim for the same service by a provider or billing company, or submission of the claim to more than one primary payer at the same time. Inappropriate reporting of the units of service also can contribute to duplicate billing.

E

"Effective" Compliance Program   The requirement according to the federal sentencing guidelines that an organization have established compliance standards and procedures to be followed by its employees and other agents to receive sentencing credit for an "effective" compliance program.

Electronic Health Record (EHR)   Generic term for all electronic patient health care systems, or a comprehensive or longitudinal collection of a patient's entire health history.

Electronic Medical Record   A medical record in electronic, digital, or computerized format. The terms electronic medical record (EMR), electronic health record (EHR), and computer-based patient record (CPR) are often used interchangeably. However in some definitions, an electronic medical record is a subset of the EHR, which is generally considered a comprehensive or longitudinal collection of a patient's entire health history. Definitions also vary in the extent of the computerization of a medical record. For example, some consider a computerized medical record a completely paperless, computer-generated medical record. Others consider an electronic medical record as scanned images of the paper record or portions of the medical record that are immediately available electronically by authorized users.

Emergency Room—Hospital   A portion of a hospital where emergency diagnosis and treatment of illness or injury are provided.

Encoder   A computerized system that assists the coder at arriving at an appropriate code. There are two basic types of encoders: book-based and logic-based.

Encounter Form   A form that is used to capture services and diagnoses of a patient's health care visit. Also referred to as a "superbill."

Extrapolation   An inference about the whole (the universe) based on a smaller subset, or what is known.

F

False Claims Act   A federal law that allows individuals to file legal actions against anyone who has defrauded the U.S. government. There are numerous provisions under the act, including *qui tam* or whistle-blower provisions, and definitions of false claims. Also referred to as the "Lincoln law."

Federal Health Care Program   Generally, any plan or program that provides health benefits, whether directly, through insurance, or otherwise, that is funded in part or in whole by the U.S. government. Includes Medicare, the Federal Employees' Compensation Act, the Black Lung Benefits Act, and the Longshore and Harbor Workers' Compensation Act. Also, any state health plan, including Medicaid, receiving funds from block grants for social services or child health services.

Federal Register   The official daily federal government publication for rules, proposed rules, and notices of federal agencies and organizations, as well as executive orders and other presidential documents.

Fee Schedule   A complete listing of fees used by health plans to pay doctors and other providers.

Female Only Diagnosis or Procedure   In the Medicare Code Editor, a diagnosis or procedure that should be assigned only to a female patient.

Fiscal Intermediary   A private company that has a contract with Medicare to pay Part A and some Part B bills. Also referred to as "intermediary."

Fraud   The intentional deception or misrepresentation that an individual knows, or should know, to be false or does not believe to be true and makes, knowing the deception could result in some unauthorized benefit to himself or herself or to some other person(s). Also, to purposely bill for services that were never given or to bill for a service that has a higher reimbursement than the service produced.

Fraud Alert   Notices issued when there is a need to advise Medicare carriers, fiscal intermediaries, law enforcement, quality improvement organizations, beneficiaries, and providers about an activity that resulted in the filing of inappropriate or potentially false Medicare claims. The various types of fraud alerts include national Medicare fraud alerts (fraud activity that has the potential to be widespread or that focuses on a particular scheme or scam) and central office alerts (related to issues that are politically sensitive or those that are about to be publicized in the national media).

G

Grouper   A software program that assigns similar patients to a payment group or classification. The purpose of the software is to emulate the payment grouping that may be assigned by the payer.

H

Health Care Clearing House   A public or private entity that processes or facilitates the processing of nonstandard data elements of health information into standard data elements.

Healthcare Common Procedure Coding System (HCPCS)   A Medicare coding system for all services performed by a physician or supplier. HCPCS is based on the American Medical Association's physicians' CPT codes and other codes for physician and nonphysician services and supplies, commonly referred to as HCPCS Level II codes. The combination of CPT and HCPCS Level II codes are used to describe HCPCS codes.

Health Care Financing Administration (HCFA)   Former name of the governmental agency now called the Centers for Medicare & Medicaid Services (CMS).

Health Care Provider   A person who is trained and licensed to provide health care services. Also, a place licensed to provide health care. Examples of providers include physicians, nurses, hospitals, skilled nursing facilities, home health agencies, and assisted living centers. It can also be a provider of services, either medical or other health service, and any other person furnishing health care services or supplies.

Health Information   Any information, whether oral or recorded in any form or medium, that

a) is created or received by a health care provider, health plan, public health authority, employer, life insurer, school or university, or health care clearinghouse and;

b) relates to the past, present, or future physical or mental health or condition of an individual, the provision of health care to an individual, or the past, present or future payment for the provision of health care to an individual.

Health Insurance Portability and Accountability Act (HIPAA)   Sometimes referred to as the "Kassebaum-Kennedy Act," passed in 1996. The law expands health care coverage if an individual loses his or her job or moves from one job to another. HIPAA also protects individuals and families who have preexisting medical conditions and/or problems getting health coverage. Portions of HIPAA also cover health care privacy, security and coding, and transactions.

Health Maintenance Organization (HMO)   An entity that provides a comprehensive package of health care services to enrolled individuals for a fixed capitation payment. The term "Medicare HMO" includes all types of HMOs that contract with Medicare.

Health Plan   An individual or group plan that provides or pays the cost of medical care. This may include a group health plan, a health insurance issuer, a health maintenance organization, Part A or Part B of the Medicare program, the Medicaid program, a Medicare supplemental policy, a long-term care policy, an employee welfare benefit plan, health care plans for active military personnel, veterans' health care programs, the Indian Health Service, and the Federal Employees Health Benefits Program.

High-Risk and High-Volume Areas   Services or items that are determined to be high-risk because of the volume or cost of the services provided.

Home Health Service   Defined by Medicare as skilled nursing services and other therapeutic services provided by a Medicare participating home health agency.

Hospice   A facility, other than a patient's home, in which palliative and supportive care for terminally ill patients and their families is provided.

Hospital-Acquired Condition   A condition that a patient develops that was not present on admission into the hospital.

I

ICD-9-CM and ICD-10-CM   The International Classification of Diseases, Clinical Modification, 9th and 10th revision. The code set adopted under HIPAA for reporting diagnoses for physician and facility claims.

ICD-9-CM Official Guidelines for Coding and Reporting   The official guidelines for reporting ICD-9-CM diagnosis and procedure codes for inpatient, outpatient, and physician services. The guidelines are developed and approved by the cooperating parties for ICD-9-CM that include the American Hospital

Association, American Health Information Management Association, Center for Medicare and Medicaid Services, and the National Center for Health Statistics. The guidelines are considered official under the HIPAA regulations.

Inpatient Hospital   A facility, other than psychiatric, that primarily provides diagnostic, therapeutic (both surgical and nonsurgical), and rehabilitation services by, or under, the supervision of physicians to patients admitted for a variety of medical conditions.

Inpatient Prospective Payment System (IPPS)   The CMS prospective payment system for acute care hospital inpatient stays under Medicare Part A.

Inpatient Psychiatric Facility   A facility that provides inpatient psychiatric services for the diagnosis and treatment of mental illness on a 24-hour basis, by or under the supervision of a physician.

In Re: Managed Care Litigation   A class action suit filed by physicians against major commercial health insurers that resulted in multimillion dollar payments plus commitments to modify physician payment practices.

Intermediary   An organization selected by providers of health care that has an agreement with the Department of Health and Human Services to process and pay institutional claims and perform other functions under Medicare's health insurance program.

Intermediate Care Facility   A facility that primarily provides health-related care and services above the level of custodial care to mentally retarded individuals but does not provide the level of care or treatment available in a hospital or skilled nursing facility.

International Classification of Diseases, 9th Revision, Clinical Modification (ICD-9-CM)   The classification based on the World Health Organization's Ninth Revision, International Classification of Diseases (ICD-9). The official system of assigning diagnosis and procedures codes for health care services.

International Classification of Diseases for Oncology (ICD-O)   The coding classification system used in tumor and cancer registries for reporting the site (topography) and the histology (morphology) of neoplasms.

J

Joint Commission   An independent, non-for-profit organization that accredits and certifies health care organizations and programs in the United States.

L

LCD Reconsideration Process   The process a local Medicare contractor or carrier uses to allow providers and others to request reconsideration to a coverage policy.

Local Coverage Determinations (LCDs)   Policies developed by Medicare contractors that explain determinations of medical necessity for services.

Logic-Based Encoder   An encoder system that leads the user to a code or codes through a series of questions.

Long-Term Care Facility   A general term that describes a "stay" in a long-term care facility. Stays are measured in terms of days of residence in a facility. Types of long-term care facilities include licensed nursing homes, skilled nursing homes, intermediate care facilities, retirement homes, domiciliary or personal care facilities, long-term care units in hospitals, mental health facilities, assisted and foster care homes, and institutions for the mentally retarded and developmentally disabled.

M

Male Only Diagnosis or Procedure   In the Medicare Code Editor, a diagnosis or procedure that should be used only on a male patient.

Managed Care   Plans that include health maintenance organizations (HMOs) and competitive medical plans (CMPs) that provide health services on a prepayment basis. Under Medicare, these plans may also be called Medicare Choice programs.

Mandatory Exclusions   Federal guidelines that outline exclusionary periods. Mandatory exclusions must be applied under the law.

Manifestation Code   A code that describes the manifestation of an underlying disease, not the disease itself. Manifestation codes are generally not first-listed or principal diagnoses.

Maternity   In the Medicare Code Editor, maternity diagnoses may be used on any woman between the ages of 12 and 55, inclusive.

Medicaid   A jointly funded federal–state health insurance program for certain low-income and needy people. Provides coverage for individuals under three main categories: parents and children, the elderly, and the disabled and blind. Commonly, there are three types of Medicaid eligibility groups: mandatory, categorically needy, and medically needy.

Medically Necessary   Services and supplies that are proper and needed for the diagnosis or treatment of a medical condition.

Medically Unlikely Edits (MUEs)   A project implemented by CMS to detect and deny unlikely Medicare claims on a prepayment basis to stop inappropriate payments. MUEs limit the units of service that can be "likely" billed during a single encounter.

Medicare   The federal health insurance program for individuals 65 years of age or older, certain younger people with disabilities, and people with end-stage renal disease (permanent kidney failure with dialysis or a kidney transplant, sometimes called ESRD).

Medicare Administrative Contractor (MAC)   A Medicare contractor that is responsible for the receipt, processing, and payment for both Part A and Part B services in a regional area.

MS-DRG   Medicare Severity Diagnosis-Related Group used in the inpatient prospective payment system.

N

National Correct Coding Initiative (NCCI) Edits   CMS coding policies developed to promote national correct coding methodologies and to control improper coding leading to inappropriate payment for Medicare services. The NCCI edits are maintained by an independent contractor, Correct Coding Solutions, LLC.

National Coverage Determinations (NCDS) or Policy   A policy developed by CMS that indicates whether a service is considered covered under the Medicare program. Policies may be included in CMS regulations, published in the *Federal Register*, contained in a CMS ruling, or issued as a program instruction.

National Provider Identifier (NPI)   The unique identifier for health care providers.

National Uniform Billing Committee   The organization that maintains the UB-04 institutional billing from.

Newborn   In the Medicare Code Editor, a newborn is defined as 0 years.

NCD Reconsideration Process   The process that Medicare uses to allow providers and others to request reconsideration to a national coverage policy.

"Never Events"   Serious and costly errors in the provision of health care services that should never happen. Never events include surgery on the wrong body part, surgery on the wrong patient, wrong surgery performed, and mismatched blood transfusion.

Noncovered Service   A service that does not meet the requirements of a benefit, including statutorily excluded services and items or services that are not reasonable and necessary.

Non-Physician Provider   A provider of health care services who is not a physician, such as a physician assistant or nurse practitioner.

Nursing Facility   A facility that primarily provides to residents skilled nursing care and related services for the rehabilitation of injured, disabled, or sick persons or, on a regular basis, health-related care services above the level of custodial care to other than mentally retarded individuals.

O

Office of Inspector General (OIG)   The office under the U.S. Department of Health and Human Services (HHS) mandated under Public Law 95-452 to protect the integrity of the DHHS programs as well as the health and welfare of the beneficiaries. The OIG conducts audits and evaluations to review the effectiveness, efficiency, and integrity of governmental programs.

OIG Compliance Guidelines   The Office of Inspector General (OIG) publishes compliance recommendations, discusses risk areas and provides guidelines for providers on issues related to coding, billing, and proper reimbursement for Medicare services.

Omnibus Budget Reconciliation Act (OBRA)   Federal law of a given year that directs how federal monies are to be expended. Amendments to Medicaid eligibility and benefit rules are frequently made in such acts.

Outcome   Measures that refer to the observable, measurable results related to preventing and detecting violations of a compliance program.

Outcome Indicator   The desired target following a process. Outcome indicators are usually measurable characteristics that can be used to assess how well a program or process is performing.

Outpatient Hospital   A portion of a hospital that provides diagnostic, therapeutic (both surgical and nonsurgical), and rehabilitation services to sick or injured persons who do not require hospitalization or institutionalization.

Outpatient Prospective Payment System   The method of payment under Part B for Medicare outpatient services for most hospitals or community mental health centers.

Overpayment An improper or excessive payment made to a health care provider as a result of patient billing or claims processing errors for which a refund is owed by the provider.

P

Part A Services provided for inpatient hospital stays, care in a skilled nursing facility, hospice care, and some home health care.

Part B Services that include physician, outpatient hospital care, durable medical equipment, and some medical services that are not covered by Part A.

Payer An entity that makes payment for medical services.

Payment System Any system that functions to settle financial transactions between a health care provider and a payer.

Pediatric In the Medicare Code Editor, a pediatric patient is a child 0–17 years, inclusive.

Period of Review The time period that is involved in a review, either internally or externally (for example, by the OIG).

Permissive Exclusions Federal guidelines that outline exclusionary periods. Permissive exclusions are partially discretionary.

Physician Quality Reporting Initiative (PQRI) A system established and implemented by CMS under the Tax Relief and Health Care Act of 2006. The act provides additional payment to physicians who successfully report quality measures as defined by CMS.

Physician Query A form or process whereby a physician is asked to clarify documentation in the medical record.

Preauthorization Similar to precertification, a process whereby the insurance company is notified prior to a service being rendered.

Precertification A process whereby the insurance company is notified before a service is rendered or a patient is admitted into the hospital.

Principal Diagnosis Defined in the Uniform Hospital Discharge Data Set (UHDDS) as "that condition established after study to be chiefly responsible for occasioning the admission of the patient to the hospital for care."

Process The manner in which a compliance program seeks to prevent and detect violations of the law.

Professional Ethical Standards A system of moral standards, values, or ethics commonly expressed in professional standards or standards of conduct.

Program Safeguard Contractors (PSCs) Contractors who identify cases of suspected health care fraud. All fraud cases developed by PSCs are referred to the Office of Inspector General (OIG) for review and initiation of any prosecution or monetary penalties.

Prospective Payment System A method of reimbursement in which payment is predetermined and fixed. Prospective payment systems include MS-DRGs for hospital inpatient services and APCs for hospital outpatient services.

Prospective Review A review of claims data and coding prior to the submission of the claim and before adjudication.

Provider In compliance program guidance, any individual, company, corporation, or organization that submits claims for reimbursement to a federal health care program.

Public Law 104-191, Health Insurance Portability and Accountability Act (HIPAA) The law that requires the Department of Health and Human Services to establish national standards for electronic health care transactions, national identifiers for providers, security, and privacy.

Q

Quality Improvement Organization (QIO) Private, not-for-profit organization contracted by CMS to perform reviews of medical care. QIOs access data on the quality and efficiency of health care and provide recommendations for improving quality outcomes.

Quality Measure The National Quality Measures Clearinghouse, sponsored by the Agency for Healthcare Research and Quality (AHRQ) provides evidence-based health care quality measures and measure sets. These quality measures are used to compare health care quality data and provide guidance on health care decisions.

Query A means of communicating with a provider on issues related to documentation, clinical significance, medical necessity, or other issues.

Questionable Admission Certain diagnosis codes that usually are not sufficient justification for admission to an acute-care hospital.

QUI TAM An abbreviation for the Latin phrase "*qui tam pro domino rege quam pro sic ipso in hoc parte sequitur*," or "who as well for the king as for himself sues in this matter." *Qui tam* is a provision of the Federal False Claims Act and is commonly referred to as the whistle-blower provision.

R

RAT-STATS   A statistical software package utilized by the OIG to develop random samples.

Recertification   The process of re-obtaining certification, for example, maintaining continuing education units to retain credentials as a certified coder.

Reconsideration Process   A mechanism by which interested parties can request a revision to a local coverage policy or determination.

Recovery Audit Contractor (RAC)   A program required by Congress to be implemented under the Tax Relief and Health Care Act of 2006 to identify Medicare overpayments and underpayments to health care providers.

Relative Value Unit (RVU)   A measure of the work, practice expense, and malpractice costs for most physician services. RVUs are used to calculate the physician fee schedule payment amount for a service.

Resource Utilization Group Version III (RUG-III)   A patient classification system used to classify nursing home residents into homogeneous patient groups according to common health characteristics and the amount and type of resources they use.

Retrospective Review   A review of claims data and coding after the claim has been filed and adjudicated.

S

Sample Size   In reference to medical record review, the number of total records reviewed. The sample size relates to the measure or degree of confidence desired in the results of the review.

Sampling and Auditing Methods   Any number of ways to sample and audit health care data for assessing coding, billing, documentation, and reimbursement accuracy.

Sanction   Any of a number of administrative actions that Medicare may impose when addressing questionable, improper, or abusive practices of providers, practitioners, and suppliers.

Sex Conflict   In the Medicare Code Editor, an inconsistency between a patient's sex and any diagnosis or procedure in the patient's medical record.

Skilled Nursing Facility   A facility that primarily provides inpatient skilled nursing care and related services to patients who require medical, nursing, or rehabilitative services but does not provide the level of care or treatment available in a hospital.

Social Security Act Amendments of 1965   The act that created Medicare and Medicaid.

Stark Law   The law that prohibits physician self-referral and defines health care financial relationships including physician employment, independent contractor arrangements, group practice compensation, administrative service contracts, leasing agreements, retirement plans, and other financial arrangements.

Structure   The capacity of a compliance program to prevent and detect violations of law.

Superbill   A form used to capture services and diagnoses of a patient's health care visit. Also referred to as an "encounter form."

T

Tax Equity and Fiscal Responsibilty Act of 1982 (TEFRA)   Permits states to cover under Medicaid disabled children under age 19 who live at home who would have been eligible if in an institution. States must determine that institutional care would have been required, that home care is appropriate, and the estimated cost of home care is no more than institutional care.

Template   Generally referring to an automatic standardized display of headings, criteria, or checklists used in creating medical record documentation.

Transactions   Health claims or equivalent encounter information and health claim attachments.

U

Unacceptable Principal Diagnosis   One of selected codes that describe circumstances or conditions but not a current illness or injury. Codes that are not specific to describe a specific illness or injury.

Unbundling   According to Medicare, the practice of using separate billing codes for services that have an aggregate billing code. Also, the practice of billing multiple procedure codes that are covered by a single comprehensive code.

Upcoding   Billing and/or coding a service at a higher level than was documented and provided. Also, misuse of standardized codes to obtain more money than allowed by law. Sometimes referred to as "upcharging."

Index

StudyWare™ to Accompany A Guide to Coding Compliance

Minimum System Requirements

- Operating systems: Microsoft Windows XP w/SP 2, Windows Vista w/ SP 1
- Processor: Minimum required by Operating System
- Memory: Minimum required by Operating System
- Hard Drive Space: [something]
- Screen resolution: 800 x 600 pixels
- CD-ROM drive
- Sound card & listening device required for audio features
- Flash Player 9. The Adobe Flash Player is free, and can be downloaded from http://www.adobe.com/products/flashplayer/
- [Other software requirements]

Setup Instructions

1. Insert disc into CD-ROM drive. The StudyWare™ installation program should start automatically. If it does not, go to step 2.
2. From My Computer, double-click the icon for the CD drive.
3. Double-click the setup.exe file to start the program.

Technical Support

Telephone: 1-800-648-7450
8:30 A.M.-6:30 P.M. Eastern Time
E-mail: delmar.help@cengage.com

StudyWare™ is a trademark used herein under license.

Microsoft® and Windows® are registered trademarks of the Microsoft Corporation.

Pentium® is a registered trademark of the Intel Corporation.

IMPORTANT! READ CAREFULLY: This End User License Agreement ("Agreement") sets forth the conditions by which Cengage Learning will make electronic access to the Cengage Learning-owned licensed content and associated media, software, documentation, printed materials, and electronic documentation contained in this package and/or made available to you via this product (the "Licensed Content"), available to you (the "End User"). BY CLICKING THE "I ACCEPT" BUTTON AND/OR OPENING THIS PACKAGE, YOU ACKNOWLEDGE THAT YOU HAVE READ ALL OF THE TERMS AND CONDITIONS, AND THAT YOU AGREE TO BE BOUND BY ITS TERMS, CONDITIONS, AND ALL APPLICABLE LAWS AND REGULATIONS GOVERNING THE USE OF THE LICENSED CONTENT.

1.0   SCOPE OF LICENSE

1.1   Licensed Content. The Licensed Content may contain portions of modifiable content ("Modifiable Content") and content which may not be modified or otherwise altered by the End User ("Non-Modifiable Content"). For purposes of this Agreement, Modifiable Content and Non-Modifiable Content may be collectively referred to herein as the "Licensed Content." All Licensed Content shall be considered Non-Modifiable Content, unless such Licensed Content is presented to the End User in a modifiable format and it is clearly indicated that modification of the Licensed Content is permitted.

1.2   Subject to the End User's compliance with the terms and conditions of this Agreement, Cengage Learning hereby grants the End User, a nontransferable, nonexclusive, limited right to access and view a single copy of the Licensed Content on a single personal computer system for noncommercial, internal, personal use only, and, to the extent that End User adopts the associated textbook for use in connection with a course, the limited right to provide, distribute, and display the Modifiable Content to course students who purchase the textbook, for use in connection with the course only. The End User shall not (i) reproduce, copy, modify (except in the case of Modifiable Content), distribute, display, transfer, sublicense, prepare derivative work(s) based on, sell, exchange, barter or transfer, rent, lease, loan, resell, or in any other manner exploit the Licensed Content; (ii) remove, obscure, or alter any notice of Cengage Learning's intellectual property rights present on or in the Licensed Content, including, but not limited to, copyright, trademark, and/or patent notices; or (iii) disassemble, decompile, translate, reverse engineer, or otherwise reduce the Licensed Content. Cengage reserves the right to use a hardware lock device, license administration software, and/or a license authorization key to control access or password protection technology to the Licensed Content. The End User may not take any steps to avoid or defeat the purpose of such measures. Use of the Licensed Content without the relevant required lock device or authorization key is prohibited. UNDER NO CIRCUMSTANCES MAY NON-SALEABLE ITEMS PROVIDED TO YOU BY CENGAGE (INCLUDING, WITHOUT LIMITATION, ANNOTATED INSTRUCTOR'S EDITIONS, SOLUTIONS MANUALS, INSTRUCTOR'S RESOURCE MATERIALS AND/OR TEST MATERIALS) BE SOLD, AUCTIONED, LICENSED OR OTHERWISE REDISTRIBUTED BY THE END USER.

2.0   TERMINATION

2.1   Cengage Learning may at any time (without prejudice to its other rights or remedies) immediately terminate this Agreement and/or suspend access to some or all of the Licensed Content, in the event that the End User does not comply with any of the terms and conditions of this Agreement. In the event of such termination by Cengage Learning, the End User shall immediately return any and all copies of the Licensed Content to Cengage Learning.

3.0   PROPRIETARY RIGHTS

3.1   The End User acknowledges that Cengage Learning owns all rights, title and interest, including, but not limited to all copyright rights therein, in and to the Licensed Content, and that the End User shall not take any action inconsistent with such ownership. The Licensed Content is protected by U.S., Canadian and other applicable copyright laws and by international treaties, including the Berne Convention and the Universal Copyright Convention. Nothing contained in this Agreement shall be construed as granting the End User any ownership rights in or to the Licensed Content.

3.2   Cengage Learning reserves the right at any time to withdraw from the Licensed Content any item or part of an item for which it no longer retains the right to publish, or which it has reasonable grounds to believe infringes copyright or is defamatory, unlawful, or otherwise objectionable.

4.0   PROTECTION AND SECURITY

4.1   The End User shall use its best efforts and take all reasonable steps to safeguard its copy of the Licensed Content to ensure that no unauthorized reproduction, publication, disclosure, modification, or distribution of the Licensed Content, in whole or in part, is made. To the extent that the End User becomes aware of any such unauthorized use of the Licensed Content, the End User shall immediately notify Cengage Learning. Notification of such violations may be made by sending an e-mail to infringement@cengage.com.

5.0 MISUSE OF THE LICENSED PRODUCT

5.1   In the event that the End User uses the Licensed Content in violation of this Agreement, Cengage Learning shall have the option of electing liquidated damages, which shall include all profits generated by the End User's use of the Licensed Content plus interest computed at the maximum rate permitted by law and all legal fees and other expenses incurred by Cengage Learning in enforcing its rights, plus penalties.

6.0 FEDERAL GOVERNMENT CLIENTS

6.1   Except as expressly authorized by Cengage Learning, Federal Government clients obtain only the rights specified in this Agreement and no other rights. The Government acknowledges that (i) all software and related documentation incorporated in the Licensed Content is existing commercial computer software within the meaning of FAR 27.405(b)(2); and (2) all other data delivered in whatever form, is limited rights data within the meaning of FAR 27.401. The restrictions in this section are acceptable as consistent with the Government's need for software and other data under this Agreement.

7.0 DISCLAIMER OF WARRANTIES AND LIABILITIES

7.1   Although Cengage Learning believes the Licensed Content to be reliable, Cengage Learning does not guarantee or warrant (i) any information or materials contained in or produced by the Licensed Content, (ii) the accuracy, completeness or reliability of the Licensed Content, or (iii) that the Licensed Content is free from errors or other material defects. THE LICENSED PRODUCT IS PROVIDED "AS IS," WITHOUT ANY WARRANTY OF ANY KIND AND CENGAGE LEARNING DISCLAIMS ANY AND ALL WARRANTIES, EXPRESSED OR IMPLIED, INCLUDING, WITHOUT LIMITATION, WARRANTIES OF MERCHANTABILITY OR FITNESS FOR A PARTICULAR PURPOSE. IN NO EVENT SHALL CENGAGE LEARNING BE LIABLE FOR: INDIRECT, SPECIAL, PUNITIVE OR CONSEQUENTIAL DAMAGES INCLUDING FOR LOST PROFITS, LOST DATA, OR OTHERWISE. IN NO EVENT SHALL CENGAGE LEARNING'S AGGREGATE LIABILITY HEREUNDER, WHETHER ARISING IN CONTRACT, TORT, STRICT LIABILITY OR OTHERWISE, EXCEED THE AMOUNT OF FEES PAID BY THE END USER HEREUNDER FOR THE LICENSE OF THE LICENSED CONTENT.

8.0 GENERAL

8.1   Entire Agreement. This Agreement shall constitute the entire Agreement between the Parties and supercedes all prior Agreements and understandings oral or written relating to the subject matter hereof.

8.2   Enhancements/Modifications of Licensed Content. From time to time, and in Cengage Learning's sole discretion, Cengage Learning may advise the End User of updates, upgrades, enhancements and/or improvements to the Licensed Content, and may permit the End User to access and use, subject to the terms and conditions of this Agreement, such modifications, upon payment of prices as may be established by Cengage Learning.

8.3   No Export. The End User shall use the Licensed Content solely in the United States and shall not transfer or export, directly or indirectly, the Licensed Content outside the United States.

8.4   Severability. If any provision of this Agreement is invalid, illegal, or unenforceable under any applicable statute or rule of law, the provision shall be deemed omitted to the extent that it is invalid, illegal, or unenforceable. In such a case, the remainder of the Agreement shall be construed in a manner as to give greatest effect to the original intention of the parties hereto.

8.5   Waiver. The waiver of any right or failure of either party to exercise in any respect any right provided in this Agreement in any instance shall not be deemed to be a waiver of such right in the future or a waiver of any other right under this Agreement.

8.6   Choice of Law/Venue. This Agreement shall be interpreted, construed, and governed by and in accordance with the laws of the State of New York, applicable to contracts executed and to be wholly preformed therein, without regard to its principles governing conflicts of law. Each party agrees that any proceeding arising out of or relating to this Agreement or the breach or threatened breach of this Agreement may be commenced and prosecuted in a court in the State and County of New York. Each party consents and submits to the nonexclusive personal jurisdiction of any court in the State and County of New York in respect of any such proceeding.

8.7   Acknowledgment. By opening this package and/or by accessing the Licensed Content on this Web site, THE END USER ACKNOWLEDGES THAT IT HAS READ THIS AGREEMENT, UNDERSTANDS IT, AND AGREES TO BE BOUND BY ITS TERMS AND CONDITIONS. IF YOU DO NOT ACCEPT THESE TERMS AND CONDITIONS, YOU MUST NOT ACCESS THE LICENSED CONTENT AND RETURN THE LICENSED PRODUCT TO CENGAGE LEARNING (WITHIN 30 CALENDAR DAYS OF THE END USER'S PURCHASE) WITH PROOF OF PAYMENT ACCEPTABLE TO CENGAGE LEARNING, FOR A CREDIT OR A REFUND. Should the End User have any questions/comments regarding this Agreement, please contact Cengage Learning at Delmar.help@cengage.com.